ECONOMIC GLOBALIZATION AND THE CITIZENS' WELFARE STATE

T0314764

For Miki, Asato, and Yuki

Economic Globalization and the Citizens' Welfare State

Sweden, UK, Japan, US

HIROTO TSUKADA
Yamaguchi University, Japan

Routledge
Taylor & Francis Group

LONDON AND NEW YORK

First published 2002 by Ashgate Publishing

Reissued 2018 by Routledge
2 Park Square, Milton Park, Abingdon, Oxon OX14 4RN
711 Third Avenue, New York, NY 10017, USA

Routledge is an imprint of the Taylor & Francis Group, an informa business

Publisher's Note
The publisher has gone to great lengths to ensure the quality of this reprint but
points out that some imperfections in the original copies may be apparent.

Disclaimer
The publisher has made every effort to trace copyright holders and welcomes
correspondence from those they have been unable to contact.

A Library of Congress record exists under LC control number: 2001087940

ISBN 13: 978-1-138-70285-1 (hbk)
ISBN 13: 978-1-138-63099-4 (pbk)
ISBN 13: 978-1-315-20698-1 (ebk)

Contents

List of Figures

List of Tables

Preface

This book questions the condition of the Welfare State today and how we can improve it.

The Welfare State that has developed in the post World War Two era has been challenged by pro-market and economic globalization trends. How it finds its balance between market and state or market and society itself is a major question today.

Having passed the 20th century, we now face fear and hope today. The fear is that our life is still difficult to live in the contradictory affluent society. The hope is that we know it. Although plagued by the cold war, civil life in the western world might have had more hopes until the early 1970s. But since then, many things have changed, the major one probably being in the total structure and atmosphere of society. Our conception of it - what a society is, and what it should be – has changed in *some* way. And so has the structure of it, too.

We will address this problem from the Welfare State view. We have witnessed the progress of the Welfare State until the 1960s and 1970s, a halt and retrenchment since the 1980s and a somewhat reactionary trend today. The nightmare of the 1970s – simultaneous inflation and depression – seems to have been the first watershed. Recent acceleration of economic globalization seems to be the second. And the problem is that these recent developments in economy and politics do not seem to have ensured us of a stable and hopeful prospect for our lives today. What it has given us, even when the economy appears to be as prosperous as in the late 1990s in the UK and the US, seems to be rather the opposite: insecurity and anxiety – insecurity of work, life, and even human relationships as well.

We will consider this problem from the viewpoint of the relation between market and society, and their proper balance. Market mechanism is one of the most powerful devices ever invented for human happiness. But as with fire and atomic energy, it is so powerful that it must be properly harnessed. Most of all, it should remain as a servant for human happiness, not its lord. The Welfare State has been thus devised to meet this shortcoming. The major question for a society is economic distribution and redistribution. As is observed in human history, how to harmonize distribution with the progress of productive capacity has always been the core question for any society. When it succeeds in this task, it is at peace.

The highly redistributive Welfare State had been an answer in the post-war period for a few decades. But it was cut short to recover the 'proper balance between distribution and economic growth', which meant directing income less toward wages and welfare and more toward profit and investment. It was argued that it was necessary to recover the proper balance between investment and consumption. Whether and how much this prescription was right needs to be given a full consideration. And how to strike a balance between these two goals today – or if market mechanism cannot realize the 'ideal' balance how much the government must still interfere – is another important question.

Theoretically, a democratic society determines its policies for the benefit of the greatest happiness of the greatest number. It also has the sovereign power to regulate everyone and everything toward this goal today, with market mechanism being no exception. But how to regulate market mechanism is a most complicated and difficult question. And so the experiment continues. By regulating bargaining conditions in the market – as by labour laws – and by correcting the uneven distribution by the market – as by social welfare provisions – we continue to try to find the proper balance in a society. And we will consider this question here with a concern that the recent two decades of policy changes – or the movement toward stronger market mechanism and less state intervention – may have lessened rather than promoted human happiness.

The difficulty in this consideration rests in its many-sidedness. The question of the Welfare State includes almost everything in social sciences. We have to deal with the people and social structure at the same time. Each of them is itself complex. We have to deal with people's thoughts, wills and sentiments. And we also have to address economic and political problems of society. In this sense, such an exploration as in this book is always an adventure but a challenge we cannot avoid today.

Society, economy, politics, and satisfaction will be the key words in this study.

First we will address the major question of this book and what has been argued about it (Chapter 1). To make progress in this argument, we need to be able to identify the related problems. We will address the key understanding of what a *society* and a civil society are, and how a Welfare State is positioned in this framework. We will look at a Welfare State as a complementary device for market mechanism (Chapter 2). We will then see the underlying layer of society, or the *economic* sphere; the recent trend of Welfare States in terms of economic policies (Chapter 3). Following that we will look at the *political* ideas that reflect and also drive them; the ideas of political leaders and opposing ideas (Chapter 4). Then we will consider the *satisfaction* or the *attitudes* of the peoples from and to these developments, for it is this that will determine social development in the long run (Chapter 5). Finally, we will arrive at the logical answer to the original question, inferred from the findings in the preceding chapters. That answer will provide us with the alternative society feasible in the present economic and political conditions that can best correspond to the people's will today (Chapter 6).

This book expects as its readers scholars in economics and sociology, college teachers and students, particularly those interested in the Welfare State theory and its problems today. Those who are already well acquainted with the past arguments in this theory can skip Chapter 1, section 4 and Chapter 3, section 1.

Acknowledgements

This book originated in my pursuit of the theme of the possibility and responsibility of market economy as a social system. Since the collapse of the socialist countries in Europe, market economy has become the major social system in the world. Thus, what it is, and what it will be, have become more important questions today. This book tries to answer them, drawing on the traditional analytical viewpoint of the Welfare State. In doing this, it adds another analytical viewpoint of three virtues in a human society: efficiency, equity, and human fellowship.

Particular thanks are due to Vic George and Peter Taylor-Gooby, who have greatly helped me study about the Welfare State. I am grateful to Susan Long, Pranab Chatterjee, Terry Hokenstad, Sang-Hoon Ahn, Peter Gundelach, Jorgen Elm Larsen, and Peter Abrahamson, who have provided me with useful ideas in discussions, and Kim Dae-Hwan, Chan Se-Jin, Hiroo Higuchi and Sook Jin Sung, who have given me useful comments on the draft. I am also grateful to my colleagues in the Faculty of Economics in Yamaguchi University, many of whom have long helped me with discussions and ideas. Lastly, I am grateful to John Rawls, who, through his book, *A Theory of Justice*, 1971, has inspired me in the possibility of the analysis of our civil society today and has provided me with useful viewpoints for this task.

Hiroto Tsukada

Yamaguchishi, Yamaguchiken
August 2001

1 Questions

This chapter questions what has been and should be argued about the Welfare State today.

1 QUESTION – Weaker welfare state?

Neo-liberal policies and economic globalization have been the two major causes for social change in the past two decades. In many industrialized countries, policies for economic growth and globalization are vigorously pursued today. One common characteristic of the current argument seems to be the larger weight given to growth than to welfare.[1] As such changes are worldwide and fast, they often appear as something irresistible for the citizens in each country. In the turbulent past two decades, the peoples in industrialized countries have experienced both good and bad times. No single country has enjoyed continuous prosperity throughout this period. As globalization proceeds, on the one hand some people are gaining much more wealth and safer lives, while on the other a large number of people are suffering from fear of loss of job opportunities and a weakening state welfare. This contrast is the same even in the currently prosperous countries such as the UK and the US. Even if this new trend should turn out to be favourable for the majority of workers 'in the end', it is not yet so today.

How long this era of turmoil will last is not clear yet. From past experience, we can infer that large social changes often fail to ensure the benefits of the change to everyone concerned. Inequality among the people and countries, for example, has appeared gradually in the labour market over the past decade in the industrialized countries. The various reforms of welfare provisions in the meantime have also affected the people unevenly. Such serious social changes might continue. But if we aim at a compassionate society for many more years to come where no one falls into

---

[1] Globalization has advanced in many spheres of life, social, political, economic, etc. In some cases it represents desirable phenomena, such as people associating with foreign people more frequently, and governments and private organizations cooperating for mutual goals more than ever before. From these different aspects I will use the word globalization mostly in the economic sense in the argument below. Economic globalization has desirable and undesirable effects on peoples' lives. For example, it is desirable if a larger quantity of capital moves faster to developing countries, but it is undesirable if the same capital causes financial crises by being withdrawn quickly. In this book, globalization is mostly addressed from the viewpoint of its destructive effect to the balance of societies.

insecure positions or misery, we must not fail to ensure security for every citizen in today's difficult social conditions.

We are on the brink of entering an age where the value of a socio-economy (a society closely related to its economic structure) is judged by firms' points of view more than ever. Globalization based on the firms' necessity and strategy has become the top priority in many countries. This is a fundamental change in the social framework or social structure. We must not just accept a social change, which means a 'new deal' of the game being played with a new rule, or the merits and demerits of this change in a passive manner, but should also take an initiative in this change.

The welfare society seems to be the major and most effective system that the peoples in industrialized countries have developed to meet the problems derived from an originally irresponsible market mechanism. Although the 'Welfare State' 'acquired an international as well as a national popularity', 'the concept of the Welfare State ... defies precise definition' (Barr, 1998, p. 6). In this book it is tentatively defined as a country that has a state system to ensure a decent living standard for its citizens. This system is understood to ensure security in major spheres of life, such as health care, old age pensions or support to people on a low income. It also includes employment policies, for job opportunities and equitable bargaining conditions between the employers and employees are also important devices to improve the shortcomings of the market mechanism, which often fails to provide people with both of them.

To counteract the heavy globalizing pressures, we will need to maintain and strengthen the Welfare State. Firms and market mechanism are the tools for us to use. But when left untouched, useful tools often turn their teeth against humans. The history of market economy in civil society has been the history of human efforts to keep its power under their control by taming its cyclical business fluctuations and reducing poverty among its population. The state welfare system in recent decades has been one of the most successful attempts for these purposes. But the new growth of market mechanism is again threatening to surpass the power of human beings today. Facing this challenge, we must now examine how this problem is being developed and how we can cope with it.

Until the 1970s, as market mechanism threatened the jobless and the weak, two policies were introduced as the components of the Welfare State: employment and social welfare policies. But in the past two decades, these policies have both been weakened by a counter movement. It has been argued that they should be curtailed for four reasons: to reduce public deficit (and its negative effect on private investment), to reduce the harmful-effects on the production system (again on private investment), to increase external competitiveness (by alleviating the burden on firms), and to increase work incentives. Such was the anxiety since the late 1970s and many policies were

2

implemented in this direction. But the resulting society we see today appears to be no securer than before. Many opinion polls in the countries studied show that this new trend has not necessarily been welcomed by the general public.

The sharp decline of consumption in Japan in 1997 was a good example. A sharp decline followed when consumption tax was raised from 3 to 5% and a new medical fee was introduced to decrease the government budget deficit. It happened when its economy was trying to 'adjust' to the new 'globalization' movement. This sequence clearly shows how people were, and probably still are, anxious about the present and prospective effects of this new trend and its effect on their spending. The prolonged depression after that incident cost Japan's economy dearly.

Japan's case is not an exception in today's rapidly changing condition. Faced with instability in the labour market and the opacity of the newly emerging society, people's insecurity increases. Uncertainty could mean a chance for the few, but risk and anxiety for the many. Being anxious about their jobs, people try to cling to their present jobs or up-grade their working abilities. It is true that such instability of life was also prevalent in the past, but people could have some expectation of the Welfare State answering the problems. Thus it had played the role of the safety net in the market society, which was not doubted until the 1970s. Of course, what is unfolding before our eyes today is not exactly a sheer regression to the pre-World War Two days, but it is also true that we now feel that we cannot rely on the state any more as before. Thus we have to answer the following question today: what should we do about the growing insecurity of our life and the weakening Welfare State?

2 FOCUS OF THE QUESTION – Trade-off between growth and welfare

After the 1970s, with the industrialized nations shifting to lower economic growth, the core question facing society has been the distributive problems: income distribution between profit and wage and resource distribution between private and public, both of which have had to do with government decisions. Even the distributive question between profit and wages, for example, is much affected by the government's attitude toward labour laws. What the governments have chosen to do, which of course has been the outcome of people's choices, has influenced and determined the state of society for the past two decades. The major question that runs through these questions is the weight given to growth and welfare or economic growth and social welfare provisions in the respective countries. The predominant argument has been that too many resources were consumed by welfare, which caused lower economic growth and lower competitiveness.

The difficulties in the 1970s – inflation, depression, government and trade deficit – were more or less attributed to too strong labour power and too much welfare expenditure. 'Too strong a Welfare State creates too much wage and welfare pressures and deteriorates the economy and export competitiveness'; this perception became popular in the UK and the US. As the two countries took up the counter measures to push back this 'big government' trend, other countries followed this path, too, for fear of being left behind in world competitiveness.

It was so even in the countries where the Welfare State had not yet grown so big, an example of which was Japan. Although she had just started to become a Welfare State, the increase of anti-welfarism and a higher competitiveness ethos acted as a restraint upon expanding the content of a Welfare State. In 1973, older people were given the right to receive free medical treatment and old age pension benefits were raised significantly, thus the year was called the First Year of Welfare. But this was also the end of its high growth economy period. Faced with the growing government deficit in the following turbulent years, the next three decades have been a period of struggle between competitiveness and social welfare.

The argument in an academic circle in Japan in 1979 shows that the central question since the 1980s in the industrialized countries has been this balance between economic growth and social welfare. The Japan Economic Policy Association met to discuss in that year the main topic of 'economic policies of efficiency and equity'.[2] This conference proposed the question of what should be the alternative direction of Japanese society when it became difficult to enrich social welfare by economic growth. This question was posed theoretically as how to find the balance between efficiency and equity. This proposal reflected the general atmosphere of that age in many industrialized countries. Already in Europe and the US, in the stable growth until the 1960s albeit accompanied by persistent poverty in society, the argument of how to re-establish such criteria as fairness and justice in socio-economy was being addressed. The widespread influence of John Rawls' *A Theory of Justice* in 1971 reflected and supported the spirit of this age. Although fundamental in its character, with the rise of anti-welfarism since the 1980s, it was inevitable that this question of social balance became the central area for the major battle between the right and left.[3]

Before we discuss the following arguments, the first thing we should understand about the Welfare State question today is that we now face a very fundamental question of what a society is. Apart from the 'golden' period when both economy and social welfare provisions grew together, we are

---

[2] Japan Economic Policy Association, Annual Report, 1980.

[3] George and Wilding's *Ideology and Social Welfare* (1974, 1985) was another example of the interest in this question. Being one of the best forerunners about this issue, apart from Rawls, their focus not only is on the systematic structure of ideas but extends from human nature to concrete social welfare policies, thus providing an anatomy of the welfare state ideas.

challenged today by a conscious choice of where to direct our resources most. This is often a trade-off question and requires that we make a precise judgement between the good and bad of the choices. In answering this question, we need to understand what are economic efficiency and social welfare, and what balance would we hope for between them.

Yuichi Shionoya argued that to revitalize economics it was necessary to address the question of distributive justice that had long been neglected under the name of scientific objectivity.[4] He pointed out that the paradigm of the past neo-conservative economics was an analysis based on one particular value called (economic) efficiency, but the significance of other values such as justice – or equity and welfare in the context here – should also be considered. He proceeded that it was necessary to reconsider the past premise of 'economic man' of neo-classics who sought for the maximum utility for himself, and instead pay more attention to the collective orientation of humans to form institutions, rules or restrictions. He emphasized that this orientation should be studied by analysing the tendencies, incentives and motives of humans, who after all live on moral values.

Whenever we consider and study social issues, we cannot avoid dealing with some social ideals. Unlike studying natural sciences, we cannot escape from value judgments from the very beginning, as when we choose our topics. Even for the most objective social scientist, subjectivity cannot be escaped in choosing one's theme. In social sciences it matters much because, for example, if the poverty problem is not taken into consideration, it will be totally ignored. And from what perspective a poverty problem is studied, whether based on sympathy for the poor or indifference, will affect the result and policies deeply. Likewise our perspective of human nature is important. Whether we view humans as selfish or altruistic affects the resulting social ideal. It is high time to consider, or reconsider, such fundamental questions today, as great thinkers used to do in earlier days. Today, we must face the question of human nature and the problem of social balance.

Shionoya's reference to the social institutions (a public system of rules) is closely related to this understanding. Social and human ideals in people appear in the social institutions. He referred to the propriety of institutional premises that construct the background of economic activities. Thus, like Rawls, by directing our attention to the background structure of our society, he tries to set up a broad analytical framework for our society. This emphasis is the most natural and useful when we need to deal with our social framework itself. Institutions are actually the embodiment of social ideals or social consent. From this perspective, he argued that the conception of justice should be taken into consideration as one of the basic institutions, not

---

[4] JEPA, Annual Report, op.cit.

as a given premise as most welfare economists had done. Until the 1970s, although the development of the Welfare State had been partly concerned with these social ideals, they had not been fully addressed. But in the adverse conditions, both economic and ideological, they have to be clarified: what kind of society or what balance between growth and social welfare would we wish for today.[5]

The influence and significance of institutions is quite clear. Who in the society become rich or poor or happy or unhappy depends much on the social institutions. In a market economy, too, these institutions affect the social members' success mainly by distributive institutions such as labour and welfare laws. How we are dealt with by the social institutions before we enter the labour market and what kind of distributive rules we have for products affect our lives significantly. The question of institutions has thus the utmost importance in human society. Being revitalized in the low growth economy in the 1970s, this argument has been given another stimulus by the ever-increasing economic pressures of globalization and its influence on the Welfare State. Lower economic growth and increasing globalizing pressures are the twin major problems today.

3 VIEWPOINTS

Below are addressed what countries and with what concerns we will deal with.

Advanced capitalist countries: When we look back on human history, we learn that different types of society have existed. They include capitalist and socialist types by the criterion of type of ownership of productive means, totalitarian and democratic types by the criterion of the extent of democracy and industrialized and developing types by the extent of industrialization. In this book it is presupposed that human society progresses toward both higher productivity in economy and higher democracy in politics. People are supposed to pursue both goals at the same time and do not trade them with each other. At present, it is presumed that these two goals are most highly realized in advanced capitalist countries. Socialist countries of today, however, do not seem to have high economic power equivalent to capitalist countries and it is not clear either if their political democracy is more highly developed to counter this defect as a whole. In addition, most of the population in the world is living in capitalist, free market regimes, which do not seem likely to change into socialist ones in the near future. Based on these observations, in considering the Welfare State problems, it is most appropriate to focus our attention on the possibilities and difficulties within

---

[5] Tsukada (1998) examines the fundamental ideas such as equitable distribution of products and human fellowship, etc.

capitalist, free market economies.

Difference among the Welfare States: Advanced free market nations launched their progress toward the Welfare State in the 1930s during the depression and unstable years. Its essential purpose has been to establish social security for the disadvantaged, or the economically weak, which consists of the unemployed and the needy. The measures for this purpose were income security and social service assistance. Income security includes full employment policy, unemployment benefit, old age pension, income support, etc., and social service includes medical insurance, elderly care, etc. The details differ between countries, but it is common that the government is responsible for the security of the people in these aspects. In this sense, every advanced free market society today has in common many of the characteristics of the Welfare State despite the differences in their achievements. Some countries prefer to think of social welfare based on a citizen's right, which includes provisions for the middle and upper class beneficiaries, and some more on the principle of relief for the needy.

Two extremes among them are the US type lower welfare, lower burden state and Scandinavian type higher welfare, higher burden state. At present the US type stresses growth more, putting the first priority on raising firms' profit rate by lower wages and lower welfare (which correspond to lower firms' and people's burdens). As a result, the US is changing toward a society with a greater income difference. The Scandinavian type thinks much of firms' profit and has aimed at promoting higher mobility of labour force based upon higher stability realized by higher welfare. Thus, developing higher productivity industry, together with higher welfare, has made their burden comparatively heavier. Neither type has shown a decisive, significant advantage over the other in the post-war years, sometimes enjoying prosperity and sometimes downturns. For the past decade the US type has shown higher records in terms of economic growth and lower unemployment rate. In between these two types are located the continent of Europe with its high rate of unemployment, and Japan with its growing unemployment.[6]

Sovereignty of the states: Meanwhile the influence of the US type society seems to be spreading among the others, and this process includes an important question of the sovereignty of a society – sovereignty by the citizens of the country in determining its course. In recent years, particularly in the 1990s, with the growth of worldwide mobility of firms under globalization, the necessity of attracting firms to stay and establish themselves within the national borders by luring them with higher profit rate is being emphasized. When the firms were not capable or not eager to move around in the world, they were counted on as the responsible 'citizens' of a

---

[6] At present the influence of the US type welfare society seems to be gradually spreading even to Scandinavian type societies as discussed later.

country. But today they are 'easy riders' and have to be lured to stay inside a country by attractive prizes. This new phenomenon proposes a fundamental question about what a firm or an entrepreneur is. While this question is being addressed, the critical necessity of keeping them based in a country has come to affect the structure of the Welfare State, particularly in its revenue side. In such an age, the US type smaller Welfare State, which can contribute to firms' higher profit rate by ensuring lower tax and lower social contribution by the firms, is of course more advantageous in competition. The existence of front-runner countries in this sense cannot but move others in the same direction. This means it has become more difficult for a country to choose its own social ideal based on its own social values. But whether this 'pressure', which is rather economic, is something to be restricted politically or should be left alone, remains a fundamental question in addressing this problem.

The future of the Welfare State today seems to be being determined not as a result of calm consideration by sovereign peoples of respective countries but by the pressing economic forces from the advantageous powers of the firms strengthened by the US type society.

Competition and insecurity: As mentioned before, our fundamental question is the social balance between growth and welfare. A guide to considering this question today seems to be the serious insecurity problem prevailing over our lives under the growing competitive atmosphere mostly originated from the firms' behaviours. Competition is the nucleus and principle underlying our lives in a market economy and has been particularly emphasized since the 1980s. It's true that competition stimulates our productive effort. But it's also true that too much competition ruins human life. In this originally competitive market society, the device formulated to keep the balance between the competitive urge in the market and security in a civil society has been the Welfare State. Workers' lives in a market economy often used to be compared with a rat race. This excessive competition has been ameliorated and restricted by the Welfare State. We have to give attention as to whether this old question is again coming back to the fore of our society.

Purpose and measures: In approaching this question, the balance in our society between growth and security, or between market mechanism and the Welfare State, we can divide it into two parts: firstly, a question of purposes – for whom; and secondly, a question of measures – how. The measure question is reduced to finding the most rational way to a fixed purpose and is rather easy to start with. The more difficult is the purposive one. This question, for whom or what kind of life for them, will eventually be settled by the number of people with a common interest, according to the fundamental utilitarian rule of 'the greatest happiness for the greatest number'. But this question is often difficult to answer for we are usually not very sure of what would be our best welfare as we become more affluent and more sensitive to spiritual satisfaction.

But this utilitarian rule seems to be being realized steadily with the progress of history. As humans recognize that knowledge is more useful than violence, the general rule for a social change has become 'for the benefit of a greater number of people'. One significant example of this rule is observed in the progress from feudal to civil society. Political suppression and low economic progress characterized the feudal age. The social change that led to a civil society opened the door to equality under the law and freedom to pursue one's own happiness. In order to arbitrate the conflicts of freedom among the citizens, the rule of the supremacy of public welfare, or for the greater number of people, was established. In this new society, as the greater majority of people attain more knowledge and increase in political power, societies that do not match this utilitarian goal either tend to be discarded or improved.

Thus, in considering the Welfare State questions, too, we can ultimately rely on this principle: when a society changes, if it is to continue, it must realize a better condition for a greater number of people. But we face a difficult question in realizing this goal. Political happiness is easier to deal with than economic. Political rights such as equality under the law are universal advantages given and ensured to every citizen with no exception, and thus they are easily tackled. But how much economic welfare is to be secured for the members of society is difficult to answer. Take, for example, the distribution of natural resources, especially the land. The abandonment of the feudal right to the natural resources, especially to land, was a prerequisite for entering a civil society, but this also meant the abandonment of a stable life for many, namely the farmers. The new life in the new society must assure the many a life that would not be worse than before. Although a few centuries have already passed, this principal contract between the civil society and its members still remains unfulfilled for many.

4 PAST ARGUMENTS

Taking account of the above viewpoints, we will now review the past arguments concerned with the question of the social balance between growth and welfare and of the directions of the present Welfare States. We will first briefly look at the social contract view and then see the Welfare State arguments.

4.1 *Social Contract Theory – Rawls*

John Rawls's social contract theory provides a useful clue for tackling the question of social balance in our society today. He tried to establish just distributive principles for a civil society (actually described as market economy society in his book). He regarded the distribution of social and economic products, including civil rights, as the basis for a society. By thus focusing on the distributive principles he succeeded to a great extent in presenting the basic framework of social structure. As today, when we face the question of the shift of a social paradigm, especially of the proper distributive balance between growth and welfare, such a bird's eye view provides us with a useful tool by which to start our analysis of the social framework for the Welfare State.

His idea is evaluated in two ways. First, his idea is above all useful because he has succeeded in providing a practical answer to how to deal with fundamental social structure. He focused on the two fundamental facets of society: productivity and distribution. This was his important contribution to the modern social analysis in the post-war years. However his idea had a serious flaw so, secondly, we must evaluate how he has not succeeded in providing a sufficient answer as to how to construct the agreeable distributive rule. The fatal shortcoming in his theory is his supposition of the 'veil of ignorance'. He came to this conclusion in trying to solve the question of unanimous consent. For him a distributive rule that is stable enough should be reached unanimously among the social members. The most basic rule, he reasoned, must be agreed by the members and it can only be realized in this way. The rule that is chosen separately from anyone's particular interest is fair and just, and so is kept by everyone, he concluded. But this way of reasoning was wrong, because it demanded an impossible thinking for each member to discard his/her own characteristics. No one is living in such an imaginative world. We have our own interest according to our particular characteristics; where and from whom we are born, what endowment we have, etc. Unanimous consent is an impossible condition. We should abandon such a notion and start from our actual, concrete conditions.

When we choose this way of concrete analysis about distributive rules, the question becomes more complicated but it becomes more realistic. We can judge if the present rule is a stable one or not by analysing the judgment of the actual people. In thinking about this question, what is important is our group-orientation. In our actual life we need to focus on the opinions of social groups, of race, sex, income etc., instead of separated individuals as in Rawls's method. Rule making or law making is often the result of group conflicts rather than conflicts among countless numbers of individuals. Secondly, we are living in an age when conflicts are settled by democratic discussions, not violence. So, what kind of distributive rules would they choose to have in such a condition?

The precise answer is left to each society but a common tendency is observed: first, the tendency toward collective use of natural resources and secondly the tendency toward 'distribution toward equality of certain degree'. Natural resources have come to be used more collectively because of and for the purpose of the growth of productivity; for example, large-scale production demands collective use of land, air and fossil fuels. We cannot escape from this collective use of them. Secondly, more equal distribution than in the feudal age is more probable than 'toward larger inequality'. It can be so argued because of three reasons: self-interest, fairness and human fellowship. Self-interest: the growth of productivity is an inevitable by-product of human life and it unavoidably accompanies the growth of division of labour. This means we have to depend on the work incentive of other people in order to improve our own life. Thus self-interest necessitates our support of other people. Social welfare is also supported by self-interest in an age of higher mobility of jobs or houses. Fairness: self-interest in a democratic age also demands fair distribution of products and this leads to the rule of distribution according to contribution. Distribution according to the ownership of productive resources will come to play a smaller role as a means of product distribution. Human fellowship: the growth of division of labour and contact among human beings nourishes close feeling among them and this leads to their stronger support to social welfare. Global scale problems such as ecology and nuclear weapons also nourish this fellow feeling among people. The significance of the drive for income difference produced by market mechanism must be contrasted with these factors.

In critically developing the Rawlsian type theory, we need to address one more question in his theory. As we saw above, the purposive question is always the basis of social analysis. How we regard human nature affects the whole theoretical structure. In his analysis he tried to replace the past human model of the self-interested person, which had long been supposed by traditional economic thought since Adam Smith, by a new human model with self-interest (indifference to others) and human fellowship. He tried to depict the probable social contract on this two-step assumption. He assumed the 'veil of ignorance' and concluded the two principles of distribution (usually known as difference principle). But he did not succeed in this new experiment. His major supposition about human nature – the presumption of indifference in the original position and allowing it to be revised if it would contradict the other half of human nature, which is human fellowship – made his theory inconsistent. Rawls first ignores human fellowship but there is no assurance that the later introduction of this condition can really revise the already reached agreement. If he is to value human fellowship, he has to start with the two human natures from the very beginning. To correct this inconsistency, we have to assume the co-existence of both self-interest and human fellowship from the beginning of our reasoning.

This assumption of a mixed human nature of both partly self-interested and partly sympathetic should be our starting point. This way of analysis will require a two-tier distributive method in a sequence; equitable distribution among the co-workers first and then distribution based on human fellowship.

11

In Chapter 2 we will address this analytical framework.

4.2 *Welfare State Theory*

Arguments concerned with the Welfare State are more closely related to the question of social balance such as between investment and consumption, or growth and redistribution. It is directly related to the composition of government expenditures and to labour's share in the national income. Combined together, this choice of balance determines the content of a society or a nation, and who prospers and who perishes there.

An OECD report (1981) shows how this question of social balance came to the fore and how the viewpoint toward the Welfare State changed over the 1970s. The report understood the difficult economic situation in the 1970s as the result of the excessive growth of the Welfare State. It argued against the increased wages in the 1970s and for the necessity of restraining it and securing profit for the firms. It clearly stated that the measures to achieve social objectives should not undermine the economic system that produced its means (p. 9). Another OECD report (1983) pointed out the necessity of realizing proper profit by adjusting wages. It argued that if the basic productivity and employment conditions should change drastically, as in the 1970s, high and rigid wage rates would become a cause of high unemployment, and that in the times when major social conditions changed, what would be necessary is an adjustment in real wages elastic enough so that a proper profit rate could be obtained for maintaining recovery and investment for employment (p. 144). It argued that behind the high unemployment rate was a high standard of social security and it must be restrained. The report said that unemployment benefit should be at the level that was socially agreed upon, and generous right to it often raised expectations for higher wages and would be a factor to reduce the incentives for the beneficiaries to actively look for jobs (op. cit., p. 94).

Heclo (1990) and Block (1987) pointed out that facing the hardship of the 1970s the public in general were not ready to present alternative ideas for the social balance owing to the over-dependence on the privileged postwar years. Heclo tried to understand the problem by setting it in a historical perspective. He divided the development of the Welfare States into four stages: experimentation of the 1870s to 1920s, consolidation of the 1930s to 1940s, expansion of the 1950s to 1960s, and reformulation of the 1970s and after. The experimentation period is characterized as the time for dispensations for the deserving poor and when social insurance was invented; consolidation was characterized by integration of social expenditures with demand policy, consensus on postwar reconstruction and risks shared by all citizens; expansion was a period when growth acted as the solvent of economic trade-offs; and reformulation in a period of recession and inflation was characterized by ad-hoc attempts to subordinate social policy to a new situation (pp. 386-7). He argued that the rapid and unexpected postwar economic growth made possible the growth of the Welfare State and this fact made people think that the Welfare State depended on economic growth and a luxury allowed by it (p. 403). This indication of unconscious imprinting in the growth era may explain much of the absence of new ideas in the past two decades. Economic growth can surely become a source for welfare spending, but it does not logically mean that the former is a prerequisite for the latter. But in an age when abundant resources seemed to provide almost every answer to welfare demand, this misinterpretation naturally suggested itself to society's mind. Having been used to this economy-and-welfare growth pattern, it is understandable why the people were late in coping with this new situation. Thus, Block argues, 'In a time of affluence, they [advocates of welfare expansion] were willing to argue that the society could afford some reduced efficiency as a means to greater justice. As the economy became increasingly troubled, this argument was no longer viable. But no argument emerged to fill the gap' (p. 155).

Mishra (1986) presented a typological analysis of the Welfare State and argued that the Welfare State would evolve into a corporatist type. He showed two types of Welfare State, pluralist and corporatist. The pluralist type is characterized by economic regulation from the demand side, autonomous social welfare, and a polity of interest group pluralism (p. 28). The corporatist type is characterized by regulation from the demand and supply side, interrelated policy of the social and economic, and a polity of centralized pluralism. He also showed another criteria for classifying the Welfare States, which was for which part the government was responsible: full employment, universal service, or relief of the poor. He concluded that the corporatist model of the Welfare State 'possesses distinct advantages over the PWS [pluralist Welfare State] and that it may well represent the next stage in the evolution of welfare capitalism' (p. 31). Such a prospect had been based upon the good economic performances of such countries as Sweden in the 1980s. Although we cannot argue today for its dominance as optimistically as he did, such classification and comparison among the Welfare States have produced many useful insights.

George and Wilding's analysis of ideologies of social welfare (1985) contributed much to the understanding and sorting out of the ideas behind opinions about the Welfare State (George, Peter, 1985, p. 33). What this book contributed to the Welfare State arguments was its provision of a map of the battlefield where attitudes to social welfare are presented, closely connected to the overall ideological views of a society. They have depicted this map so clearly that it has convinced people of the usefulness of understanding ideologies in dealing with the Welfare State problems. Ideology consists of a few basic values and subsequent ideas that flow up to the surface of a society

13

or the actual policies.[7] Ideologies do contain some overlapping ideas. When we locate the conflicting ideas about social welfare, except for the basic few fundamentals, these ideas can be discussed, evaluated, and settled in concrete terms. Once we come up to the overlapping concrete questions, such as whether larger government budgets increase unemployment or not, we can argue about them in positive terms. And even when the fundamental ideas are at issue, if we succeed in showing them and their respective consequences clearly, we can settle the conflict by democracy, by the majority choice.

Apart from various differences about the basic ideas about society, the focus of the question today is being converged into the relationship and trade-off between economic growth and welfare provisions. Whatever social ideas we might have, we judge societies by their overall outcome, the overall satisfaction we get from them. Thus, when we think about this trade-off question, our interest is directed toward the aggregate effects of various Welfare States. When we have gone through this task, we can choose and vote for our preferred Welfare State.

In discussing the usefulness of ideological analysis, we should heed the point that in recognizing and creating the social images that correspond to the various types of Welfare State, we should not pay too much attention to economic figures so as to obscure the ultimate criterion, our overall satisfaction. One important viewpoint from which to look at the Welfare State issue is the balance between production and consumption, welfare provisions being part of the latter. Although it is actually a matter of shifting tangible resources between the two, we should pay due attention to the shift of overall satisfaction as its result. Increase in aggregate goods could sometimes mean reduced satisfaction for a society through a particular distribution. Especially is this so when a large group of people are losing their say as reflected by labour's decreasing power caused by the anti-labour policies in reaction to the 1970s – the understanding and measurement of society's satisfaction become difficult, because its voices is not heard effectively.

We can assume, first, that different types of Welfare State could meet the problems differently, secondly, that we should create the total image of a society to consider social welfare and the Welfare State, and thirdly that the intangible factor of satisfaction should be taken into account in comparing various types of Welfare State. We have to analyse the actual societies and various combinations of resources to economic growth and social welfare to

---

[7] The bottom layer of ideology may be described as aims of our life. Barr interprets ideology as the choice of aims. As he says, when we confine our argument to social matters, the most important issue about aims would be the trade-off between social justice and economic efficiency (Barr, 1998, p. 98).

choose among different types of societies.[8]

Among the relations between social welfare and economy, that between government deficit and higher interest rate was one of the widely discussed issues concerning state expenditure. Focusing on US society, faced with neo-conservative criticism of the federal budget and welfare expenditures' negative effects on economic growth, Block (1987) also examined various cause-effect relationships. As for the relationship between government deficit and productivity, Block quoted and criticized the US 1984 report of the White House Conference on Productivity. The report said, 'Further increases in government borrowing relative to the supply of funds will add to the upward pressure on already high interest rates. Higher interest rates "crowd-out" private investments that would add to the productive capacity of the economy' (White House Conference on Productivity: 1984, Report on Productivity Growth, p. 19). He disagreed with this reasoning and argued about the importance of output level: '... productivity gains are strongest when output is rising fastest'; 'Instead of the "realist" remedy of limiting government spending in the hope that private investment would increase, an expansion of social welfare spending would strengthen purchasing power among working people and the poor, which could contribute to faster growth and more rapid gains in measured productivity growth' (p. 127). Under certain conditions when inflation is not probable this argument can hold true, and particularly so when the economy suffers from excess capacity and a shortage of purchasing power. And this was the case, he argues, in the 1981-82 recession. He referred to the effect of deficit spending in the 1980s US economy and agreed that the Reagan administration's deficits were extremely effective in pulling the economy out of the 1981-82 recession (p. 136). Thirdly, the relationship between productivity and employee security was addressed. Even the Conference on Productivity admitted, 'There is a close connection between productivity improvement and employee security' (pp. 151-2). These arguments suggest that we have to be careful in discussing the positive and negative effects of government spending.

He also suggested the sustainability of a high tax and high growth economy: '... the evidence ... is overwhelming; many European nations have prospered with much higher tax rates, and even Japan had a far more progressive tax system than the United States'. However, this argument seems less convincing as a general remark in the new situation of the 1990s when these countries suffered lower growth rates. Concerning this point, he referred to the strong influence of international competitiveness and the effect of low wages. First, the influence of globalization was mentioned that

---

[8] An early work of which was that of George and Wilding (1984) about UK society. They introduced and emphasized two points in this regard, the positive effect of social welfare to economic growth such as that of education and training and the negative effect such as that of wage rises to lower profit.

it has become one of the major forces against the Welfare States: '... when faced with intense competition from Japan and from a wide variety of low-wage countries, the United States has little choice but to accept a reduction in living standards – in order to be able to compete effectively. Of all the arguments against the Welfare State, this one is probably the most potent'. But he also argued that the effect of wage factors should not be exaggerated. In this argument he paid attention to the limited effect of wages and the growing effect of the service sector: 'The debate about international trade is still carried on as though goods production were the entire economy and as though the major determinant of the international competitiveness of a country's goods were the direct (wages) and indirect (government social programs) costs of labor.' 'The presumption is widely shared that those countries that do best in lowering wages and public provision will do best in international trade. Neither of these assumptions has much to do with reality. First, success in international trade has very little to do with the price of labor; second, the growing centrality of services in modern economies renders much of the goods-based analysis obsolete' (p. 139). But this argument about service sector and wage and welfare burden must be considered carefully. As for wage and welfare burdens on firms, although it is wrong to deal with them as though they were the only factors to affect the competitiveness of firms in a country, they are nevertheless still important factors. As for the weight of the service sector, it is right that its growth should be paid more attention to when we deal with the competitiveness of a whole country's economy. And it will also be true that we have to pay due attention to wage cost in this sector as its cost structure is more dependent on wages.

As for the actual effects of the anti-Welfare State policies, Klein and O'Higgins (1988) argued that the Welfare State had survived through the 1980s because of the popular support from the middle class: 'Despite the political rhetoric of rollback and the extent of economic disruption, the attack on social policies has, in most countries, been largely blunted.' 'It is precisely because the middle classes benefit from so many of the welfare programs that ... their political base [was] wider than anticipated by governments of the Right' (p. 204). '... the Thatcher administrations have failed in the light of their original intentions. Real public spending has grown by an average of between 1.5 percent and 1 percent annually since ... 1979' (p. 215). 'These failures accurately reflect the government's inability to maintain popular support for reductions in social responsibility' (p. 216). Rather, they argue, we should pay attention to the shift of the burden among groups. The right wing government succeeded in this: 'Although conservative administrations have generally been unsuccessful in effecting major cuts in social programs, they have been ... successful in shifting the burden ... onto lower income-groups' (p. 207). As we observe the widening cleavage of income and stability between the rich and poor in the following years, we have now a serious problem arising from this trend: a disintegrating society.

Esping-Andersen (1990) argued for the coexistence of different types of Welfare State, focusing on the class coalitions and their influences on the development of the Welfare States. He followed the Mishra-type approach that considered employment, wages and overall macro-economic steering as its integral components in the Welfare State complex: 'The leading theme in our account ... is that the history of political class coalitions is the most decisive cause of Welfare State variations' (p. 1); '... Welfare States are not all of one type' (p. 3); 'Sweden, Germany, and the United States may very well be heading towards three diverse "post-industrial" welfare-capitalist models' (p. 229).[9] This view is useful when we observe the possible diversity among the countries. But when we consider the growing trend in economic globalization we should also pay attention to the converging side of the problem, too.

Ginsburg (1992), through his comparative study that dealt with welfare provisions of Sweden, Germany, the US and the UK, characterized Sweden as a social democratic Welfare State, Germany a Welfare State in the social market economy, the US a Welfare State in the corporate market economy, and the UK a liberal collectivist Welfare State. He characterized the US, FRG and Sweden in line with Esping-Andersen, and the UK as a hybrid (p. 28). As for the effects of the neo-liberalist policies, he argued like Klein and O'Higgins that liberal collectivism survived through the 1980s: '... since 1979 ... the Thatcherites attempted with some success to move towards a more centralized version of the US Welfare State with more or less publicly regulated private welfare provisions'; '... despite the significant shifts in such directions under Thatcherism, it can still be argued that important elements of Liberal Collectivism have survived' (p. 190). But he also added that it was not likely that the Welfare States today go back to the postwar-type strong regime: 'The future of all four of the Welfare States examined here, viewed from 1991, looks increasingly uncertain. There seems little likelihood of a return to the political and economic conditions which sustained the post-war expansion of the Welfare State' (p. 194). As we consider in the following chapters, this posture has become the mainstream in the 1990s even among the social democrat governments. Among them the

---

[9] Concerning the typology of welfare state, Ninomiya (1997) pointed out the significance of the number of earners in families. He argued that whether a country is a one-income or a two-income type affected the type of the Welfare State. This factor is deeply connected with the long, traditional cultural style of a society. The former type includes Germany, the UK, and France, and the latter, Sweden or Denmark. He sums up that in the latter type, 'traditional communal works as family or regional nursery to old age care become impossible' and 'a systematized social service becomes necessary to secure them' (p. 77).

UK Welfare State is even sometimes regarded as approaching the US-type one.

As the two extreme types of economic performance appeared on both sides of the Atlantic, one focus of the Welfare State arguments was directed to the evaluation of them. Deborah Mitchell (1992) pointed out the growing inequality in the US-type Welfare State. She examined the differences among the Welfare States in the 1980s' difficult conditions and argued that although inequality in market incomes increased in all of the quoted countries around 1980 and 1985 – Australia, Canada, the Federal Republic of Germany, the Netherlands, Sweden, the United Kingdom and the United States – the US leads the others in the income inequality, with its Gini coefficient for disposable income from 0.317 to 0.328, while the UK was rapidly catching up with it, from 0.266 to 0.304 (p. 76). But she also argued that at this stage the UK was not actually very close to the US yet: 'While there is some evidence that the United Kingdom is moving away from policy outcomes akin to the continental European countries, it is not sufficient at this stage to place it in the same group as the United States. Although income inequality clearly increased in the United Kingdom during the 1980s, the Welfare State appears to have continued to act as an effective "safety net" at the lower end of the income distribution' (p. 89).

The effect of large cultural changes, globalization for one, on the Welfare State is being addressed. In an effort to understand the fundamental social changes generated by this trend, Giddens (1994), in line with Ulrich Beck, discussed the Welfare State issue from the viewpoint of 'reflexive modernization' (p. 80). It is meant to be modernization in which every member of the world mutually influences each other as, for example, through an 'instantaneous global communication' system. It is 'a world of intensified social reflexivity' in which 'Globalization means much more than the internationalizing of economic competition' but also 'detraditionalizing in everyday social activity', and 'an acceleration of the reflexivity of lay populations'. Thus he challenged the traditional presumptions of our way of thinking, including the traditional suppositions for the Welfare State. He argued, 'Keynesianism ... presumes a citizenry with more stable lifestyle habits than are characteristic of a globalized universe of high reflexivity' (p. 42), and globalization was changing the conditions of the background people of the Welfare States in which the concept of collective class had changed into individual, isolated classes.

Class, one of the most important building blocks of the postwar Welfare State is thus regarded as a changeable factor: 'Class used to be connected to communal experience and action in several ways ... regional division ... common occupational experience'. 'Many such traditional communities, particularly working-class communities, have become broken up. New modes of regionalization, the result of globalized stratification divisions, rarely produce the same class solidarities'. 'Class for the most part is no longer experienced as class. ... Class becomes individualized and expressed through the individual's "biography"; it is experienced less and less as collective fate' (p. 143).[10] And he would rather respond to the problem by proposing a new type Welfare State, a 'social investment state' (1998, p. 117) that would invest vigorously into 'positive welfare' for 'wealth creation', into which the old type 'economic maintenance' Welfare State would change. A classless, but positive and wealth-creating new state is thus being proposed. Although whether the traditional class solidarity would again recover its power is yet to be seen, this 'third way' idea is actively being pursued under the new Labour Party in the UK.[11]

In line with the interest of Mitchell, Fitoussi (1996) paid attention to the difference in job and wage conditions between the US and Europe. Although the positive relationship between smaller government spending on the one hand and higher growth rate and lower unemployment rate on the other had been widely discussed, she pointed out that the real question was between two types of poverty, and by this criterion the US-type Welfare State had not proved itself advantageous over European style ones. First she pointed out the converging trend to lower wages and working conditions: 'In particular, the fiercest challenge comes from those economies characterized by low labor cost and poor social protection mechanisms. Given the fact that capital and technology can be transferred fairly easily, the only effective competition seems to take place in labor markets. Hence, Western economies need greater labor market flexibility and this in turn implies a reduction, (if not the complete removal, of the artificial) imperfections that hamper its free and efficient functioning. ... The conclusion seems straightforward: society at large could keep its level of affluence (and full employment could be reached) if workers could be forced to accept lower paid and more precarious jobs' (pp. 330-31).

Then she argued that the US type's 'success' was really not a success, compared to European type: 'Apparently, each side of the Atlantic has chosen different ways to cope with a common problem. On the one hand, Europe ... has been experiencing a positive trend of unemployment growth for the last twenty years ... And this difference could be traced to Europe's

---

[10] Beck's view (*The Risk Society*, 1992, originally 1986), although he too argued about reflexive modernization, looked at the problem from a somewhat different perspective. He had more of an ecological point of view, focusing on the impact of technological progress that is about to bring both nationwide and worldwide disastrous risks, and thus he hoped for an emergence of new politics rather than traditional welfare states. This emphasis on parting from old politics has similar resonance with Giddens' view.

[11] Whether 'Trade union membership has gone up for the first time in 19 years' (TUC General Secretary John Monks, *The Guardian*, 11, September, 1999) means the resurgence of labour power is yet to be seen.

inability to abandon its highly ideologies [sic] view of the Welfare State'. 'However, it would be too hasty to conclude from this that the American way is painless or even necessarily successful. ... [In the US] during the last twenty years, the cost of unskilled workers has decreased in real terms by something like 30% relative to the cost of skilled workers while in Europe, an opposite trend has been observed. ... The real trade-off is not between unemployment and somewhat lower wages for the unskilled: instead, it is between two kinds of poverty, one arising from unemployment, the other arising from insufficient wage' (p. 331). Denying both types as ideal, she referred to the German and Japanese-type Welfare State as the models to achieve both economic success and social cohesion: 'Among the most developed countries, Germany and Japan are the ones that have suffered less from unemployment or poverty. They are also economies with a highly compressed income distribution' (p. 338).[12] This last comment, however, does not hold true for Japan in the 1990s. Her economic performance has been poor for the past decade.

Rhodes (1996) also thought much of social cohesion. He addressed the necessity for securing time to realize it. He argued 'reform and adaptation to the global economy is contingent on the ability of each to invest in new technologies ahead of their competitors' (pp. 311-2). This is true both for entrepreneurs and the employed: '... if social standards are driven down in western countries, and if industries are not given time to adjust, then more militant pro-protectionist movements and legitimacy problems will emerge' (p. 323). This question may overlap with the sovereignty question referred to before. Under the overwhelming economic changes, sovereignty or adjusting time seems to be being neglected. While this legitimacy question is being raised at the individual level and people come to feel that their lives are driven by a mysterious but irresistible economic power, they might not only become protectionist but also even fall into disruptive behaviours.

The strength of the globalizing trend has also been referred to in the highly advanced Welfare States such as Sweden. Olsson Hort (1997) discussed the critical change in Swedish welfare policy in the early 1990s that produced an unprecedented high unemployment rate: 'Full employment has been the over-riding objective in Sweden and at least up to the early 1990s the government seemed to unfailingly adhere to it.' However, with 'the deep recession of the first half of the 1990s, unemployment increased to levels hitherto unknown since the 1930s. Such a dramatic development in a few years' time poses a challenge to the idea of the Welfare State. In the early 1990s, Sweden reached a point where the welfare system – except

---

[12] 'Growing disparities in income and consequences of the globalization of national economies are now being addressed by various scholars who point to the success of capitalism of a non-Anglo-Saxon tradition capitalism' (Misztal, 1996, p. 223).

20

unemployment insurance – stopped growing. It remains to be seen if this is just a temporary break or the beginning of a new retrenchment trend' (p. 334). As for EU, the situation seems to be similar. Tezuka (1996) pointed out that the growing competitiveness among the nations was working against the regional integration of the EU. He discussed the reluctant attitudes of governments toward equalizing labour conditions, in spite of the EU's original aim of integration, for fear of losing their advantageous position through lower wages (p. 272).

Pierson (1998) described the current arguments on the Welfare State today as follows: 'We are told that, in anything like its traditional form, the Welfare State cannot survive. But, as yet, the workable alternatives are quite unclear' (p. 1). He comments on some prominent arguments, such as: 'the Welfare State is incompatible with a healthy market-based economy', the postwar period was only an exception (p. 3); 'the processes of globalization … have undermined the circumstances for the promotion of national Welfare States. ... The Keynesian Welfare State is incompatible with this new international political economy'; 'The post-war Welfare State represented a "historic compromise" between the powers/interests of capital and organized labour. That "compromise" has now broken down'; 'The development of Welfare State has transformed the class structure of advanced capitalism … to undermine the class basis for its own continuation. Most significantly, these changes undermine that alliance between middle and working classes … upon which the Welfare State was built' (p. 4); '… the expansion of consumer choice/affluence within Western industrialized economies engenders increasing dissatisfaction with state-administered welfare' (pp. 4-5). These arguments could be titled as 1) 'conflict with market' theory, 2) 'pressure of globalization' theory, 3) 'historic compromise' theory, 4) 'self-contradiction' theory, and 5) 'demand for higher quality' theory, which have been discussed in the arguments above.

Pierson also argues the serious impact of globalization: 'Facing the heightened international mobility of capital … competition to attract capital encourage governments to establish … flexible labour markets, low social costs and low taxation' (p. 64). In evaluating these arguments, he concluded that major questions about the future of the Welfare State are yet left unanswered: 'For many, the crisis was real enough, but is now passing. For others, the crisis looms in front of us, brought on by "irresistible" changes to the global economy or the "unmanageable" aging of the population. It is certainly true that many of the most difficult … decisions about welfare lie in the future … [and] have to be addressed anew' (p. 208). In foreseeing future development, he suggests possibilities for EU social policies. 'In the West European context, … whilst the pressures of globalization may be common, they call forth differing sorts of responses in the several regime types that Esping-Andersen and others have identified' (p. 181). 'Despite much talk of the "social dimension", evidence of an emergent "European Welfare State" is extremely scarce. If, however, we focus not upon positive enactment but upon the extent to which EU institutions have constrained the social policy autonomy of constituent states or the ways in which enactment in other policy fields have had a social policy effect, the role of the European Union will look much extensive.' 'European Court of Justice determinations have had a significant policy-making impact in areas such as working hours, equal pay, pension rights and parental leave' (p. 205).

In such a mixture of both pessimistic and optimistic arguments for the maintenance or growth of current Welfare States, the recognition that has become more common through the arguments of the 1990s is that the globalizing trend is inevitable, has been intensifying, and its effects must be seriously taken into account in examining the future of the Welfare State. One apparent influence of this trend on the Welfare State is that the larger costs of firms in one country compared to others will be thrown away. Facing this threat to the welfare fund, George and Miller et al. (1994) posed a challenging question on newly increasing demand for social welfare. They analysed British welfare demand conditions today and concluded that it would continue to increase because of a growing ageing population and single-parent families. As they argue, welfare demand arising from demographic and social change does seem to be inevitable in other countries, too. Although such welfare provisions as unemployment benefit could be largely cut by higher employment, their proportion is not necessarily large enough to offset the increase in such expenditures. Furthermore, if higher employment were only achieved by lower wages, the poor population would remain the same proportion and increase the welfare demand. Such a risk is looming large in the presently 'high employment' US or UK in the late 1990s. As such these phenomena also make the prospect of the future Welfare State still unclear. For the goal of devising the most desirable Welfare State one thing is for sure, that we do not yet have a single panacea Welfare State model to answer the various particular problems in different countries.[13]

Some Concluding Remarks for this Section

As seen above, major arguments about the Welfare States after the 1980s have included three topics; 1) typology of different groups of Welfare States,

---

[13] George and Miller et al. perceive the possible exit in the new idea of 'citizens' welfare state' which will be supported by the increased burden of the electorate. Chatterjee (1999) also regards the critical question today as lying in the willingness of people to accept higher tax rates. 'For the most part, the welfare state depends on the ability to transfer income from the middle and the working classes'. 'Without expanding the tax base, the only alternative is to reduce welfare state benefits' (p. 170).

2) the social and economic significance and impact of the Welfare State in society as a whole, and 3) the alternative designs of the Welfare State today. With the intensifying globalizing movement swiftly eroding the traditional Welfare State ideas and policies, the major task at present is to clarify the possible alternatives between growth and welfare. When it is done, then respective societies (countries) can choose the best-fit answer for their own priorities. To achieve this goal we need to answer such questions as what combinations of resource distributions to economic growth (profit and production) and social welfare (wages and welfare provisions, or consumption) will generate what kind of social conditions and possibilities, and among these alternatives to which one we would give our first priority. In considering the former question we will need to deal with the political possibilities under the pressures of economic globalization. Helped by the insights and suggestions shown in the arguments above, we will discuss these questions: what choices we have today and what choice we should take.

5   OUTLINE OF ARGUMENT

We'll explore these questions in the following chapters; 1) what combinations of resources to economic growth (higher profit and production) and social welfare (higher wages and welfare provisions, or consumption) will generate what kind of social conditions and possibilities, 2) among these alternatives which one we would like to choose – our will – and 3) what are the political possibilities achievable under such economic pressures as economic globalization. In addressing these questions, this book intends to clarify some of globalization's impact on the Welfare States and to discuss the alternative Welfare State. It will explain globalization's impact on tax and social contribution funds, on the ideas of political leaders, and on the people's spiritual welfare. It also aims to explain the inevitability of proceeding to an alternative Welfare State. Our deeper understanding of the problem and the necessity for this alternative way would be the first necessary step, and the major task of this book.

Chapter 2 – First we will see the basic structure of a society and the significance of the Welfare State; what makes up a society and a civil society and how the Welfare State has been formulated. We will start from the fundamental three virtues for a society: efficiency, equity, and human fellowship, and see how their balance is subject to erosion in a market mechanism. We will then see that in a market economy, these three virtues are re-established by the Welfare State.

Chapters 3 and 4 – Based on such an analytical framework of the Welfare State, we will then see the problems we are facing today. The Welfare States have different characteristics in each country and are unique in their respective structures. Although we can observe a converging trend for some characteristics, nation states are still the major playing fields for each nation's citizens. As such, the Welfare State will remain unique in its main features in different countries, and so we will need to study the respective cases to examine the present and future prospect of the Welfare States. Sweden and the US seem to be located at the two poles in the Welfare State spectrum. The UK, another typical Welfare State, and Japan, a newly developing Welfare State, seem to be experimenting between the two extremes and currently more or less seem to be approaching the US type. Even the Swedish type seems to be affected by the US type these days. But still there is a big difference between the two extremes and among the four. In looking at these countries together, we may be able to obtain an insight into the limits and effects and prospect of the US-led welfare reforms and economic globalization. First, we will look briefly at the formative process of the Welfare State in four countries, Sweden, the UK, Japan, and the US up to the 1970s. Then we will look at the 'setback' process of the Welfare States for the past two decades by following policy changes and their effects on the economy and social welfare in these four countries (Chapter 3). And then we will see the underlying views of the political leaders of these countries, by which we will be able to see that although they all share some fear about social disintegration, though with Sweden to a lesser extent, they are determined to proceed toward the 'competitive' US-type society (Chapter 4).

Chapters 5 and 6 – In contrast to the leaders' views, we will see here the different preferences for the prospective Welfare State in people's attitudes. We will examine their attitudes first explicitly by opinion polls and next by 'hidden preferences' in related social problems or pathological social phenomena (Chapter 5). Based on the understandings of the possibilities – namely a strong tendency towards a competitive Welfare State, and thus a lower burden state, contrasted with the conflicting desire of people for a higher security state – we will consider what solution we will have today. The possibility and inevitability of solving this question through the citizens' Welfare State is discussed (Chapter 6).

The conclusion of this chapter: With the 1970s as the first watershed, the Welfare State has entered an era when we have to seek a proper balance between economic efficiency and social welfare. In trying to answer this question various studies have been presented: on the typology of the Welfare States, on the social and economic impact of the Welfare State, and on the new designs of the Welfare State. This book will address these problems by studying the analytical framework for the Welfare State (Chapter 2), clarifying the setback processes of the Welfare States (Chapter 3), analysing the leaders' and writers' ideas on the prospective future of the Welfare State (Chapter 4), analysing the explicit and implicit will of the people (Chapter 5), and proposing an alternative Welfare State, a citizens' Welfare State, that can satisfy the people's will in the unfavourable economic and political conditions (Chapter 6).

2 Civil Society and the Welfare State

This chapter questions how the Welfare State problem should be studied.

1 CIVIL SOCIETY – Three virtues

We, in this book, regard a society as a 'socio-economy'. In general, a society includes several major spheres as cultural, political, economic, etc. 'Socio-economy' is a category to conceptualise a society as a two-tier structure; its first layer, the economic part and the second layer, the rest of the society, on top of it. Thus this word aims at showing whereby our attention is directed to a society. Although this synthetic word is not popular in ordinary social sciences, it is meant to be similar to Max Weber's dichotomy of culture and economy.[1]

The formation of a society is as the formation of cooperative relationship. The fundamental but most difficult task is the construction of this cooperative relationship among humans. The core of this relationship is the distribution of social goods or the advantages and disadvantages produced in a society. This relationship was once determined by violence in the past, but not in a modern society. In modern democratic societies it is decided through democracy, and the major distributive rules today are meritocracy and some distribution by need. These rules are not noticed or are often taken for granted when a society is in good condition. But they need to be addressed or improved when a society is in disturbance. Today is actually such an age when we need to review the fundamental building blocks of our society, the ways and rules of distribution such as between economic growth and social welfare.

In addressing this distributive question, we need to understand that human beings can secure their lives only by forming a society, and that three pillars are necessary for the continuance of a society in general: efficiency, equity, and human fellowship.

Efficiency: Efficiency in cooperative production is the first condition for a society. Efficiency here means economic productivity of the society as a whole. Humans need many goods to live by and can obtain them more readily by producing them together. This becomes the fundamental reason

---

[1] Cf. 'Die Protestantische Ethik und der »Geist« des Kapitalismus', 1904/05.

for the formation of a society. Thus in order for a society to be conceptualised, a certain level of efficiency is necessary that ensures more products for the members than when the members produce them in isolation. Division of labour is one of the best inventions for this purpose.

Equity: Secondly, a rule for distributing the products of this efficient production is necessary, which is called equity. It ensures that the produced goods are distributed in an agreeable manner to those who participated in the production. Equity is also necessary for the distribution of natural resources. Natural resources here include resources such as land, natural advantages, inheritance, etc. They are defined as those that are not the results of anyone's labour but distributed to a person by socially recognized rules. This question about natural resources has not been answered fully in our societies. Take land, for example. In one case land was distributed by the first-comers' claims, and in another it was redistributed equally. Today, some people own a piece of land but there is no established account for their right. The right to hereditary assets such as money or natural advantages is another example. These assets have usually been regarded as belonging to the descendants, but taxation on them is also widely accepted. Modern market economy society has not answered this question fully yet either.[2]

Equity in product distribution concerns the division of the products between the cooperating people, and particularly between the employer and employees today. As had been the case for a long time, the bargaining powers of these two groups of people tend to be more tilted toward the employer because of the disadvantaged position of the employee. It can often cause an unfair bargain. Thus, to correct it to the genuine fair bargaining conditions social supports for the employed from outside the market become necessary.

Human fellowship: Efficiency and equity were the main focuses of Rawls but he did not deal satisfactorily with a third factor, namely, human sentiment applied to distribution. To maintain a society we need a third criterion for distribution, human fellowship for those who are unable to work or earn enough. It is necessary because we are emotionally deeply connected with other people even if they are not fit for productive cooperation. Here, we will call this sentiment human fellowship. So this third factor, human fellowship, is necessary in a society. Through physical incapacity or merely a lack of opportunity, some people often lack their chances to participate in production. To support those needy people is a strong disposition of humans and so must be institutionalised in the social structure.

There seems to be a relationship between these virtues of a society, in that the fulfilment of equity helps human fellowship to be expressed fully.

---

[2] As Kotaro Suzumura argues, in a market economy society, 'Competitive mechanism itself does not have the function to correct the original conditions.' (Nikkei, 21, March, 1999).

This relationship is described as follows. Although humans belong to one species and potentially are sympathetic to each other, the latter sentiment can flourish in a larger number of people only when they form a society in a cooperative manner. This cooperation can be only maintained when the products are distributed in an equitable way. When it is so distributed, the participants come to understand and confirm their common character as humans and their fellowship comes to the fore. It is embedded in human nature, and is recognized and flourishes on the basis of equitable distribution. Thus, full equity helps human fellowship to be realized fully. As it is often difficult to confirm whether this major distribution of products in a market economy between management and labour is appropriate or not, human fellowship is at a disadvantage in this society from being fully realized at the individual level.

To incorporate these three virtues into the social structure is always the imperative and fundamental for a society. For imaginary convenience we may call it a tripod structure of a society. And one very significant character of this is that these three pillars, efficiency, equity, and human fellowship, as each supports the base of a society, must be in good proportion to each other. As efficiency grows, so must the other two virtues. When more goods are produced by higher efficiency, equitable distribution must keep up with it, and so distribution by human fellowship. As far as human beings are human fellows or members of one species rather than detached entities from each other, it is inherent in human nature, so it seems, to maintain a good balance. We can probably recognize its existence by observation, and also by studying historical progress from the age of slavery to civil society or from a laissez-faire survival market economy to a modern Welfare State.[3]

Some may say that equity and human fellowship are concepts that are usually related to values, and values are individual matters and not subject to be studied in social sciences. It is right that we should not arbitrarily press others to have the same views on values. But it is also right that for some values we have to make a consensus about how to institutionalise them, or else we cannot create a society. Thus, we need to consider these concepts, equity and human fellowship in order to establish the rules how to distribute social goods to the participants and the non-participants in production. As they regulate the allocation of socially produced goods, both political and economic, they are the most fundamental rules to determine our life prospect.

---

[3] In many religions, human fellowship is expressed as God's sacred teaching as 'neighbourly love' or 'mercy'. In a religious life, some human beings find the answers to the questions of life and death by the existence of God. Some of them might obey such orders of kindness in return for their expectation of eternal life. But apart from such religious behaviours, there seems to be an inherent disposition of human sympathy that gives birth to mutual help. It is observed in the fact that many people behave kindly to others even if they have not been taught religious orders.

So they are to be studied: what opinions are there, and which one is to become prevalent. By understanding and comparing different views, people can further revise or confirm their own. We can and have to reach some kind of consensus to carry on our society, although the chosen rule is not unanimously agreed. It is such values and ideas that have formed the basic framework and starting point of our societies. A society cannot exist or start without these values. Values cannot only be studied but must be studied. They stipulate the ways humans propose to create their relationships, the most important of which are the distributive relationships. The principles of private property, freedom to pursue one's own happiness or public welfare are all main categories of these relationships. Through the conflict among various individual and ambiguous ideas about values a socially chosen one emerges. These virtues become most influential when they are materialized into laws and institutions. As the legislative process affects the contents of laws, it is also important to secure the political rights and will of the people. When the realized rules truly reflect the virtues held by the people, people are ready to obey them.[4]

The pair of words more familiar in the discourse of social sciences than the three virtues introduced above are probably freedom and equality. In a political sense they are in the same dimension, freedom describing the range of action left to individuals and equality the equal right in forming the laws. The freedom to pursue one's own happiness is an important example of the former and also, to some extent, of the latter. Drawn from the feudal experience, this political freedom was emphasized in civil society. But almost any pursuit of happiness concerns tangible consumption goods except when it is obtained in the mind alone. Rules of distribution become necessary and so the concepts of the three virtues become useful, being able to deal with these problems. Thus we use the two concepts, equity and human fellowship, instead of equality to directly and concretely address the distributive question of a society.

Finding the best rules to materialize them and the best balance between them in a human society are difficult tasks. It is easily observed from the rise and fall of many rules in the history of civil society. Starting with democratic political rights in the early days of this society, and gradually proceeding to various economic rights in the following centuries, we may say that the whole structure of rules for these three virtues are still under construction. Our civil society started to construct such rules in its early days. It only started with the hints from the negative images learned from the feudal society. But the opposite of the negative images did not necessarily ensure

---

[4] As such, the legislative process is very important. As King and Waldron summarize, Rawls contends that a society is just if we can show that its institutions satisfy certain principles that people would have agreed to as basic terms of cooperation, had they been given the opportunity to decide (King and Waldron, 1988, p. 440).

sufficient answers, and even what was right and what was wrong in the old images has not been always clear. For example, as for the problem of inequality; even though many would easily agree that inequality of birth should be corrected, whether inequality from natural advantages or hereditary assets should be accepted or not still remains a difficult question.

Figure 2.1 Feudal society   **Figure 2.2 Civil society**

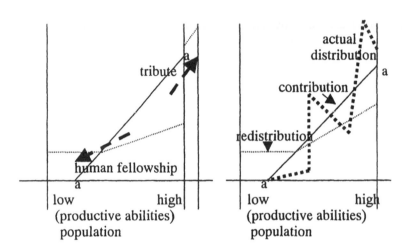

Line a–a shows the efficiency of the society – or the area between the solid line and the horizontal axis.

Equity, discussed only in civil society, is defined here by the extent of coincidence of the two lines, actual distribution (heavy dotted line) and contribution (solid line).

Human fellowship is shown by the redistributed amount from richer to poorer population.

To help obtain a clear image, we can draw the following picture. We assume that a person judges the desirability of society by having an overall social image. A person's satisfaction with social life is influenced first by efficiency, or the aggregate product of the society – how much it can produce – and second by his/her share of the product or equity and human fellowship. His/her share of burden will also be important. Efficiency, equity and human fellowship can be depicted by the above figure. Figure 2.1 shows feudal society and Figure 2.2, civil society. On the horizontal axis are placed the social members from left to right according to their productive abilities. The vertical axis shows the amount of their distributive and contributive shares. The lower ability people, some of whom are often unable to manage to produce by themselves the minimum amount of goods necessary, are positioned closer to the left end of the horizontal line. But it should be noted

30

that these abilities in Figure 2.2 are only those counted in a market mechanism. The lower ability person may be positioned higher in a different type of society. In this sense the higher ability or the rich people today are those with the abilities of 'better-fit-for market mechanism'.

Thus, efficiency of a society is shown by the sum of each member's produce. Equity can be understood to be the extent of coincidence of efficiency curve or the true contribution (before redistribution) and actual distribution curve. For example, in Figure 2.2, as the actual distribution curve does not coincide with the contribution curve shown by the solid straight line, equity is eroded by the extent of this discrepancy. Human fellowship is shown by the extent of transfer shown by the amount between the contribution curve (the solid line) and the redistribution curve (closely dotted line).

Figure 2.1 shows that in a feudal society a certain amount of produce is compulsorily transferred to the rulers and also an amount is transferred to the poorer members by human fellowship. Figure 2.2 shows that in a civil society the compulsive transfer to the rulers disappears but instead a new problem of difference between contribution and reward appears. It should also be noted that the differences in productive abilities owe much to the following two 'differences in birth' even in a civil society.

Table 2.1 Differences in birth

Feudal society	Civil society
Differences in	differences in
birth by rank	–
birth by family	birth by family
birth by ability	birth by ability

The shapes of these lines and the amount of areas are determined by the distributive rules the people adopt for their society. In a civil society, first their opinions differ whether they adopt market economy or planned economy, and second what type. For example, although many peoples live in market economies today, their content has changed a lot in the past centuries. Most of all, they have taken in some planned economy elements. In this sense Figure 2.2 only shows the general idea common to any civil society. The specific locations of these lines shift according to the socially reached consent in each particular society. Our question about the Welfare State concerns how the shapes and positions of these lines and areas should be and which combination would create the greatest happiness of the greatest number.

In many cases introductions and reforms of various rules and policies gradually form the overall framework of these virtues. Among the three virtues efficiency is a criterion that people can recognize relatively easily, such as by GDP figures, so that it tends to get excessive attention. Equity and human fellowship are not tangible and so are less addressed. These intangible virtues among human beings are relatively easily achieved within the smaller circle of close people, as in a kinship, but need to be fortified by social institutions as their contact spreads to a larger number of people, as from family to village people and to the nation, etc.

How to keep good balance between efficiency and equity and human fellowship, particularly to keep the first from overgrowth and the second from being neglected, is the major problem in a market economy. The basic balance we have chosen is contained in the expression of the predominance of public welfare over individual freedom. As economic efficiency is usually pursued in individual efforts for wealth creation, the social balance orders the balance of public welfare and individual freedom. Today, in most of market economies this predominance of public welfare is stipulated in the Constitutions.[5] But this is only a general rule and often fails to answer the daily conflicts.

An ideal society from the viewpoint of the three virtues would be realized by maximizing the total satisfaction from both total production (efficiency) on the one hand and equity and human fellowship in distribution of products on the other. The question lies in the fact that these virtues all need resources and thus are in trade-off relationship with each other. If we put much in productive goods, the consumptive goods to be divided will be smaller, at least in a short run. If we put much in consumption, the total products will be smaller, if not offset by some unexpected by-product such as productivity growth. If we put much in human fellowship – that is higher redistribution to the needy – it will be the same, too. And the difficult question is that even though the total amount of goods may become smaller, the total satisfaction of the society may become larger. If we pay attention to the differential characteristics of each country, we'll also need to take them into account, too.

Between equity and human fellowship the latter is more difficult to grasp. The category of equity is more manageable. Although we need to scale the contribution of each participant, it is basically a matter of judging if two concrete figures coincide. But the question of how much we are willing to spare for the needy is a matter of our heart and mind and more difficult to handle. Concerning this, we may say that the long-term trend of human fellowship is supposed to be increasing when it is measured by the ratio of

---

[5] For example, people should 'refrain from any abuse of these freedoms and rights and shall be responsible for utilizing them for the public welfare' (Japanese Constitution, Article 12). Freedoms of residence, movement and choice of occupations will be protected only 'to the extent that it does not interfere with the public welfare' (Article 22). 'Property rights shall be defined by law, in conformity with the public welfare' (Article 29).

welfare provisions to the total income of a society. Generally speaking, when productivity grows, we have two choices, either to curtail our working hours – thus to live by self-interest – or to work the same hours and distribute more to the needy – thus by human fellowship. The increasing share of welfare spending for the past half a century may suggest the latter trajectory (Figure 2.3).

Figure 2.3 Productivity and human fellowship

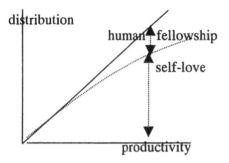

2 MARKET ECONOMY – Overwhelming competition

We have seen the fundamental structure of a society. We will now focus on the danger of exaggeration of the virtue of efficiency in a market economy. We will first start by looking at the classical view of Adam Smith on market mechanism and competition. We will then look at the views of Alfred Marshall and John M. Keynes. Following their views in a sequence, we will be able to see where they have found problems and remedies for the market economy.

Adam Smith showed both hope and caution about market mechanism. He recognized such sentiments as pity, compassion, sympathy or fellow feelings in human beings, but he felt that these were often insufficient and not strong enough to be the basis of a society. He thought that a warm sympathetic feeling of others was a supreme happiness for a human being, but he could not observe this capacity sufficiently belonging to everyone.[6] He then ceased to regard sympathy as the main keystone for a society and adopted justice as the main pillar for a civil society. Lack of sympathy or dominance of self-interest did not mean that a society could not be constructed, he thought. Justice in exchanging goods in a market mechanism would construct a functionable society; this was his prospect for the

---

[6] He pointed out in an imaginary example the indifference of an English citizen to the disaster of Chinese people in an earthquake.

emerging civil society. [7] If fair or equitable exchange of goods would prevail in the market, which was economic justice, it would enable the market mechanism to grow steadily. Then it would bring forth competition among the producers for price, which would not only generate increasing wealth for the advantaged but also be beneficial for the disadvantaged, who would enjoy abundant goods at lower prices, he reasoned. He thus expected that even if humans lacked enough sympathy or human fellowship, self-interest would eventually create happiness for everyone.

As for the safety mechanism preventing this society from displaying too much self-interest, he presented one condition – the notion of impartial spectator. He argued that the market behaviours had to be those that would be admitted by the impartial spectator, or the common sense of the ordinary people. He expected and believed that fair trade in a market economy would prevail and bring about affluence for everyone, but it was only with this assumption. If the competition became too harsh and unscrupulous, he thought the majority of people would not follow those extremes. His idea was right, but the problem was firstly that it was often difficult for the spectator to judge if the behaviour of competitors was excessive or wrong, and secondly that often the spectator's voice was small and powerless compared to the wealthier participants.

The problems grew. Firstly, however cheap the goods became, people needed money to buy them. But the fluctuating business cycles constantly created unemployment, thus the lack of purchasing power for the goods. Secondly, the majority of people were workers and not just content to be able to buy goods. They also had to be content in workplaces, but the constant pressure for the employers to compete with other producers compelled the latter to provide cheaper and miserable working conditions for the workers. The vague anxiety of Smith thus became true. It became clear that market mechanism brought demerits and had to be regulated by some force outside the market. These difficulties had to be addressed by the citizens or the workers themselves and so they did gradually for the following two centuries. [8]

The understanding of the market mechanism, its demerits and their remedies, gradually made progress. A century after Adam Smith, at the end of 19th century, having experienced the problems of business fluctuations and tenacious poverty problems and class structure, Alfred Marshall (1890)

---

[7] Smith, 1976A, Book II, Part II, Chap. 3.

[8] A strong supporter of market mechanism, F. Hayek supports market economy with a condition that improves the majority of human beings in the best way. He says that market economy 'was allowed to exist because it was expected to improve the needs of all or the majority of people' (1976, pp. 64-5). Hayek tried to prove its desirability by comparing it with a socialist economy. But after market economy has become the predominant economic system in the world today, the absolute merit of its functions is at issue and needs to be proved.

considered the merits and demerits of market economy but was reluctant to emphasize them. His view was still rather optimistic, similar to Smith, focusing on the positive side of the market economy. As his view still seems to reflect the majority opinion which sometimes preoccupies our thoughts today, it will be useful to look at it closely in order to understand this question.

He describes the merit of competition in a market economy in contrast with monopoly. When 'competition is arraigned, its anti-social forms are made prominent; and care is seldom taken to inquire whether there are not other forms of it, which are so essential to the maintenance of energy and spontaneity, that their cessation might probably be injurious on the balance to social well-being.' 'In many cases the "regulation of competition" is a misleading term, that veils the formation of a privileged class of producers, who often use their combined force to frustrate the attempts of an able man to rise from a lower class than their own' (p. 8).

He is conscious of the accusation that competition increases human selfishness, but hesitates to emphasize it. He refers to the possibility of an alternative, less selfish world, but remains cautious. 'No doubt men, even now, are capable of much more unselfish service than they generally render: and the supreme aim of the economist is to discover how this latent social asset can be developed most quickly, and turned to account most wisely. But he must not decry competition in general, without analysis: he is bound to retain a neutral attitude towards any particular manifestation of it until he is sure that, human nature being what it is, the restraint of competition would not be more anti-social in its working than the competition itself' (p. 9).

And he rather argues against a society that idealists wish for, 'Men would think only of their duties; and no one would desire to have a larger share of the comforts and luxuries of life than his neighbours. Strong producers could easily bear a touch of hardship; so they would wish that their weaker neighbours, while producing less should consume more. Happy in this thought, they would work for the general good with all the energy, the inventiveness, and the eager initiative that belonged to them; and mankind would be victorious in contests with nature at every turn' (p. 9). And just as Smith did, he also discards this idea as impractical against human nature. 'Such is the Golden Age to which poets and dreamers may look forward. But in the responsible conduct of affairs, it is worse than folly to ignore the imperfections which still cling to human nature' (p. 9).

Denying the possibility of putting human fellowship at the basis of a society, he goes further to say that the present-day market society has not worsened human nature or human behaviour after all. Instead, he argues that human ties have rather improved. 'In a modern society, the obligations of family kindness become more intense, though they are concentrated on a narrower area; and neighbours are put more nearly on the same footing with strangers. In ordinary dealings with both of them the standard of fairness and honesty is lower than in some of the dealings of a primitive people with their neighbours, but it is much higher than in their dealings with strangers. Thus it is the ties of neighbourhood alone that have been relaxed: the ties of family are in many ways stronger than before, family affection leads to much more self-sacrifice and devotion than it used to do' (p. 6). Such a statement is, as it is concerned with moral feelings, not easy to prove or refute, but it is also true that such judgement of social improvement does count much in judging the overall condition of a society. And after having been through the one hundred years since Marshall, this merit that he argued market mechanism had generated has not necessarily flourished yet. After all, he took the view that market economy was not creating the serious problem of disintegrating society, which is often repeated in today's arguments, especially in the views of conservative speakers.

Marshall's cautious words and protective attitude toward market and competition were challenged by J. M. Keynes in the 1920s even before the great depression. The affirmation Marshall gave to market mechanism was not acceptable to Keynes. To his eyes the darker side of market mechanism was what had to be addressed. 'If we have the welfare of giraffes in mind, how could we overlook the pain of the short-necked ones ... or the ugly greediness with its bare fighting instinct?' (1926, section 3, paragraph 6). After experiencing the 1930s Great Depression, Keynes's understanding and judgement became the spirit of the age. Not the merit but the demerit of market mechanism or laissez-faire capitalism became clear to everyone. If the harmonization of self-interest and common good was the fundamental purpose of civil society, the development of pure market mechanism up to the 1930s proved that it could not achieve this. What the historical process showed was that the spectator's restraint to the excesses of market mechanism and resulting miseries would not be realized within its own mechanism. It proved that if we were to follow Smith's advice, we had to realize it from outside the market mechanism.

Market mechanism allocates resources to the most profitable areas and thus achieves the maximum satisfaction with the given distribution of purchasing power. But it is all it can do. It does not question the original distribution of purchasing power, its equity or desirability. It functions best when price mechanism works fully. Competition is its engine. It can then work best to produce the demanded goods cheapest. It is so far the best mechanism to connect supply and demand, with the smallest effort for the largest result. But that is all it can do. It is an efficient machine but efficient as far as it presumes the given starting point and destination. After all, what counts is the overall condition of a society, which includes the entire structure of our lives. Market mechanism presumes given supply and demand. It does not concern itself with the spread of them. The spread of effective demand is the ultimate condition to determine our life and death. But in the long effort of civil society the rules to determine this spread properly is still under construction. We should not leave this task to the market mechanism that is rather biased toward competition and efficiency.

And this problem is created by the market mechanism itself. The urge of competition promotes efficiency (investment) more, and equity (profit-wage distribution) and human fellowship (social welfare) less. The remedy would not be sufficiently provided by the good intentions of individual entrepreneurs trapped in this mechanism, for every resource in the producers' hands is ordered to be invested for higher competitiveness, and less and less toward the employee and the needy. However good hearted an entrepreneur is, he/she would perish if he/she were generous. By lowering wages, paying less for the raw materials, often dismissing a large number of workers and moving his/her factories to lower wage and lower tax countries, he/she pursues his/her goal of maintaining his/her firm. This irresistible order of market creates conflict between profit and wages, rich and poor, productive goods and consumption goods, and supply and demand. Occasional individual charity does not solve the problems, including poverty. Once the entrepreneur has achieved success, he/she might think that 'now I can afford to contribute to the society. I will be beneficent.' But his good-hearted charity might be compensating only a part of the hardship he had created. This is ironical, but market mechanism with its competitive nature often makes this happen. It is not the outcome of any ill will of any entrepreneur, but the inevitable outcome of the system itself.[9] The root cause of this is the competitive ethos itself that is an indispensable part of market mechanism. If it is so, and if we cannot find any other better mechanism as the basic tool for production and distribution for our society at present, it is necessary to find a way to complement it.

In reference to human fellowship, when left alone, market mechanism can pursue the less redistributive society. How much we should change it to a highly redistributive society has been one of the major questions. What has to be borne in mind is that market mechanism and its competitive nature always threaten to override the other two virtues by preferring efficiency or economic competitiveness.[10]

---

[9] As Christian Bay expresses it, 'even if peoples in modern nations are harsh to the disadvantaged people in and outside their countries, it cannot be explained by the defect in "the plain humanity". Rather, the cause lies in the fact that in certain societies, human anxiety and motives are incorporated in a wrong manner' (Toronto University, 'Crisis and Future Prospect of Modern Society', 1984, p. 57). '… it encourages one to use its power solely for oneself. The capitalist system itself creates this behaviour … treats people not as ends, but as means" (Winter and Joslin, 1972, pp. 12-13, Tawney, 1923, p. 48).

[10] The negative effect of market mechanism seems to grow larger with the growth of productive power. When it keeps growing unreined, it could mean even the collapse of society

3 WELFARE STATE – Recovery of social balance

The Welfare State is the counter-measure to such a danger of the market economy. When we call it the welfare 'state' we usually already have a relatively clear image of both its ideological and institutional structure. It usually declares the public welfare of the people as the ultimate goal of state policies. It often has a clear objective of realizing and elevating the minimum welfare level for all citizens. It then enacts relevant laws and institutions to realize it: labour laws, various social welfare provisions, etc. But we should also note that this systematic structure is only the culmination of long term and diverse piecemeal efforts toward this goal. (We can see it in the chronology in Chapter 3.) Piecemeal counter-measures were proposed by the workers, the poor or their supporters and have gradually crystallized into the Welfare State, rescuing the most needy, restricting working conditions, giving the employed stronger bargaining power, and even creating jobs for the unemployed. The aims have been assisting the disadvantaged and regaining the social balance between the social, but rather economic virtue – efficiency – and the other two social virtues – equity and human fellowship.

As for human fellowship, state intervention is particularly necessary in a market economy because this economy, as mentioned before, often restrains the natural tendency from being expressed fully, especially in economic downturns. In a market economy the instability of life because of the frequent rise and fall of firms and jobs nurtures a tendency to earn and save for oneself, thus creating an obstacle to the full expression of natural human fellowship in an apparently contradictory affluent society. The general uncertainty of market transactions lies behind this anxiety and saving tendency. In the impersonal mechanism of market, what a social member can directly recognize is limited to the transactions before his/her eyes. The future and stability of one's market transaction – whether one's jobs will last or commodities produced will be sold tomorrow – is not at all certain. The Welfare State with the institutionalised redistribution of income becomes necessary to offset this unnatural fluctuation of human fellowship.

Thus we have today the Welfare State to effectively complement the shortcomings of a market economy. As Mishra (1990) says, the relationship between market economy and the state today lies in this complementarity. 'The capitalist market economy seeks to maximize efficiency and profit through competition', through which the economy becomes unequal and amoral. It also 'tends to be supernational'. The countervailing movement is gradually formed through the movement of the majority people for political right and economic security. It has been materialized in the state laws and

---

itself. 'If the bonds of community giving are broke ... the vacuum is filled with hostility and conflict' (Titmuss, *Commitment to Welfare*, 1968, p. 199).

policies. Thus the responsibility for correcting this trend today rests in the state. 'The political order is firmly rooted in the nation-state'. 'It may pursue such objectives such as social security, equity and environmental safety, which are of national concern.' 'Harmonizing economic and social objectives appears as a major task in all modern industrialized economies' (pp. 10-11). We are not sure if there will appear any other countervailing powers to market economy, but so far the Welfare State has been the most effective, and we cannot foresee any other better alternatives yet today.

Corresponding to the two major difficulties that market mechanism originally has, two major policies are necessary in the Welfare State: equalizing the bargaining power of labour (for equity) and creating a safety net for the needy (for human fellowship). Labour laws aim to secure the bargaining power of the employees in order to realize fair contracts. High employment policy also helps attain this goal by creating scarcity of labour and thus strengthening labour's bargaining power. This policy helps to realize the equity in distribution in Figure 2.2, thereby matching it to the line of distribution by contribution. Safety net was first established to save the worst-off people without job or money and has grown today to cover a larger number of people and a higher standard of living, though with significant difference in its levels among countries, as we will see in the comparison in Chapter 3.

One by-product of such policies of the Welfare State is its effect toward adjusting demand and supply. The redistribution of income among the rich and the poor functions to adjust the total demand and supply. As market mechanism has the tendency to overproduce by its 'addiction' toward investment for higher productivity under competitive pressures, this function is usually effective, and particularly when the gap widens in a depression period of a business cycle. We might say the relatively smooth economic growth in the post-war years owed much to this adjusting effect.

Figure 2.4 Welfare State and three virtues

resource distribution→product distribution 1→product distribution 2

(among the members)	(among the participants)	(to the needy)
equity	equity	human fellowship
↑	↑	↑
restriction on property rights	labour law, full employment policy	social welfare (income support, etc)

The relationships between the policies of the Welfare State and the two fundamental virtues of a tripod society are shown in Figure 2.4. Among the Welfare State policies the restriction on property rights counteracts the unfair starting point for individual efforts for market competition. It defines what advantage each citizen can obtain from natural and inherited resources. The rules for equitable and human fellowship distribution, realized by such policies as labour laws, full employment policy and social welfare policies assure citizens of larger fairness and stability in the insecure market life. As already mentioned, the first of them, equity in resource distribution, has been less addressed than the other two. Equity in resource distribution would provide, say, an equal amount of access to natural resources such as land, sea, etc for each social member, thus a fairer chance to succeed in a market society. Why this is still to be addressed may be because the present structure of ownership of natural resources is so closely connected to everyday reproduction, and a radical change may be feared to be destructive. But still this question will remain for a truly equitable civil society. After all, the Welfare State functions so that the favoured virtue of market mechanism, efficiency or increase in productivity, should be realized in a more harmonious way with the other two virtues of society.

Such are the fundamental tasks of the Welfare State. The goals are to fortify equity and human fellowship in a market economy. Based on this understanding of this structure, we need to proceed from these two virtues to the concept of 'security'. Although conceptually important, these two virtues are not ordinarily observed or recognized in our consciousness. These are so to say the underlying criteria for the purpose of recognition by reason. We can recognize their importance by reason but to apply them directly to our everyday life is not easy. The reactions we usually have in response to our social life are rather the emotional ones of 'being satisfied', 'anxious', 'optimistic', etc. The most relevant emotional category for the questions of equity and human fellowship seems to be the feeling of security. After all, the two categories, equity and human fellowship, can be described as the sub-targets for the ultimate goal of the security of human life. Affluence or efficiency is deemed important also by its possible contribution to this notion of security.

As our interest in equity and human fellowship is most keenly expressed when we feel our lives insecure, our first approach whether our society today, the Welfare State, is the best possible one or not should start from this question: how our lives are secured by the Welfare State today. As referred to above, this insecurity occurs in a market economy through the uncertainty of market transactions and its over-emphasis on competitiveness for survival. Security of jobs and incomes – including provision of social services – is the ordinary criterion people have for judging society today. Whether the Welfare State today ensures it to the citizens is the first focus of the question. When this question is fully analysed, we'll have the clue to how to approach the cause of the security problem – imperfectly realized equity and human fellowship – and how seriously we need to study them.

To consider this security question, we should note that we have two kinds of insecurity today. One is the traditional insecurity accompanying market mechanism, the above-mentioned uncertainty in the market transaction. Human life appears there as if it were an attendant to the price mechanism, not its master. Market mechanism is thus intrinsically discouraging for people in this sense. What the Welfare State can do against this fundamental problem is the provision of a safety net to ameliorate the resulting anxieties. The other is a new phenomenon, the reactionary resurgence of insecurity for the 1980s and 1990s. It is happening under the accelerated rise and fall of firms, their changing locations in the world, and inadequate welfare provisions for these trends. Thus we have today the traditional and modern insecurity, both being generated from the market mechanism, the former from its general layer and the latter from its modern upper layer.

The focus of this book will be on the effects of these two-tier competitive pressures and insecurity for the citizens in general today, especially under globalizing economic competition. There are four hypotheses to consider: first, market mechanism has intrinsic insecurity in its nature; secondly, the Welfare State has helped ameliorate this insecurity; thirdly, state policies after the 1970s and economic globalization in the 1980s and 1990s are aggravating this insecurity; and fourthly, the Welfare State must strengthen itself to meet this growing insecurity.

As most of the increase in the Welfare State provision means also an increase in resources for it, the fourth consideration will naturally lead to the question of how to increase the necessary fund to strengthen the Welfare State. As this shift of resources means the redistribution of income among the economic entities – firms, the employed, the needy, the rich etc – it poses the choice between larger redistribution and economic growth. When it is done through transferring resources from productive goods to consumer goods, it tends to decrease the rate of economic growth, or the pace of the increase of the aggregate goods produced and redistributed. One level of redistribution determines one level of economic growth. The choice among these combinations becomes the fundamental question for the Welfare State. Although we usually seek two goals, economic growth and redistribution together, the optimal satisfaction from them becomes an important social issue. To find this best mix becomes particularly important today when we cannot expect as high a growth as before, when it could realize both economic and welfare growth. The present fluctuation of politics between 'right' and 'left' in these two decades in many industrialized countries shows the difficulty of this question of understanding the possible alternatives and their own preferences in the changing conditions.

The dominant idea for the past two decades for the overall social balance has been that the Welfare State should be contracted and changed toward a more pro-firm, pro-production, and pro-'supply side' society. And we should consider this course of progress in the light of the above-mentioned analytical framework: the balance between efficiency and equity and human fellowship, competition and security, or economy and society. This welfare setback argument first occurred in the US and the UK, who had experienced severe stagnation in internal growth and external competitiveness, and also in better-off countries like Japan who enjoyed high competitiveness but whose public deficit had grown large. In the 1990s, as the previously socialist countries in the main joined the regime of market economy society, the rapidly growing world market grew still larger, making worldwide economic competition harsher. This has made the question of the Welfare State more difficult today. The countries that have taken the pro-firms, or pro-productive, high economic growth course, such as the US and the UK, are enjoying low unemployment on the one hand but suffering from enlarged income difference and weakening social ties on the other. As has been seen in the past arguments, the overall score sheet does not indicate a clear-cut answer as to which type of the Welfare States is superior.

As we will often deal with the balancing problem in terms of resource allocations toward growth or welfare, it will be useful to have a quantitative image of this question in the following way. The two figures below show the relations among the conflicting factors for resources. The basic formula is the same as in Figure 2.2. Here, welfare policies are represented by minimum income support, health care benefit, and pension benefit policies. We will first look at the welfare provisions in Figure 2.5.1, and then other public expenditures in Figure 2.5.2.

Figure 2.5.1
Welfare State in quantity (1)

Figure 2.5.2
Welfare State in quantity (2)

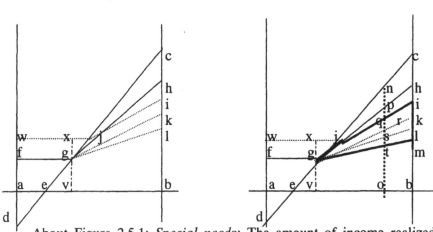

About Figure 2.5.1: *Special needs*: The amount of income realized through the market is shown by the area *ebc*. The area *ead* shows that the people from a to e do not only produce no goods but also need to consume special goods as shown here. *Minimum income* is secured by transferring *ghc* to *gdf*. *Health care benefit* is secured both by transferring *jih* to *jgfw* and through contribution *gkij*. It is supposed here that those from v to b pay the expenses for public medical care for themselves according to their earning abilities and most of them also for lower income people. *Public pension* is secured by *glk*. Here people from v to b pay the contribution also according to their earning abilities.

About Figure 2.5.2: Modern society needs expenditures for *other government activities* than social security, which amount is secured by *gml*. Here, to focus on the conflict in bearing the social burden between the firms and citizens, the taxpayers are classified in two groups: *ao*, indicating *individuals*, and *ob*, *firms*. Firms' original income was *obcn* and the final disposable income left for firms after taxes to invest is *obmt*, and similarly, disposable income for individuals, *otgfa*.

By these figures, we can confirm the idea that the qualitative question is focused on the welfare as redistribution and growth as the total production, as shown in Figure 2.5.2. The amount of *obmt* becomes the fund for a new investment, thus the source of economic growth. The proportion of the total consumption, *eon* (or *opjwa*), to the total productive goods, *obcn*, shows that of supply and demand. By changing the transferred amount and proportion, the economic circulation is influenced. These major trade-off questions and the sub trade-offs among the different welfare expenditures, such as between medical care and pensions, are still to be answered.

The major question about the resource allocation in the Welfare State today, for more welfare spending or for higher economic growth, is depicted by the balance between firms' burden, *tmcn*, and firms' profit, *obmt*, or the impact of this balance on the total production, *ebc*. The argument from the pro-growth supporters is, firstly, that the Welfare State had overgrown by the 1970s so that firms' profit had decreased beyond bearable limit, thereby weakening firms' activities and reducing the economic ground of the Welfare State. The logical conclusion then becomes one to restrict the quantity of welfare spending, re-balancing the society toward more growth. This is the first type of anti-welfare argument (welfare vs. growth theory). The second line of anti-welfare argument in the 1990s emerges as a measure to cope with economic globalization and the moving out problem, which argues for the reduction of firms' burden to retain firms within the country. This argument focuses not on the balance between welfare and growth but between welfare and competitiveness (welfare vs. competitiveness theory). These two arguments have different origins, but have the same effect, which is to retrench the traditional Welfare State.

Figure 2.6 shows the dynamic causal relationship between the socio-economic factors in the Welfare State and helps us have a clearer

Figure 2.6 Anti-welfare argument

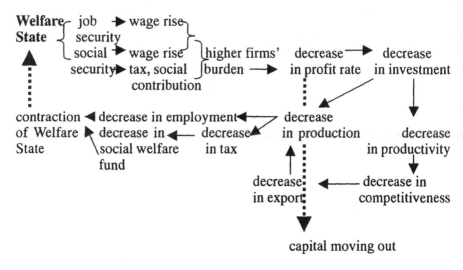

image of the question. In this figure, the welfare vs. growth theory emphasizes the negative effects of welfare provisions on firms' burdens, lower production and employment. The welfare vs. competitiveness theory emphasizes the negative effects on competitiveness and then on lower production and employment. Both aim at raising the profit rate, but the latter theory, setting the criterion on relative competitiveness, has no absolute theoretical limit. It could result in an endless tax-cutting competition among the countries. In this sense, the latter has the possibility of becoming a bigger threat to the social balance in the Welfare State.

Such a diagram helps us to gain an overview of the question about the Welfare State, but one important question remains, which cannot be shown in this figure. That is the question of the overall satisfaction of the citizens. As has been referred to, the difficult question is to know what choice will bring us how much satisfaction. This question is difficult because we have to compare the two kinds of satisfaction; one from the tangible factors such as income, goods and benefits, and the other from the intangible, such as redistribution, working conditions, safety of society, etc. To invent an accurate scale to make possible such calculation will probably be very difficult. But as hinted in Bentham,[11] a rough scale might be obtained more easily. We will be able to judge whether the society as a whole is heading for a 'right' or 'dangerous' direction just as our ancestors could when they chose to change the old feudalistic society. Even if it proves difficult to discern, small changes in individual leaves, it should be easier to see if the entire tree

---

[11] Bentham (1948).

is in good condition or not.

Although this task for the Welfare State is not easy, we will have to keep seeking and achieving the social balance, which seems to be deteriorating in today's market society. This is the basic understanding when we examine the present conditions and problems of the Welfare States. A society needs a balanced mixture of efficiency, equity, and human fellowship in order to exist in a stable manner. And a society based on a market economy needs a balance between competitiveness and security. The Welfare State is a countervailing measure to complement the often-weakened equity and human fellowship in a market economy. This task is complicated and difficult, but without it our market economy society will never work properly. Based on this analytical framework, in the following chapters we will see the growing power of market mechanism concerning economic policies in Chapter 3 and concerning ideologies in Chapter 4, then the people's reactions and responses to this trend in Chapter 5, and a feasible alternative to the present Welfare State in Chapter 6.

ADDITIONAL NOTE – Some presumptions

North vs. south: The argument in this book presumes that there will not occur significant redistribution between the northern and southern hemisphere as once occurred in the oil shock years.

Worldwide growth: A second problem about the background conditions of the Welfare State that we can foresee in the near future is the shortage of resources when we try to realize the present level of living standards for every country. As other countries catch up in productivity, there is no assurance of the present advanced countries being able to secure the amount of resources they get today. Serious economic competition might occur for scarce resources, which might well change the presumptions of the argument here.

Environmental restraint: The third problem is the limit posed by the environmental problems. The report of the United Nations Environment Programme, Global Environment Outlook 2000, warns of a serious environmental crisis in the near future. It argues that such a crisis can only be averted by reducing the consumption of natural resources by the minority, industrialized countries, to one tenth of what it consumes today. It even warns that time has already run out (BBC online network, September. 15, 1999).

We will discuss the questions above by assuming that the amount of available resources for the Welfare States will not change significantly in the near future. But in the longer run, as the developing countries catch up in education and productivity, the competition for scarce resources will be harsher. The limit imposed by the envronmental problems will add to this problem.

The conclusion of this chapter: We should study the Welfare State question by recognizing that 1) the Welfare State is also a type of civil society, which means that it must satisfy three virtues: efficiency, equity, and human fellowship; 2) the Welfare State has been a counterbalance to meet the defect of market mechanism, which tends to push the balance toward too much efficiency; and 3) the criterion for the justification of the Welfare State should rest on the proper balance between market and state, or growth and welfare.

3 Setback of the Welfare States – Sweden, UK, Japan, US

This chapter questions if the Welfare State has been in its setback since the 1970s.

In Chapters 3 and 4 we will see the shifting trend between growth and welfare in the market economy. In this chapter we will see how this process was attacked by the two movements: 'welfare vs. growth' and 'welfare vs. competitiveness' or globalization. In Chapter 4 we will see the ideas of government leaders and other arguments of both pro- and anti-Welfare State and pro- and anti-competitive state. By looking at the leaders' ideas we will be able to see that the present anti-welfare, pro-competitiveness trend will still continue for years to come.

In these chapters we will deal with the social balance problem by referring to the developing and contracting processes of the four Welfare States – Sweden, the UK, Japan, and the US. The US and Japan are at a similar level in the proportion of GDP allotted to social security benefit but Japan is placed before the US through having a universal health care system. Sweden and the US are supposed to be the two extreme types of the Welfare State. They are quite different in terms of the extent of social welfare provisions in the national economy and the underlying ethos for social welfare. The UK was also a leading Welfare State, but since the 1970s it seems to be changing into a hybrid of the Swedish and the US type. Japan was once regarded as a 'welfare pluralism'-type state (Gould, 1993).[1] Although it has also incorporated some of the European-type welfare system, as in health and pension areas, in a relatively short period of time from the 1960s to 1970s, now it also seems to be adjusting its system toward a more competition-oriented Welfare State, such as the UK. By dealing with these countries together we will be able to understand their conditions, problems and prospects better, especially between the two types of countries: the more market and competition-oriented ones such as the US, the UK and Japan and the more security-oriented one, Sweden.

---

[1] Gould (1993, pp. 8, 249) discussed 'Japanization of welfare state'. The force that had other countries look to Japan then was its competitiveness.

In this section we will look briefly at the development of the Welfare State up to the 1970s. In the post-war years until the 1970s in most of the industrialized countries, social welfare provisions improved and the number of beneficiaries increased; the amount of pension was increased, health insurance was introduced or strengthened and child benefit and family allowance were introduced. Accompanied by the growing contributions of the people in general in terms of higher income tax, social contributions, higher fees, or through higher consumption taxes, the total welfare system grew until the 1980s when this trend was halted and sometimes even reversed.

The origin of the Welfare State can be traced back to the very beginning of civil society, when the nation state had to provide the minimum public goods to maintain itself as a united country (Smith, 1776). Public goods are divided into pure public goods (defence, roads, etc) and quasi-public goods (education, medical care, etc.). They are divided by the criteria of non-rivalry and non-excludability. The pure public goods were necessary for public safety and economic efficiency of the overall society, and the quasi-public goods, for the purposes of national strength and also human fellowship. Social welfare policies were already partly introduced in industrialized countries before the 19th century to cope with the poverty problem. They developed in the 1930s' economic depression and the post-war years. In the 1930s, securing jobs for those who wished to work came to be recognized as an integral task of the government, too.[2] The success of Keynesian policy in the 1930s and two post-war decades incorporated a high employment policy in the Welfare State regime.

The development of social rights, from the realization and protection of civil rights such as the political right to vote to that of social rights as health care and pensions, shows the epochs of the development of social welfare in a broad sense (Marshall, 1963, pp. 70-4; Pierson, 1991, p. 23). In the 17th and 18th centuries, when modern nation states were established, people sought for liberation from oppression; hence it first led to the establishment of the rights of liberty, especially the security of the individual. In the late 19th century to 20th century, as the destabilising forces accompanying capitalism developed and became apparent, it became clear that the rights of liberty alone could not secure the lives of social members. Several palliatives

---

[2] The Welfare State has adopted the goal of full employment since the great depression in the 1930s. As Worswick says, employment is important not only in terms of income but also of self-respect or sense of attachment to the society: 'By Full employment, I mean a state of affairs in which everyone who wants to work, can'; 'Someone who is able and willing to work, but unable to find a job, is being denied a basic human right in a civil society' (Worswick, 1991, p. 4).

were introduced by poverty laws etc, but it was not until the 20th century that it was generally understood that the market economy must be complemented by state intervention in poverty and health problems. This new thought that the state should protect individuals' lives by restricting laissez-faire capitalism materialized in the Weimar Constitution in Germany in 1919. Although it admitted property rights and the individual's economic freedom, the necessity for restricting them for the public welfare was made explicit.[3]

The Universal Declaration of Human Rights in 1948 shows the general goals of social welfare in human society today. We should note that social security is not only important by itself but is also valued as a measure for human dignity. The right to work and social help in need are explicitly stated in Articles 23 and 25.[4]

Article 23: Everyone has the right to work ... to just and favourable conditions of work and to protection against unemployment.
Article 25: (1) Everyone has the right to a standard of living adequate for the health and well-being of himself and of his family ... and the right to security in the event of unemployment, sickness, disability, widowhood, old age or other lack of livelihood in circumstances beyond control.

National and international efforts are called for to realize these goals. But as stated in Article 22 as 'in accordance with the organization and resources of each State', the development of the related conditions of each state is supposed to be the major key.

Article 22: Everyone ... has the right to social security and is entitled to realization, through national effort and international cooperation in accordance with the organization and resources of each State, of the economic, social and cultural rights indispensable for his dignity and the free development of his personality.

These are human rights but become effective only when individual nations legislate laws and institutions to embody them. These principles

---

[3] This new thought spread among countries during the 1930s and after the Second World War. Its landmarks were the 1935 Social Security Act of the US, the 1938 Social Security Act of New Zealand, the 1942 Beveridge Report, ILO's *the Road to Social Security* of the same year, the 1944 Philadelphia Declaration, the Recommendations on Income Security and the Recommendations on Medical Security of the same year, the 1945 Preface of the UN Charter, Article 25 of the 1948 Universal Declaration of Human Rights, etc.
[4] ILO defines that 'Social security ... is the protection for the members provided by the society through public measures to meet the economic and social hardships caused by the cease or serious decrease of income' (website). Thus employment (and enough wages) and social assistance for the needy form the two major parts of this goal.

have been expressed first in the Constitutions of most of the industrialized countries and then in the respective laws for labour and social welfare to actually realize them.[5]

We can have a rough idea about when the respective parts of the Welfare State have been constructed in the four countries by looking at the years of introduction of minimum wage, health care, old age pension, etc (Table 3.1). Minimum wage is related to the bargaining scene in the labour market, with some labour laws deeply concerned with it, too. The other five items in Table 3.1 below are social security programmes run by taxation or insurance contribution. Table 3.1 shows the time difference between the first group (the UK, Sweden) and the second group (the US, Japan). Many of the landmarks for the first group occurred in the late 19th and early 20th centuries, while those of the second group are around the great depression in the 1930s and after the Second World War. Apart from the items listed in the table, full employment policy is also an important measure for the overall welfare of the society. This policy has developed in almost every industrialized nation after the 1930s depression. It is either publicly announced as in the 1946 Employment Act of the US or is pursued in practice without such an announcement. But as it seemed to push up wage levels and led to inflation in the 1960s and 1970s, it was gradually discarded as one of the first priority policies.

Table 3.1   Some landmarks in the development of the Welfare State

	Minimum wage	Health	Old age	Industrial accidents	Unemployment	Family allowance
Sweden	–	1891	1913	1918	1934	1947
UK	1909	1911	1908	1897	1911	1945
Japan	1959	1922	1941	1947	1947	1971
US	1938	1944[*]	1935	Each state	1935	–

[*] Old age health insurance is from 1956, and maternity from 1912.

Sources: Susumu Sato, *The System of Social Security Laws*, Pt. 1, p. 16. Jiten Kanko Iinkai, 1989, p. 720. Pierson, *Beyond the Welfare State*, 2nd ed., p. 104.

Focusing on the trend of the ratio of social security benefit to GDP from the 1960s to 1980s, (Table 3.2) we can observe two more different

---

[5] This is exemplified in the Labour Standards Act of Japan, for example, where Article 1 and 2 provide: 'Article 1, Labour standards must be the kind ... that is suitable for a human being. Article 2, Labour conditions ... should be determined by both the employer and the employee on equal positions.' These complementary measures become necessary because of the intrinsic imbalance in the power between management and labour.

characteristics among the four countries. One is the difference in the level of benefit among the countries, and the other is the common change in their trends in the 1980s. First, the ratios of the four countries increased till the 1970s.[6] Sweden was positioned at the same level as the UK in 1959, which was double the figures of Japan and the US. But the following years of uneven development put the UK in the relatively lower ratio group.

Table 3.2 Social security benefit, % of GDP

	Sweden	UK	Japan	US
1959	10.7	10.2	4.5	6.3
64	–	11.0	4.6	6.5
65	13.4	–	–	–
66	–	5.1	7.3	–
67	15.6	12.7	5.0	7.7
68	16.9	13.0	4.8	8.2
69	17.6	13.1	4.8	8.8
70	18.4	13.2	5.0	9.8
71	20.1	13.3	5.0	11.2
72	20.3	13.7	5.4	11.6
73	21.0	13.6	5.5	11.7
74	23.9	15.2	6.6	12.4
75	25.6	16.3	7.8	13.1
76	26.7	16.3	8.6	12.9
77	29.7	16.3	8.9	11.3
78	29.6	16.7	9.5	11.6
79	29.7	16.9	9.8	12.2
80	31.1	17.2	10.0	12.1
81	32.0	18.8	10.4	12.9
82	31.6	19.5	10.9	13.2
83	29.4	19.4	11.2	12.9
84	29.4	19.6	11.1	11.9
85	29.5	19.1	10.9	12.0
86	30.1	19.0	11.4	12.1
87	33.2	17.8	11.5	11.9
88	33.9	16.8	11.2	11.7
89	33.6	16.2	11.1	11.7

Source: ILO, *The Cost of Social Security,* 1976, 1979, 1981, 1985, 1988, 1992, and 1996. Fiscal years.

---

[6] 'During the 1960s and early 1970s, there was very rapid growth of social expenditure: on average across the OECD area public social expenditure doubled from 10 per cent of GDP in 1960 to 20 per cent in 1980' (OECD, 1999, *A Caring World*, p. 40).

Although not exactly moving together, the rates have stopped increasing (Sweden, Japan) or started decreasing (the US, the UK) in the beginning of the 1980s. In the US and UK the peak years are relatively clear as in 1982. Apart from the figures presented in Table 3.2, the figure of social security transfers as a percentage of GDP also shows that this decreasing trend occurred mainly in 1983 in Sweden (from 18.3% to 17.6%) and in 1984 in the UK (from 14.0% to 13.9%), Japan (11.2% to 11.0%) and the US (11.9% to 11.0%).[7] The early 1980s is thus marked as the beginning of the changing trend of social security development.

Below are added brief characteristics and developments of welfare policies in these four countries up to the 1970s.

SWEDEN

Characteristics

Although having experienced the hard treatment of the poor in the former centuries as in the other countries, its growth toward a Welfare State after the development of the labour movement at the end of the 19th century was significant and gathered force after the Second World War. It could not help following a restrictive budget policy after the worldwide decline of economic activities because of the ever-growing closer relationship with the world market, and this led to the review of some of the welfare policies, particularly of the high employment policy. But except for this, the high achievements in the post-war years are mostly maintained still today.

Chronology

18th century	second half – beginning of the decomposition of farmers enclosure movement, vagrancy
1763	Poor Law, carried on by villages
1862	relief of the poor, by communes
19th century	industrial revolution, serious poverty first half – inferior labour conditions
1871	relief, the responsibility of the state
1880s	emigration promoted (a quarter of the population emigrated in 40 years)
Late 19th century	labour movement, Social Democratic Party (SAP), universal right to vote

---

[7] OECD, 1992, *Historical Statistics*, p. 67. Social security transfers consist of social security benefits for sickness, old age, family allowances, etc., social assistance grants and unfunded employee welfare benefits paid by general government (ibid., p. 75).

1913	old age pension
1917	SAP, coalition government
1918	Labour Protection Law
1928	Per Albin Hansson, 'The house of the people'
1938	Salziobaden agreement
1935	basic pension, by state fund
After WWII	constructing a fully-fledged Welfare State: full employment, social service, from selective to universal, and rationalization of industrial structures
1976	conservative centre, to power

(Tilton, 1991; Okazawa, 1991; Shibata, 1996)

UK

Characteristics

The UK has a strong tradition of liberalism as an important role of government. A part of it could be traced back to the factory laws in the first half of the 19th century. In contrast to Sweden, the Liberal Party became a counterpart of the Labour Party in improving the workers' conditions from the turn of the 20th century. When in government both parties had an important role in addressing these goals. As Rose says, 'Britain combines two distinctive traditions: liberalism that places a high value on individual freedom and responsibility ... and trust in government that has much more in common with solidaristic Scandinavian societies than with the United States'[8] (p. 80). But this broader national consensus seems to have been changing since the 1970s. At present, both Conservative and Labour Parties are experimenting with the next image of the Welfare State.

Chronology

Medieval age	mutual assistance in the guilds of merchants and craftsmen in cities
	Church, encouragement of the relief of the poor
14 – 15th century	England, widening cleavage between the rich and the poor through the development of merchandising economy
Absolutism age	enclosure movement, executions of vagabonds, harsher treatment to the poor
17th century	The Puritan Government, relief of the poor by the district

---

[8] National Health Service, Child Benefit, social assistance, etc are much more generous policies than in the US (Walker, 1998, p. 32).

	governments
	After the revolution, a new view of regarding the poor as idle
	one fifth of the population supported by the poor law
18th century	restoration of charities, middle class's self-consciousness of the responsibility as the leader of society and appreciation of their success
	Methodist John Wesley, 'Earn as much as possible, save as much as possible, and give as much possible'
19th century	first half – Factory Law
1834	Poor Law Amendment Act, to workhouse
	Malthus, 'private charity harms less the spirit of self-help'
	second half – social work regarding the poor as the victims of society
1868, 1884	universal suffrage, First Commissioner for the Protection of the Poor
late 19th century	one third of London in serious poverty
1906	Lloyd George, 'If the government of the Liberal Party puts its effort in liberating the people from the malignant rule of the united monopoly capital ... the appeal of the Independent Labour Party to the labourers will be in vain'
1906 – 11	Reform Acts (old age pension, minimum wage, unemployment security, etc) between the wars
1919	state subsidy to council houses, subsidy to constructing labourers' houses
1920	unemployment security, wider coverage
1924	first cabinet by the Labour Party
	declaring the responsibility and obligation of local government for protection of houses
1925	old age pension
1942	Beveridge Report, Want, Disease, Ignorance, Squalor, Idleness
1943	Ministry of Housing and City Planning
1944	Atlantic Ocean Charter, article 5, 'improvement of labour conditions ... economic progress and social security'
1944	White Paper on Medical Treatment, NHS
	White Paper on Employment, Keynesian policy
	Butler Education Act
1961	proportional pension to salaries
1960s	Abel-Smith and Townsend, 'increasing poverty'
1970s	economic slump

(Takashima, 1995, pp. 18-75; Jiten Kanko Iinkai, 1989, p. 478)

JAPAN

Characteristics

One significant characteristic of Japan is that the state welfare policies only began at the end of the 19th century when it opened its doors to the western world and started to catch up with them in armament and national wealth. The development of Japanese welfare policies is divided into four periods: relief policies by the grace of the emperor at the end of the 19th century, policies for raising a stronger army in the first half of the 20th century, the introduction of democratic policies in the few decades of the post-war years, and the setback period after the 1980s. It is one characteristic that the Japanese pension system was always accompanied by a second purpose for the state – raising the war fund in the pre-war years, and raising the fund for investment and growth in the post-war years. Japan is in its transition period now, trying to follow the prescriptions of retrenching the public finance and deficit recommended by the Temporary Administrative Investigation Committee of the early 1980s. But experiencing the depression of the 1990s in the aftermath of the bursting of the economic bubble, it had to pursue a positive fiscal policy in the late 1990s.

Chronology

1874	Relief Ordinance
1909	Reformatory relief work, organizing mutual assistance
1911	Grace foundation Saiseikai
	labour movement
1917	Rice riot, Social Work introduced (reforming houses, child care on a small scale)
1922	Health Insurance Act
	welfare policies for raising a stronger army
1932	Relief Act, unemployed excluded
1934	reform of Health Insurance Act
1937	Military Assistance Act, protection of mother and children
1938	National Insurance
1941	Pension Insurance for Workers
1944	Welfare Pension Act
After the WWII	Post-war reforms start
1946	Livelihood Protection Act
1947	Workmen's Accidents Insurance Act, Unemployment

	Insurance Act, Children's Welfare Act
1949	The Disabled Welfare Act
1973	Free Medical Care for the Old
1975	Council for Fiscal Institutions: 'already caught up with western levels,' recommending restriction of social welfare

(Shibata, 1998)

US

Characteristics

In the history of US welfare policies, the policies in the New Deal years of the1930s, the resurgence of the 'war on poverty' in the 1960s, and the setback years after the1980s should be noted as its landmarks. 'The US emerged from the WWII with the basic building blocks of its current Welfare State already in place ...' Its main features were social insurance for the elderly and unemployment insurance. A social assistance programme (aid to families with dependent children, AFDC) complemented the system, directed at widowed and divorced mothers with children. The disabled were added to the social security system in 1955 (John Myles, 1996, p. 119). The US and the UK, who jointly declared the goal of freedom from poverty in the Atlantic Charter, both faced 'the re-discovery of poverty' in the beginning of the 1960s. 'The mid-1960s was an exciting time for social welfare planners and policy makers. A vast array of new social welfare programs was unfolding under the Economic Opportunity Act of 1964, the Demonstration Cities and Metropolitan Development Act of 1966, the Older Americans Act of 1965, the Food Stamp Act of 1964, the Community Mental Health Centres Act of 1963, Medicare and Medicaid in 1965, and other legislative initiatives of the Great Society.'[9] In the 1960s, states were allowed to add a programme for unemployed fathers to AFDC and about half the states did so. Income transfer model through the old age pension programme, proved the more successful and poverty among the elderly declined significantly in the US. Pension replacement rates grew. The rates for single worker with average wages in manufacturing rose from 30% in 1969 to 44% in 1980, compared to 40% to 49% in the average of 12 OECD countries in the same years. The rates for an elderly couple rose from 49% to 66% in the US, compared to 50% to 61% in the OECD countries (Myles, op. cit., pp. 121-6).

---

[9] Neil Gilbert, 1983, p. vii. 'In 1964 and 1965 major action took place along three fronts. First, Medicare ... and Medicaid ... Second, programs designed to wipe out poverty under the auspices of the Office of Economic Opportunity ... Third, a major Civil Rights Act and Voting Rights Act outlawed discrimination in employment and education on grounds of race'. (Nathan Glazer, 'Welfare and "Welfare" in America', in Rose and Shiratori, eds, 1986, p. 40.)

16 – 17th centuries the poor law, by town meeting imitating 1601 Elizabeth I's poor law in England

The late 19th to increase in poverty
early 20th century

The age of progressivism
labour laws (collective bargaining, work hours, minimum wage, compensation for workmen's accidents) The Anti-Trust Law

1886 Social Settlement

1930s from charity to obligation: F. D. Roosevelt, 'The unfortunate citizens are offered helping hands by the government, not as a matter of charity but as a matter of an obligation'

1935 Social Security Act (Federal old age pension, unemployment insurance, public assistance, social work -- not including health insurance and family benefit)

1960s War on poverty

1964 the Economic Opportunity Act

1966 the Demonstration Cities and Metropolitan Development Act

1965 the Older Americans Act

1964 the Food Stamp Act

1963 the Community Mental Health Centres Act

1965 Reform of Social Security Act, Medicare and Medicaid

1975 universal pension system

(Shibata, 1996)

The above briefly sketches the Welfare State developments in the four countries up to the 1970s. The 1960s were characterized by the renewed expectations to 'wipe out' the revived poverty and insecurity after the post-war economic growth. However, this expectation in the 1960s was not realized fully. After the three decades since then poverty in America for example still continues to be a significant percentage. The tumultuous years of the 1970s and the subsequent policy changes in many of the industrialized countries have generated somewhat different images of the Welfare State than of the 1960s. As we have seen in the previous chapter, poverty and relative income difference, and most of all a growing sense of insecurity are being regenerated in a market economy which rewards the advantaged (the more 'fitted for market society') more highly. When this trend is left unchanged, social balance will be tilted toward too much efficiency and too little equity and human fellowship, or too much insecurity. The present situation in many countries seems to show that the Welfare States, after having tried to revive the market force in the past two decades, face this question of social imbalance seriously today. We will now proceed to our main focus of this book, the setback process of the Welfare State since the 1980s, and explore its effects and alternative policies in the next era.

2 SETBACK OF THE WELFARE STATES – Since the 1980s

As viewed in the arguments of the previous chapter, the Welfare States have been in their retreating, transforming period for the past two decades. How they will change in the near future is one of the most acute questions for the peoples living in these states. As far as we observe from the various proceedings and experiments of the Welfare States in the world today, whether a new type of Welfare State emerges, which can accomplish both high employment and high security, or any other types will be prevalent and accepted by the people, is yet to be seen. As the first step to consider this question, we will study the changing process of the Welfare States after the 1980s, focusing on the relationship between economy and welfare, or competitiveness and welfare provisions. As will be clarified, this relationship seems to be the major factor for the changing processes today. And, as the Welfare State is basically based on a market economy or market mechanism, the critical question seems to hinge on the relationship between welfare provisions and profit rate. Based on a market economy, the Welfare State is much affected by the profit rate. The extent and mode of this influence of the changing relationship between them vary according to the stance of the government, hence of the citizens who support it. The two decades of the 1980s and 1990s seem to show good material for analysing this relationship. How the relative weights of welfare policies and economic growth, whose nucleus is the rate of profit, have changed in different Welfare States, reflecting the changing attitudes and political choices of the peoples, is the major question here. Thus our focus in the following part of this chapter will be put on the changing processes of economic and social policies and the relationships between them.

The major question the Thatcher and Reagan administrations posed in the 1980s concerning the size of the government was about the balance between welfare provisions and economic growth. The answer ultimately depends on the attractiveness of the type of society provided by various choices of this balance. What balance between them would create what type of society? Which way is the present balance in the US, the UK, or Sweden and Japan headed? Which balance and what type of society would maximize the peoples' satisfaction or overall welfare? The answers or the experiments of the governments will be examined next. In order to do this, first we have to consider from what viewpoints we will handle the development of policies and their effects.

2.1 VIEWPOINTS – wages, taxes, social contributions and profit rates

First, we need to understand that the underlying cause of the recent socio-economic trend for restricting the growth of the Welfare State has been the conflict between profit and its costs – wages, taxes and social contributions, etc. Since the 1980s, the Welfare State has been criticized for having grown too large and having restricted economic growth significantly, or more than necessary, through causing financial difficulties such as higher interest rates, or by reducing competitiveness through higher wages, higher taxes, and lower work incentives.

This mounting anxiety about lower economic growth, which is lower or smaller profit and lower competitiveness on the firm's side, soon joined by the export of capital argument has been the major cause obliging governments to reconsider their welfare provisions. The argument about lower competitiveness is especially gaining power today. IMD International's *The World Competitiveness Yearbook 1998* says that in today's world where firms are more and more world market oriented and there is a worldwide labour force available, the critical factors by which the firms choose either to stay in or move out of one country will be the level of wages and taxes (including social contributions) (IMD, 1998, p. 42).

Its competitiveness tables rank not the firms but the countries by their attractiveness as the object of investment by certain criteria. It counts the following factors as the components of the competitiveness of a country:

1) Dynamism of Economy, which includes size and growth rate,
2) Industrial Efficiency such as productivity,
3) Market Orientation such as how it is exposed to internal and external competition,
4) Financial Dynamism such as volume and cost of capital,
5) Human Resources such as skill and motivation,
6) Impact of State such as its size and if it supplies good resource allocating policies,
7) Natural Resources and Utilization,
8) International Orientation such as larger presence of native firms in foreign markets and of foreign firms in internal market,
9) Future Orientation such as faster technological developments, and
10) Socio-Political Stability such as fewer industrial disputes or a smaller maldistribution of income (op. cit., pp.37-57).

Of these factors, some, such as the size of a country, are not flexible but such factors as productivity, financial cost, and government size are flexible political factors. Productivity or the amount produced by a worker is affected by technological investment, and the latter, by profit. Government expenditure, when it produces deficit in a financially tight condition, can affect firms' financial cost by higher taxation and social contributions. Thus taxation and social contribution, and their background condition, namely the size of government expenditure that includes welfare provisions as one of its main factors, become the more important battlefield where pro- and anti-welfare arguments centre.[10]

As mentioned before, what this kind of argument should deal with is the balance of a society, or the balance between growth and redistribution, or investment and consumption. This should also include the productive influences that welfare provisions exert by raising educational levels or workforce ratio, etc.[11] Counting in these effects, the choice here will be reduced to the combination of investment and consumption for a larger satisfaction of society. Thus, in order to answer the question of the future of the Welfare State, we have to consider two questions: what choice we have in the combinations of this balance, and which choice we prefer most. The former means what welfare level or content corresponds to what growth level. Although this question includes many technical and positive analyses that will not be fully studied in this book, we will try to get some insight into it by following past experiences and arguments in this and following chapters. The second question, the preference of the peoples, is which mixture of growth and welfare they prefer to choose among the possible alternatives. We will address this question by paying attention to the notion of security, or social health in Chapter 5.[12]

---

[10] The absolute labour cost is not necessarily a single most important factor. It is combined with other factors and the resulting unit labour cost is what actually counts. In the US's case it was higher than that of South Korea, Thailand, and Mexico, but lower than that of India and Philippines in 1990 (S. Golub, 1995, p.142).

[11] The positive effects of welfare provisions on economic growth are not studied much in this book. Once the necessity to strengthen the Welfare State is agreed, this question will have to be studied fully to attain this goal efficiently. These effects include both macroscopic and microscopic ones. The former is the effect on the aggregate demand through redistribution of total purchasing power, and the latter is such productive effects as above.

The 'wasteful' solution to this imbalance of supply and demand, for the purpose of full employment, which was often discussed concerning the effect of military spending in the Second World War and the cold war years, is excluded in the following argument. As the cold war is over, and if we can believe in the rational human nature, that the owners of wealth or investors will not be satisfied with wasteful productions, this course of argument will not be addressed in this book.

[12] In a precise argument about adding peoples' total satisfaction we will need a refined method of calculating it, which we will not try to develop here. In arguing this question in Chapter 5, we will largely depend on opinion polls and reasoning from widely obseved social phenomena.

The diagram below (Figure 3.1) shows the outline of the possible relationship between the market and the Welfare State spheres. It is in principle the same as Figure 2.6, but the two parts of society, market mechanism and Welfare State regime, are shown clearly separated here. This diagram consists of the upper part, the economic circulation in the market mechanism and the lower part, the policies or interference in the upper part of the Welfare State. As such, every modern market economy society consists of these two parts. The two major parts in the upper part are production and distribution in the market. When profit and wages are equitably distributed so that they can both obtain the fund and incentive large enough for future investment and work, the system is maintained. But as market mechanism, when left alone, tends to, first, distribute the product in favour of the employer because of the advantageous bargaining position, and, secondly, as it tends to provide insufficiently for the disabled and weak, counter- and complementary measures are needed, hence labour laws and welfare provisions of the Welfare State. Recent critiques of this development have been twofold: first, that the balance between labour and management has tended to be much tilted toward the labour side, and second, that the welfare level has tended to become too high. Through these routes, the welfare policies are said to have reduced profit to a critical level, hence investment and competitiveness.

Figure 3.1 Two sides of modern society: market mechanism and the Welfare State

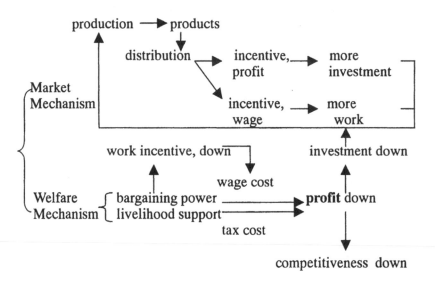

Figure 3.2 shows another view of the question. It is focused on the

Figure 3.3 Another view of the question: redistribution among the factors

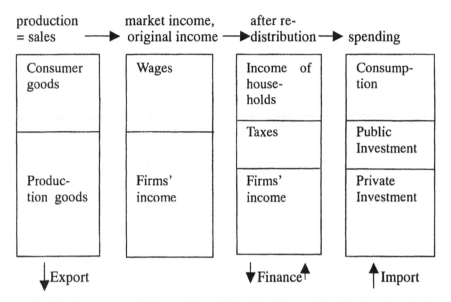

production = sales → market income, original income → after re-distribution → spending

| Consumer goods | Wages | Income of households | Consumption |
| Produc-tion goods | Firms' income | Taxes / Firms' income | Public Investment / Private Investment |

↓Export   ↓Finance↑   ↑Import

redistributive part of the product. The fund for redistribution is obtained through taxes on households and firms. (Here social contribution is included in taxes.) The redistributed fund ends up as a part of household consumption and the whole of public investment. (Subsidies to firms are ignored.) All the spending flows into either consumption or investment. Taxes here include both direct and indirect taxation. What is important in relation to firms' competitiveness is the former. Indirect taxation ordinarily accrues to end-users.[13]

The four factors – wages, corporate income tax, social contribution, and profit – are supposed to have worked in the following interrelated manners in respective periods of economic circulation.

i) 19th-century type economic circulation – under little state interference
1: In a market economy society, wages, taxes, and social contributions in later years, form important parts of the production cost for firms. At the same time they constitute the major amount of demand for consumer and production goods in the market as seen in Figure 3.2.

---

[13] Direct Tax and Indirect Tax: Both taxes give the whole private sector the same amount of impact. Direct tax is collected from realized income. Indirect tax is collected from sales, which is the same as a single rate income tax. In either case there is no escape from the burden for management and labour except through regaining the loss by enlarging their own share against the other.

2: In a usual free-competition business cycle, where price is given to individual firms, the cost of labour, whose supply can hardly be increased in a short period, increases faster in prosperity than the growth of the economy. At a certain point, the negative effect of the increasing cost, particularly of labour cost, overrides the positive effect of increasing production, or the decreasing unit cost. Then the profit rate begins to fall, which reduces investment, thus leading to recession.

3: In a recession, wages decline and less efficient firms are eliminated from the market. This downsizing of excess capacity, combined with the introduction of new technologies, raise productivity, and the profit rate starts to recover again. And so a new cycle begins.

4: Empirically, through this process, the increased poverty from unemployment was not given much attention as a social problem. Only extreme cases were met by charity.

5: At this stage, smaller government meant lower corporate tax. Tax or social contribution burden meant little to firms.

6: The relative weight of wages was the major cause of fluctuating profit rate, hence of investment and business cycle.

ii) 1930s-type economic circulation – oligopoly and state intervention

7: When the above recovery mechanism ceases to function properly for some reasons (as caused by the twofold price movements between the oligopolistic firms and the smaller firms in the 1930s US) and the depression is prolonged, government intervention for the unemployed and the needy becomes inevitable. This new policy is started by emergency relief and developed into conscious high employment and social security policies.[14]

iii) 1950s to 1970s-type economic circulation – growth of labour's bargaining power and inflation

8: The establishment of high employment and high social welfare policies gradually generates high wages, high taxes, and high social contribution burdens on the firms. Large firms, now having the power to 'set' prices, adopt the policy of shifting the increased cost to prices. Labour tries to meet it by raising wages. The distribution conflict results in a general price rise. A continuous trend of inflation occurs. This trend was accentuated by the rise

---

[14] After the 1930s, as major firms became oligopolised, many of them adopted the policy of reducing the rate of operation instead of lowering the price even in depressive years. But smaller firms could not. This polarization of prices became a heavy burden to the non-oligopolistic firms' profit, whose prices could not help but fall. The profit of oligopolistic firms was less affected than before, but in turn they themselves could not help restricting new investment while holding unused capacities. Under this pressure of low operating rate, combined with the slow recovery of non-oligopolistic firms' profit rate, the economy suffered the long stagnation of investment (TNEC reports and Tsukada 1983).

of oil prices in the 1970s.[15]

9: Under this inflationary spiral of prices and wages, government's policy to meet depression by deficit spending becomes ineffective and public deficit accumulates. The enlarged public finance (by accumulated interest), its negative-effect on private investment, anxiety about future tax increases, and the fragile credibility of government bonds come to the fore of the policy argument.

iv) 1980s to 1990s-type economic circulation – Welfare State retrenchment and globalization pressure

10: Advanced industrialized countries have taken various measures to meet the stagflation in the 1970s. One was the policy to reduce government deficit, which has been pursued largely through holding down the rapidly growing social welfare expenditures. Another is the reduction of wage costs, which was pursued through weakening the labour unions' power directly by revising labour laws and indirectly by creating massive unemployment. The shift to lower growth economies worldwide after the 1970s, with its resultant high unemployment rate, has had a significant depressive influence on the wage level.

11: The reduction of tax and social security burdens on firms and the lower wage policy are being reinforced by the pressure to increase firms' competitiveness to meet the rapidly advancing economic globalization in the 1990s.[16]

Against the background of this preliminary bird's-eye view, Section 2.2 deals with the development of policies in the four countries, focusing on their economic and welfare conditions in the 1980s and 1990s. We will see the processes in which policies, economic growth, and social welfare changed in an intertwined manner. Next, in Section 2.3, we will deal with the causal relationship between them. By following these steps we will be able to observe the actual shifting weight of the balance between economy and society or competitiveness and security.

---

[15] Keynesian policy in a market economy thus proves ineffective when it leads to inflation.

[16] MNEs' influence or control of world trade is still increasing; it already covered one third of output and three quarters of commercial technological capacity and trade in the late 1980s (Bonoli et al., 2000, p. 57). Although two thirds of imports for Europe were still from within the area during 1980-95, South East Asia's growing technology is expected to increase its share further. Foreign direct investment in developing countries increased from 24% in 1970-80 to 29% in 1991 and 1992. Although job creation in developing countries by MNEs amounted to merely 2%, 'there is ... a widespread belief that FDI (foreign direct investment) is a potent source of jobs and growth' (ILO, 1995, pp. 45-6).

2.2 ANALYSIS 1 – policies, growth, and welfare in the 1980s and 1990s

Overview of the Policies and Economic Development

The development of economic activities and policies in the 1980s and 1990s is better understood by first referring to the 1970s. Until the end of the 1960s, there was widespread confidence for rapid growth and low inflation both among economists and political leaders in the industrialized countries. But two fundamental problems were already emerging: creeping inflation and widening current-account imbalances for some countries. The former is understood to be a by-product of the 'success' of post-war active demand management policies as mentioned above, and the latter the result of the unequal economic growth among countries.

The unequal growth, especially of competitiveness, pressurized the weak currencies and gradually led them to the floating currency system. The inflation problem was more difficult to be addressed. Shaken by the oil price rise, the governments in general lost track of feasible macroeconomic policies. The task of fine-tuning between the narrow paths of unemployment and inflation was difficult but inevitable. Countries with current-account surplus were expected to practice expansionary policies, and vice versa.

Although the oil price shock was the main cause of the raging inflation in the 1970s, the preceding inflationary pressures in the 1960s had shown that the favourable conditions for high growth economy in the post-war years were fading. The recovery of the devastated countries that contributed to the high growth era was ending. The redistribution of wealth to OPEC countries pushed down the growth rate. But in most countries, the belief in continuous high growth rate still kept the expectations of both employers and employees high, and these expectations then transformed into spiralling inflation. Such expectations were also shared by the political leaders, who supported the generous spending in the second half of the 1970s. But the following recovery was weak and left an accumulated public deficit.

New answers were needed. Higher interest rate was powerless to keep inflation down when a generous budget provided ample money for raising prices. When the fundamental cause of inflation was the rivalry between the bargaining powers, of the employers and employees, the fundamental remedy within the market economy mechanism was to weaken either side. 'Changes in government in the United States and United Kingdom accelerated the process of trying out new solutions' (OECD, *Economic Outlook*, 50, December. 1991, p. 7). They changed the conventional policies. They gave the first priority to controlling inflation, not to full employment, and this was pursued by both restrictive money supply and restrictive medium-term fiscal policy.

Process of the Policies

1970s – Spending Policy

The 1970s was still the age of positive spending policy for Sweden. Until the beginning of the 1970s, corporatist type socio-economic management of society had functioned well. Investment policy to cope with business fluctuation, which was to reserve a part of the profit for investment in recessions, and active labour market policy were the strong supports for the Swedish economy.[17] The employer and employee were charged with the obligation to follow broad national goals of harmonizing production and distribution, or economy and social welfare.

To meet the worldwide depression from the 1970s to the beginning of 1980s, positive fiscal policy was adopted. The ratio of public spending to GDP had been almost the same in 1974 in Sweden and the UK, but after the positive spending policy in the 1970s, that ratio in Sweden far exceeded that of the UK in 1982. The share of general government's current disbursement of GDP increased from 33.5% (1960-73) to 60.2% (1979-83) in Sweden, but from 31.3% to 40.9% in the UK (OECD, 1996a, p. 100).

1980s – Public Deficit, Inflation and Restriction

In the 1980s the huge deficit necessitated the government to adopt tight budget and devaluation policies. By positive public spending in the 1970s, the government suffered a huge deficit from the late 1970s to the mid-1980s, reaching its peak in 1982 and continuing to 1986. The large-scale spending sustained overall economic growth in the 1980s, but it created a far bigger government than ever and a higher inflation rate, rising from 3.8% in 1960-68 to 6.0% in 1968-73 and to 9.8% in 1973-79 (OECD, 1992, *Historical Statistics*, p. 87). As the reduction of the enlarged deficit became a pressing problem, the 1982 Social Democratic Party Conference proposed the restriction of the public sector as an urgent task.

To promote larger investment and higher competitiveness, the Social Democratic government devalued the currency in 1982, and cut tax for the highest rate personal income bracket, and also corporate tax from 52% to 42% in 1982. Public spending was restricted and its ratio to GDP was

---

[17] Still today, 'Its active labour market policy absorbs 7% of the government's budget, $5 billion for a workforce of 4.4 million. More than 70% goes to training and placement programmes' (Isabella Bakker, 'Globalization and Human Development in the Rich Countries: Lessons from Labour Markets and Welfare States', UN, 1999, p. 91).

reduced to 61% in 1990 compared to 67% in 1982 (OECD, *Hist. Stat.* 1992, p. 68). Welfare spending was restricted, too. In 1982 a part of the pension sliding scale system to prices was curtailed.

Following these tight budget policies internally and export-promoting policies externally, economic recovery appeared. The GDP growth rate rose from 1% in 1981 to 1.8% in 1983, and 4% in 1984, and stayed above 2% until 1989. Unemployment rate rose to over 3% in 1982-84, but declined from 2.8% to 1.3% in 1985-89. Inflation rate also declined from 13.7% in 1980 to 4.2% in 1986 and 1987 (Appendix, Statistical Table for Sweden). Although welfare provisions suffered some cuts, Swedish society muddled through the serious depression without causing high unemployment and large welfare setback (Nagaoka, 1992; Maruo, 1994).

The economic performance in the 1980s was quite successful, but Esping-Andersen warned in 1990 of the emerging fragility of the connection between employment and wages in the Swedish-type Welfare State. One of his critiques was focused on the enlarged public employment during this course of development. The 'cost-disease problem cannot be avoided ... Expanding public employment to more than 30 percent of total employment ... will eventually be stalled by tax-ceilings.' This he called the 'Achilles' heel of the Swedish model' (Esping-Andersen, 1990, pp. 223-4). Furthermore, to 'sustain and expand Welfare State employment, government is compelled to ask for wage moderation among public employees. In Sweden, the centralized solidarity-wage policy implies that such wage moderation will have to be spread across the entire economy. It is the latter which is proving impossible and, as a result, the most serious conflicts ... in the Swedish labor market have, throughout the 1980s, occurred between public- and private-sector trade unions' (ibid, p. 227).

1990s – Joining EU, Worldwide Depression and Sky-High Unemployment

In the 1990s the 'EU' effect and worldwide depression made the government finally abandon its high employment policy. It became the policy agenda at the beginning of 1990s to satisfy Maastricht criteria of current public deficit at no more than 3 % of GDP and public debt to GDP ratio of 60% or below, and at the same time to strengthen its international competitiveness for the expected harsher competition after joining the EU in 1995. Several reforms were carried out in 1990-91 for these purposes.

Tax reform:
- 80% of the taxpayers were exempted from the state tax; the actual average rate became 31%.
- Progressive tax was changed into proportional tax, with the highest marginal tax rate at 51%.

- The objects of value-added tax and asset tax were widened.
- Double taxation on assets was abolished and asset tax rate was reduced.

Deregulation:
- Regulations on currency exchange were abolished.
- Direct investment abroad and investment in Sweden by foreign firms became possible.
- Deregulation for promoting competitiveness in the fields of the taxi industry, construction, farming, private airlines, electric power, and communications were implemented.
- Regulations on labour market were partly loosened, the workmen's fund was abolished, and some public utilities were privatised.[18]

But this was also the period of worldwide depression. From 1991 to 1993 Swedish GDP growth rate in real terms went below zero for three years. The unemployment rate rose to over 9% in 1993-94. Until then depression had been met by an increase in government employees but this policy was not taken this time under the EU-joining restrictions. The unemployment rate jumped from 1.5% in 1991 to over 9% in 1993-96. During the depression at the beginning of the 1990s, the ratio of budget deficit to GDP grew again to 15%, 13%, and 9% in 1992-94. The decrease in tax revenue and the increase of unemployment benefit made the accumulated government deficit 79.5% of GDP in 1994, increasing the burden of interest payment. The deficit grew much faster than in the mid-1980s in 1993-95. But the depreciation of the Krone in the middle of the 1990s promoted exports. The prompt investment of public money into the monetary crisis after the bursting of the bubble economy supported the recovery (Maruo, 1999, p. 46). Investment and productivity recovered from 1994 to 1996. Trade surplus has continued since 1994 until 1999.

Overall production and employment started to recover from the beginning of 1997 and unemployment decreased rapidly from the beginning of 1997 to over 5% at the beginning of 1999. The budget deficit dissolved finally in 1998 after the restrictive financial stance. Both the producers' and consumers' prices have settled down since 1992 under the restrictive policy and depression, with the rate of consumers' price rise at around 1% from 1997 to 1999. The deficit in the international balance of payments increased in 1989 and reached 2 to 3% of GDP in 1990-92, but decreased in 1993 and turned into a surplus from 1994 to 1997.

---

[18] Naomi Maruo (1999), Jun Shirota (1997), Nobutaka Nagaoka (1992).

Effects of the Policies

Economy

**Figure 3.3   Sweden: economic performance; GDP, inflation, un-
employment, 1970-96**

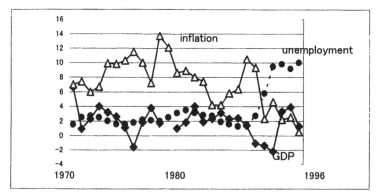

Source: Statistical table for Sweden (Appendix).

Figure 3.4 Sweden: government deficit, % of GDP, 1966-98

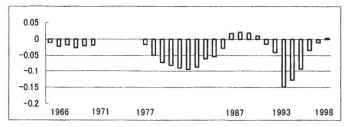

Source: Statistical table for Sweden (Appendix).

Figure 3.5 Sweden: current account, 1973-97

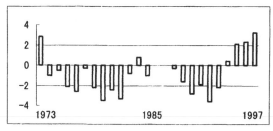

Source: Statistical table for Sweden (Appendix)

The growth rate in industrial production from the mid-1970s to 1993 and

69

1994 lagged behind OECD countries but has been rapidly catching up since then. After the serious depression of the early 1990s prices have remained low and unemployment has decreased quickly to less than 6% in early 1999 (OECD, website, *Main Economic Indicators*), although at a much higher level than before the 1980s. Government deficit and current account also recovered fast in the 1990s.

Welfare

As a result of the genuine austerity programmes in the early 1990s social welfare provisions were gradually restrained. In the 1988 election the Social Democrats campaigned on a new round of social reforms but the bubble burst and it failed to deliver on any of these promises (Stephens, 1996, p. 45). The Conservative government elected in 1991 implemented a number of spending cuts in social benefits, most of them with Social Democrat support. They reduced sick pay to 80% after 90 days; basic pension to 98% of the base amount and industrial injury insurance was coordinated with sick pay. Qualifying conditions were sharpened for sick pay and work injury; employers were now obliged to pay for the first two weeks of sick pay. A five-day waiting period for unemployment benefits was reintroduced with

Table 3.3 Social protection expenditure[*1] and total social benefits[*2] (% of GDP)

	1990	1993	1996
Sweden[*1]	32.9	38.6	34.8
[*2]	–	38.0	34.2
UK [*1]	23.1	28.8	27.7[*P]
[*2]	22.1	27.7	26.7[*P]
EU-15[*3][*1]	25.4[*P]	29.0[*P]	28.7*
[*2]	–	27.8[*P]	27.5*

[*1]: Social protection expenditure includes social benefits, administration costs, transfers to other schemes and other expenditure (p. 7).

[*2]: Social benefits include benefits for sickness/health care, disability, old age, survivors, family/children, unemployment, housing, and social exclusion not elsewhere classified (pp. 68-71).

[*3]: EU-15: Belgium, Denmark, Germany, Greece, Spain, France, Ireland, Italy, Luxembourg, the Netherlands, Austria, Portugal, Finland, Sweden, the United Kingdom.

*: EU-15 includes for 1990 Germany as constituted prior to 3 October 1990 as from 1991 as constituted from 3 October 1990 (p. 36).

[*P]: preliminary.

Source: European Communities, *Social protection – expenditure and receipts: European Union, Iceland and Norway*, 1999, pp.12, 67.

replacement rates lowered to 80%. The SAP government added to it the replacement rate for parental insurance, which was decreased from 90 to 80% (Maruo, 1999, p. 48).

During the 1980s public social protection expenditure in the percentage of GDP in Sweden remained high, 32.4 in 1980 and 33.9 in 1990, while it was 19.4 in 1980 and 20.3 in 1988 in the UK, 14.2 in 1980 and 14.8 in 1990 in the US and 10.5 in 1980 and 11.6 in 1990 in Japan (OECD, 1996, *OECD Economies…*, pp. 107-8). In the 1990s, reflecting the early 1990s depression, this figure increased first to 38.6 in 1993 but then returned to 34.8 in 1996. As seen below, social protection consists mostly of social benefits. In 1996 the figure for Sweden was the highest of all the 15 EU countries, with Denmark and Finland following next.

We can see two characteristics of Swedish welfare provisions today by looking at Tables 3.4 and 3.5. Firstly, both in Sweden and the UK two major items in social benefits are old age pensions and sickness/health care benefit. Although in most items Sweden shows a higher figure, for housing and survivors benefits the UK spends a larger share.

Table 3.4 Composition of social benefits, 1995, % of GDP

	Old age	Sickness/ health	Disabi lity	Family/ Children	Unemp- loyment	Hous- ing	Survivo- rs	Social exclusion
Sw	12.2	7.6	4.3	4.0	3.9	1.2	0.8	1.1
UK	9.2	6.7	3.3	2.4	1.5	1.9	1.4	0.2

Source: European Communities, *Social protection – expenditure and receipts: European Union, Iceland and Norway*, 1999, pp. 68-71.

Table 3.5 Gross and net social expenditure as a percentage of GDP factor costs, 1995

	Sweden	UK	US
Gross	36.4	25.9	17.1
NPMSE*	25.6	22.6	18.0
Net	25.7	26.0	24.5

*: Net publicly mandated social expenditure
Source: Adema, 1999, p. 30.

Secondly, the concept of 'net social protection' provides us with the net scale of social protection (Adema, 1999). 'Governments provide social support through the tax system, but the value of such measures is partly offset by the value of taxes paid by recipients of benefits' (p. 6). Table 3.5 shows gross and net social expenditures for Sweden, the UK and the US in terms of their percentage of GDP.

The large decrease from gross to net terms (NPMSE) for Sweden is due to the return from the recipients of benefits to the government through direct taxes and social contributions paid over public cash benefits (5.2%) and indirect taxes (5.8%), etc. These two items are much smaller at 1.2% in total for the US. The figures of the UK and the US increase further to the 'Net' (net social expenditure) by adding voluntary private social expenditure (private social cash benefits and voluntary private social health benefits) (Adema, 1999, p. 31). Swedish people receive a lot from public expenditure but pay back some amount. The US one receive a little and add some amount on their own. But we should note that the latter case is only possible for those who can afford it.

These reforms have shown a certain shift in balance toward growth and competition from social welfare in Sweden. Although the people's evaluation of this movement, shown in the 1998 election, seems to be critical, firms are determined to be against the increase of their burden and will demand its decrease for fear of losing competitiveness. Maintenance or some retrenchment of the present level Welfare State seems to be the most probable for Sweden.

UK

Process of the Policies

Central feature, profit rate As profit rate has long been argued to be the main key element of the UK economy, it would be useful to start our argument by observing its movement.

Having been a liberal-concession-type Welfare State rather than a corporatist one, the measures taken when the profit rate seemed to suffer from wage and tax burdens were harsher to the labour force from the very beginning of the 1980s. The decline of profit rate up to the 1970s was often the centre of argument for the UK economy. The profit fall in manufacturing industries had already started in the 1950s and continued until the 1970s. The main reason for the profit squeeze was wage rises supported by full employment on the one hand and international competitive pressure on the other. Growing public spending supported full employment in the 1960s (George and Wilding, 1984, pp. 152-160; Glyn and Sutcliffe, 1972). By observing the figures below, we can say that the wage factor since the 1950s, spending factor and its burden on profits since the 1960s, and increasing competitive pressures throughout the post-war period were the major reasons for profit squeeze in the UK, particularly for manufacturing industries. Manufacturing industries' net profit rate showed a constant decline since the second half of the 1950s: 25% in 1954, then declining to 12-13% at the beginning of the 1970s. In the oil shock years it fell to as low as around 5%.

Gross profit rate, measured by the rate of return on capital investment, for the whole enterprise sector for the second half of the 1950s was around 12%, which continued until the middle of the 1960s (Oughton, in Hughes, ed., 1993, p. 59). Net profit rate was around 16% and stayed that high in the 1950s, but started decreasing at the beginning of the 1960s, earlier than the gross profit rate. The latter kept decreasing to about 10% at the beginning of the 1970s in the exceptionally turbulent environment; it fell to under 7% in 1975. In 1980, it started increasing and reached over 14% in 1989. Net profit rate for manufacturing rose from the 5% low to 10 to 13% in 1988-91. Net operating surplus, the percentage of net value added in manufacturing, recovered in the 1980s from 12.3% in 1984 to 21.0% in 1989. It declined in the depression to 13.3% in 1991, but rose again to 20.9% in 1994 (OECD, *Hist. Stat.* 1996, p. 82).

Post-war to the 1950s: Post-war Recovery

Soon after the end of the Second World War, coalmines and railways were nationalized and the National Health Service was established. Business declined in the beginning of the 1950s, recovered in 1955, but overheating and over-dampening policies were repeated. The ratio of civil service spending in total government spending was still lower than that of the continental European countries in 1952 to 1956. The bargaining power of labour grew, supported by high employment. Wages grew faster in the 1950s than other costs. Many of the other European countries were under reconstruction, and international competition was not yet harsh. It gave the economy the room to delay the rationalization investment that was often opposed by the workers.

The Middle of the 1960s to the Beginning of the 1970s: The Sterling Crisis

At the beginning of 1964 the government had to face the accumulated deficit in the international balance of payment of £ 8,000 million. Avoiding devaluation or import controls, a surcharge on imports of 15% was adopted. But the pressure to sell pounds became stronger and the reserve of foreign currency decreased rapidly to sustain the pound. Restrictions on currency for travel abroad and restrictive financial policies (consumption tax was raised by 10%, wages frozen for six months) were expected to meet this problem, but the pressure to sell did not stop, and the recession caused by the restrictive fiscal policy raised the unemployment rate. Finally, in 1967, the pound was devalued from £ 2.8 to £ 2.4 to the US dollar. Government tried to restrict wage increases by the 1971 Labour-management Relations Act but the Thatcherite group opposed it and proposed leaving the wage problem to be determined by free bargaining between labour and management.

The Middle to the End of the 1970s: Stagflation

Facing the 1973 oil shock and price rise, labour unions demanded a large wage increase. A social contract policy to hold down inflation through a deal with trades unions was tried. In exchange for the self-control of wage increases, the policies for the poor (food supplement, rent freeze, and pension benefit rise) were reinforced. The profit rate of the firms after tax recorded – 0.3%. The expansive fiscal policies for the two oil shocks resulted only in stagflation. The Labour government cut corporate tax rate. With the continuous wage increases, the unemployment rate kept increasing, from 2.9% in 1974 to 4.3% in 1975, and around 5 to 6% in the second half of the 1970s. With both the increase of wages and large deficit in the international balance, the pound suffered a heavy fall. Restrictive policies were adopted, cutting public spending drastically, resulting in a temporary stabilization of the pound. Following the frequent occurrence of strikes in 1978, the Conservative Party won the 1979 election by a big margin.

From the 1980s to the Mid-1990s: Conservative Years

The new government changed the course of the nation sharply against the trades unions and social welfare. In 1979, a restrictive budget policy was adopted, aiming at calming down inflation through monetarism. In 1980 not only the inflation rate but also the unemployment rate rose steeply but the restrictive policies were continued. The Thatcher administration understood that the trades unions' power was reducing the competitiveness of the firms, and determined to weaken it.[19] It abolished the closed shop system and banned sympathy strikes. At the same time it stockpiled coal in preparation for the negotiation with the coal miners' union.

As a result of this anti-labour and deliberate depression (and deliberate unemployment) policies, workers' bargaining power fell sharply. The following figures in Table 3.6 show the working days lost in the UK. It had gradually increased from 2.9 million days in 1965 to 4.7 million in 1968, 6.8 million in 1969, and over 10 million in 1970. In the turbulence of the oil shocks it rose to 23.9 million in 1972 and 29.5 million in 1979. But in the hostile Thatcher administration years it decreased sharply to fewer than one million in 1991, the first time since 1975. It kept decreasing to 278,000 in 1994. Recently, in 1996, there was a slight rise to 1.3 million. Compared to

---

[19] Thatcher wrote, 'I never ceased to believe that, other things being equal, the level of unemployment was related to the extent of trade union power. The unions had priced many of their members out of jobs by demanding excessive wages for insufficient output, so making British goods uncompetitive' (Thatcher, 1993, p. 272).

the other three countries, the sharp decrease in the UK is conspicuous (Table 3.7).

Table 3.6 Working days lost (1000)

1970	10,980	1978	9,405	1986	1,920	1994	278
1971	13,551	1979	29,474	1987	3,546	1995	415
1972	23,909	1980	11,964	1988	3,702	1996	1,303

Source: ILO, *Yearbook of Labour Statistics*, 1975, 1980, 1985, 1990, and 1997.

Table 3.7 Working days lost by industrial disputes (per 1000 inhabitants)

	1986-88 average	1994-96 average
Sweden	47.90	28.0
UK	53.23	11.4
Japan	2.12	0.7
US	2.17	19.9

Source: IMD, 1990, 1998.

Tax and spending Alongside the large tax cuts for the purpose of revitalizing the economy, restrictive social welfare spending policies were pursued. Income Supplement was changed into Income Support, Family Income Supplement, and then to Family Credit, with the amount of benefit reduced. Additional pension was reduced in the reforms of the 1986 Social Security Act and private pension schemes were recommended. In the 1990 NHS reform, the internal market was introduced and a market relationship between the budget holder and service providers was set up in 1990. Prescription charges were increased and the beneficiaries were charged a part of the fees for dental and ophthalmic examinations. With the 1988 Education Act and 1991 White Paper, financial assistance was to be given to the universities according to the number of students. The disqualification period for those who chose to remain unemployed was prolonged. Unemployment benefit for those up to 25 years of age was reduced on the grounds that their parents could assist them. Limit to cash payments was introduced as a general restrictive measure on public spending, thus separating the power and funding in the 1988 and 1989 budgets. The increased charge on the beneficiaries restricted the usage of medical care among the lower income people (George and Miller, 1994).

Under these new neo-liberal policies, inflation was held down in 1982 and industrial productivity increased. The sell-offs or privatisation of public firms contributed to it. From 1983 to 1988 the economy grew at around 3 to 4%. The deregulation of securities transactions attracted a large amount of capital from outside the country. Repeated income tax cuts fuelled the consumption boom, especially that of houses. With the deregulation of foreign exchange, interest rates became less effective in controlling inflation, because the banks could now supply money through its foreign subsidiaries. People accumulated huge debts by buying houses, believing that prices would keep rising. The consumer boom continued with mounting consumer debt. The bubble burst in 1989 (Smith, 1992). The depression lasted longer than expected. The rate of GDP growth dropped from over 4% in 1988 to over 2% in 1989, and to less than 1% in 1990. The unemployment rate increased from 6.8% in 1990 to 10.3% in 1993. This time the downturn was the outcome of the Conservative government's policies.

After the collapse of the Smithsonian regime of 1973, a floating exchange rate system was introduced. In 1979 European countries started the European Monetary System, whose central feature was an Exchange Rate Mechanism (ERM). It set target zones for each of the exchange rates of member countries' currencies. The UK joined the system in 1990, but the large fluctuation did not stop. From 1988 the UK suffered a large deficit in its international balance of payments. Cooperation among the EU countries did not work well as Germany suffered the burden of inflation accompanying reunification. It had to raise interest rates, while other countries needed lower interest rates. Sterling and the lira were most affected and they were finally compelled to exit from the system in 1992.

After the depression the growth rate returned to 2 to 3% and the deficit in the international balance dissolved after quitting the ERM. Inflation, which was again gaining force in the second half of the 1980s, settled down after 1992. The unemployment rate started to decrease from 10.5% in 1993 to 7% in 1997.

Labour Years Since the Late 1990s

After the 18 years of Thatcherite hard policies against trades unions and social welfare the Labour Party came to power in the May 1997 election. The framework for the 'New Britain' that the Labour government pursues is characterized by its pro-competitiveness attitude as much as its predecessor and by a somewhat larger emphasis on social welfare policies. Prime Minister Blair's posture to think more of market mechanism and competitiveness than the traditional Labour policies had already been shown in his effort to delete the nationalization clause from the Party's constitution in 1995. The Conservative anti-inflation policy was also continued and reinforced when the power to decide monetary policy was shifted to the Bank of England. The serious lesson learned in the consumer boom in the latter half of the 1980s was behind this decision.

The government also sought to strengthen the relationship with

Continental Europe and to adopt the common currency at an early stage (planning a referendum in 2002 and joining the system in 2005). Although business hopes to join it as soon as possible to receive the benefits of no more exchange risks in the area,[20] the strong pound to Euro at the time of writing continues to be an obstacle.

In the sphere of social welfare, there 'are few fundamental differences between the parties in most social policy areas' (Budge et al., 1998, p. 625). 'The major difference between the parties is on the degree of selectivity, with Labour favouring higher benefit levels' (ibid., p. 84). One significant change was the implementation of the national minimum wage in April 1999. The two major problems, health care and pensions, are still not fully addressed.

Effects of the Policies

Economy

Figure 3.6 shows the economic growth rate (GDP, in real terms), unemployment rate, and inflation rate (consumer price index) in the 1980s and 1990s.

Figure 3.6 UK: economic performance; GDP, inflation, unemployment, 1977-96

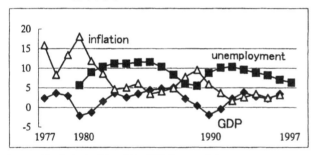

Source: Statistical table of the UK (Appendix).

Unemployment moved with GDP with a slight lag. Inflation and unemployment moved in opposite directions. Probably being influenced by the two major unemployment peaks, the inflation rate tended to decrease even when unemployment came down.

Figures 3.7 and 3.8 show the movement of the international balance of payments and financial balance of the government. During this period, the financial balance recovered up to 1989, then worsened in the depression until 1993, recovering since then. The current account was in surplus at first, and

---

[20] Cleve Thompson, the Chairman of CBI, Nikkei, 21, November, 1998.

then suffered heavy deficit up to 1988, recovering since then. We can observe large fluctuations in both indexes.

Figure 3.7 UK: government deficit, 1970-98

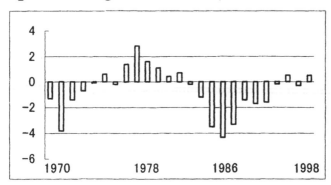

Source: Statistical table of the UK.

Figure 3.8 UK: current account, 1977-97

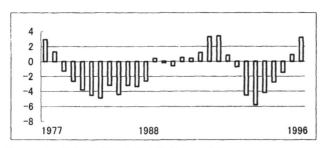

Source: Statistical table of the UK (Appendix).

Low profit rate, hence low investment was the major policy target to be tackled both by Conservative and Labour governments. Machinery and equipment investment as a percentage of GDP had not increased since the 1960s to the mid-1990s (8.4% in 1960, 8.8% in 1968, 7.4% from 1981 to 1983, 8.0% in 1984, 9.1% in 1989, 7.6% in 1991, 7.2% in 1992 and 1993, and 7.3% in 1994). Non-residential construction was even worse (6.3% in 1968, 7.4% in 1974, 5.8% in 1980, below 6% until 1987, 6.4% in 1988, 7.2% in 1990, 5.4% in 1992, 4.8% in 1993, and 3.8% in 1994) (OECD, *Hist. Stat.*, 1992, pp. 70-71, 1996, pp. 74-75).

Such movements of indexes partly reflect a decreasing share of industrial production (or the increasing share of service industries). Compared to the other three countries, the UK decreased its share drastically for these years from 42% in 1980 to 31% in 1993, a similar level with

Sweden, 30% in 1993, and the US, 27% in 1993 (Table 3.8).

Table 3.8 Share of industrial production in GDP

	Sweden	UK	Japan	US
1980	34%	42%	41%	33%
1993	30%	31%	40%	27%*

* 1991

Industries include mining and quarrying, manufacturing, electricity, gas and water, and construction.

Source: OECD, *OECD Economies at a Glance*, 1996, p.75.

Welfare

Government welfare spending ratio to GDP already showed a sharp decline in 1977-78. It decreased again from 1983 to 1988, but rapidly increased in the economic depression between 1990 and 1992, reaching a new height of well over 25% of GDP in the years 1992-96. This rise reflected economic factors such as the increased unemployment in the depression in 1990-92 and also such demographic and social factors as the constant increase of pensions, health care, and single parent families (Hills, ed., 1997, p. 9). At present, Britain spends 25% of its GDP for welfare spending as a total in the 1996/7 fiscal year. It spent 7% for the National Health Service, 5% for education, 4% for retirement, 2% for income support, 2% for incapacity, and 2% for housing. Unemployment benefit is, surprisingly, a small ratio at 0.1% (Barr, 1998, p. 8).

Table 3.9 also shows a complementary movement among the ratios of social security transfer payments, consumption expenditures, and investment in GDP for respective periods. The transfer payments consist of social security benefits for sickness, old age, family allowances, social assistance grants and unfunded employee welfare benefits paid by general government,

Table 3.9 Social security, consumption, and investment, % of GDP

	1960	1968	1974	1974-79	1980-90
Transfer[1]	6.8	8.7	9.8	10.7	13.1
Consumption[2]	66.0	63.1	63.8	61.2	61.9
Investment[3]	13.4	15.1	16.3	15.2	14.0

Sources:

[1]: social security transfers, OECD, *Hist. Stat.*, 1996, p. 67.

[2]: private final consumption expenditure as a percentage of GDP, ibid., p. 66.

[3]: machinery and equipment and non-residential construction, ibid., pp. 70-71.

etc. (OECD, *Hist. Stat.*, 1996, p. 75). It should be noted that under the restrictive welfare policies of the Thatcher administration the ratio of transfer payments still kept increasing.

Income Difference – By Taxes and Welfare

By taxes In the years through the 1980s and 1990s, the gap between the rich and the poor has widened. Between 1983 and 1997, the hourly income of the top 10% increased by 1.45 times whereas the bottom 10% only by 1.2 times. The trend of income difference changed in 1979. The share of the bottom decile group was 4.2% in 1961 and 1979, but dropped to 3.1% in 1996/97. That of top decile was 22.0% in 1961, 21.0% in 1979, and reached as high as 28.0% in 1996/97 (George and Wilding, 1999, p. 135). Through the 1980s, the male workers whose wages were less than the minimum by the European Commission's standard increased from 14.6% to 28.1%. Those whose disposable income was less than 50% of the average income increased slightly from 12.8% in the mid-1970s to 13.9% in 1985 in the European Community as a whole, while that figure for the UK increased significantly from 6.7% to 12% (George and Miller, ed., 1994, p. 44).

The first cause of this change was tax reform, or the amelioration of progressive tax rates. The maximum personal income tax rate decreased from 83% to 60% from 1979 to 1980, then to 40% in 1990. Although the rate for the lowerst also decreased from 34% to 25% in 1979, and then to 20% in 1993, the advantage was much greater for the higher income group.

Table 3.10 Income tax rates (%)

FY	1974	75	76	78	79	80	81	87	88	90	93	97	98
Lowest rate	30	33	35	34	25	25	30	29	27	25	20	20	20
Basic rate	–	–	–	–	–	–	–	25	24	23	–	–	–
Highest rate	75	83	83	83	83	60	60	60	60	40	40	40	40

Source: UK Office of National Statistics, *Annual Abstract of Statistics*, 1983, 1993, 1997, 1999.

Table 3.11 Tax burden among income groups (%)

	1	2	3	4	5
1979	4.0	11.5	18.0	25.1	41.4
1986	4.5	8.1	15.9	25.0	46.4

Source: Japan Keizai Kikakucho Keizai Kenkyujo, 1998, p. 29.

Consequently, income was redistributed from the top and bottom to the middle-income group. As shown in Table 3.11, the burden of the former two in the five income groups increased in the first half of the 1980s and that of the third group decreased, and the condition of the poorest people much worsened.

The shift of the burden from personal income tax to general consumption tax (VAT) through the Conservative administrations in the 1980s also enhanced the income-shift and increased actual inequality at the consumer level. The weight of personal income tax in the whole tax revenue decreased from 37.9% in 1975 to 27.8% in 1993, while general consumption tax increased from 8.8% in 1975 to 19.5% in 1993 to offset this decline of tax revenue (Table 3.12).

Table 3.12 Structure of tax revenue (%)

	1975	1993
personal income tax	37.9	27.8
corporate income tax	6.7	7.2
soc. sec. cont.[1] (employer)	6.6	6.6
soc. sec. cont. (employee)	10.3	10.5
general consumption tax	8.8	19.5
others [2]	29.8	28.3

[1]: social security contribution.
[2]: taxes on property, etc.
Source: OECD, *OECD Economies at a Glance*, 1996, p. 96.

By welfare The second cause was the restrictive welfare provisions that mostly affected the lower income group. The figures of transfer payments through government show that the bottom and the top two groups received less in 1986 than in 1979, compared to the second and third groups being favoured. This suggests that social welfare policy as a whole was another cause of the increase in income difference of this period (Table 3.13).

Table 3.13 Transfer payments (%)

	1	2	3	4	5
1979	30. 6	20.0	17.4	17.0	15.0
1986	26. 7	25.9	19.4	16.1	11.0

Source: Atkinson et al. cited in Japan EPA Keizai Kenkyujo ed. (1998) p. 30.

Overall we can summarise that the process of the UK-type reform of the Welfare State characterized by a harsher attitude to labour and social welfare has resulted in higher economic performance and increasing income difference in the 1980s to 1990s.

JAPAN

Process of the Policies

Although Japan has had rather low inequality in its market (pre-redistribution) income distribution, stable employment and a strong export-oriented culture, the anti-welfarism since the 1980s and its failure to meet the post bubble-burst period have created serious insecure feelings in the society.

1970s – Recession, Spending, and Deficit

Faced with the oil shocks in the 1970s, the economic growth rate (GDP in real terms) dropped from around 10% in the 1960s to around 2 to 5%. But government spending contributed to economic growth in the 1960s and most of the 1970s until 1978. By continuing large-scale government spending to meet the depression, the budget balance from the 1970s to the first half of the 1980s turned into a deficit of 3 to 5% of nominal GDP. After 1979 a restrictive budget policy was pursued.

1980s – Yen's Appreciation, Bubble and its Bursting

Export and appreciation of the yen Facing the changing trend of a high to low growth economy after the two oil shocks of the 1970s, the Japanese economy first tried to meet this hardship by expanding its exports. In the first half of the 1980s, Japan recorded a growth rate of over 3% (compared to industrialized nations of around 1%), which accompanied a large current account surplus and generated economic frictions with others. In September 1985 a major adjustment to the currency exchange rate was made by the Plaza agreement. It caused the yen's appreciation and threatened exports. Exporting firms pursued cost cutting by further rationalization and kept their competitiveness in the world market.

The report of the Temporary Administrative Investigation Committee at the beginning of the 1980s reshaped the Japanese economy and society in the following decades. This report gave the first priority to the deficit cutting of government finance and to reviving its economy by deregulation and smaller government. Reducing the deficit and stimulating the economy by monetary relaxation and deregulation became the major economic polices. The public deficit ratio to spending decreased from one third in 1981-84 to one quarter in 1985-88, and to one fifth or sixth in 1989-93. Supported by export-led prosperity in the second half of the 1980s, the budget balance turned surplus from 1987 to 1992.

The necessity to support the strong dollar and the incompetence of financial policy led Japan's monetary policy to pursue lower interest rates in the 1980s. The official bank rate was 7.25% in 1980, 5% in the first half of 1980s, and then decreased in the following three years to 3% in 1986 and 2.5% in 1987 and 1988, thus generating a significant monetary relaxation. This resulted in the provision of speculative money to the business world from 1988 to 1990. The swollen price of land and stocks of industrial firms invited more loans from banks, which were further invested into stocks and land. Firms also invested the abundant money into productive capacity.[21] Affluent loans expanded consumption, too. After the bubble burst, the interest rate was pulled down further to a super low rate of 0.5% in 1995 and 1996.

1990s – Depression and Spending

The collapse of bubble economy led to long-term depression in the 1990s. The accumulated debt caused by the bubble burst now made the upturn of business the more difficult. The next observations by OECD in 1992 describe well the situation of Japan in this period: 'In a number of countries, households and firms are still seeking to reduce high levels of indebtedness that were contracted in the buoyant asset-market conditions of the second half of the 1980s. This ongoing adjustment is leading them to increase saving and restrain investment, thereby damping aggregate demand and output ... In addition, banks and other financial intermediaries in some countries have adopted more cautious lending attitudes. Consumers are also being prudent because of fears of becoming unemployed' (OECD, *Economic Outlook*, 52, 1992, p. ix). What was serious for Japan was that this situation was to continue for nearly a decade.

Faced with the serious recession, government could not help expanding its spending. The finance turned deficit from 1993 to 1998. The ratio of accumulated central government deficit reached 48.6% of GDP in 1996 and that of general government (including local government) 90.1%.[22] With the slight recovery of the economy, a restrictive financial policy for financial reconstruction resumed in 1996. Through the rise in consumption tax rate and users' fees for the health service, reduced exports due to the Asian currency crisis and the fear of the uncollectable loans of many banks, this restrictive policy immediately stopped the recovery and reopened the serious depression in 1997 and 1998. The economy lost the chance to recover in the

---

[21] The Economic Planning Agency in Japan estimated the excess capacity for July to September 1998 to be over 85 trillion yen, as much as the new investment of all the firms for one year (Nikkei, 1999, March 22).

[22] Although the absolute amount was 438 trillion-yen in March 1998 (Ministry of Finance) it is also pointed out that the net burden to the total savings in the country is much lower in Japan than the US, Germany, the UK and France (Kato 1996, p. 228).

mid-1990s. A lost ten years became a reality.

Social welfare retrenchment The suspension of welfare growth in Japan began with the Temporary Administrative Investigation Committee Act in 1980. In accordance with its first report in 1981 and final report of 1983, which praised self-help and recommended retrenchment and higher efficiency of the welfare system, free health care for the old was abolished in 1982 and the government started to raise the fees in 1986. The beneficiary's fee of 10% of the medical cost was introduced in 1984 and the cost of meals in hospital has come to be charged since 1994. Payment by central government into national health insurance was reduced in 1986 and health insurance in 1992. Withholding of health insurance certificates for the offenders was introduced in 1986. Local government has paid a share to national insurance since 1986. Contributions for pension were significantly increased and benefit was cut in 1985.

Effects of the Policies

Economy

After the post oil-shock years, the economic performance in Japan has experienced two contrasting periods. The GDP growth rate was around 5% in the1970s, dropped to 2 to 3% in the first half of the1980s but recovered to 4 to 6% in 1988-90. With the burst of the bubbles, however, came the zero growth years of the 1990s. It showed a slight recovery in 1995-96, but dropped again in 1996-98. A new characteristic for the Japanese economy was the gradual abandonment of the firms' traditional policy of retaining the workforce within firms even in depression. The unemployment rate rose rapidly in the 1990s from 2% in 1990 to 3% in 1996, then to over 4% in 1997 and finally to 5% in the first half of 1999.[23] Having been accustomed to a stable employment culture, people experienced a great shock facing this change.

The fluctuating exchange rate induced firms to increase foreign direct investment and to the 'hollowing out' of the economy. The yen/dollar rate had changed from 360 yen to a dollar in 1965 to 299 yen in 1975, and was further appreciated to 201 yen in 1978, 159 yen in 1986, and 113 yen in 1996, thus appreciated by almost three times in three decades (Japan Keizai Kikakucho Chosakyoku, 1998, p. 32). Japanese firms tried to get over this situation by pursuing higher productivity and cutting costs by producing abroad. A rapid increase of foreign direct investment occurred in 1972, 1981, and 1986. The US had been the major country to invest in, with over 40% of

---

[23] The average unemployment period also rose to 4.2 months, the longest in postwar years (Nikkei, March 21, 1999).

the total investment, but the ratio of Asia has increased rapidly from 12% in 1985 to 24% in 1995. The largest share today in Asia goes to China and ASEAN countries (Japan Keizaikikakucho Sogo Keikakukyoku, 1997, p. 21).

Figure 3.9 Japan: economic performance; GDP, inflation, unemployment, 1970-96

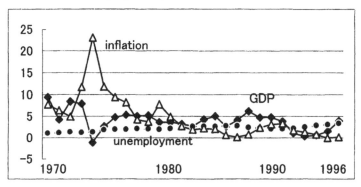

Source: Statistical table of Japan (Appendix).

Figure 3.10 Japan: government deficit, 1970-98

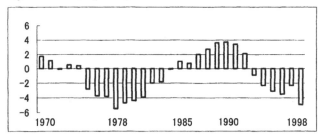

Source: Statistical table of Japan (Appendix).

Figure 3.11 Japan: current account, 1974-97

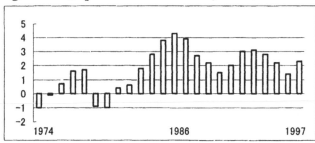

Source: Statistical table of Japan (Appendix).

85

Welfare

The Japanese government has often argued that one of the reasons for the containment of welfare provisions since the 1980s was that the welfare level of Japan had caught up with the European levels. But it is doubtful if the Japanese welfare level is sufficiently high enough yet, judging from the weak consumption attitude that has continued in the 'insecure' social atmosphere in the 1990s. Although it is catching up with the European style welfare system in health care, pensions, old age care, etc., the overall security it gives the people has not fully ameliorated their anxieties since the bursting of the bubble. It seems to testify to the necessity to strengthen the public welfare provisions when the society as a whole is being thrust into a highly 'flexible' but unstable era by economic globalization.

Income Difference

Income difference in Japan was relatively low compared to the other countries. Gini co-efficient for them before redistribution (market income level) was 31.7 in Japan (1989) compared to 43.9 in Sweden (1987), 42.8 in the UK (1986), and 41.1 in the US (1986) (Japan Keizai Kikakucho Keizai Kenkyujo, 1998, p. 27, and Atkinson et al. 1995). The figure of post-redistribution was also low in Japan at 25.2 (1984), 26.5 (1994), compared to the UK at 30.4 (1987), the US 34.1 (1986), 34.4 (1995), but the lowest were in Sweden at 22.0 (1987) and 23.0 (1995) (OECD, 1996a, p. 15; Japan Keizaikikakucho Keizai Kenkyujo, 1998, p. 25; OECD, 1999, p. 66).

Because of the difficulty in foreseeing the effect of a changing traditional culture, it is not easy to predict what type of Welfare State Japan is going to converge into. But whatever type it will be, whether it can meet the heavy anxiety prevailing in Japan will be an important factor determining its development.

US

Process of the Policies

A similar change as in the UK has occurred in the US economy in the 1980s and 1990s. It was initiated by the political change from pro-welfare to anti-welfare, more pro-market policies. In a word, the mainstream in this period has been the change of the political stance of the government from liberal to conservative (Reagan) and its maintenance under the Clinton administration. By the end of the 1970s, overcoming declining competitiveness in the world market, reducing inflationary pressure and the growing government deficit became major targets for the US. The Reagan administration, which came to power in 1980, aimed at economic restructuring by tight budget, tax cuts, restrictive money supply and deregulation.

Up to the 1970s – Declining Competitiveness

After the end of the World War Two, the US boasted high productivity in the 1950s and 1960s. But at the beginning of the 1960s the signs of an inflationary trend and rising unemployment appeared. In contrast to the recovery of other countries, similar to the case of the UK, the competitiveness of the US declined and the trade balance turned deficit in 1971. With the suspension of the convertibility of dollar into gold in 1971 and the shift to the floating exchange rate system after 1973, the value of the dollar started to go down. Government deficit accompanied this trend until the middle of the 1990s.

The First Half of the 1980s – Anti-inflation Policy, but Continued Deficit

The Reagan administration aimed at economic recovery by tax cuts and controlling inflation by restricting money supply. But as it increased military spending and also failed to cut welfare spending (see Table 3.2), the deficit grew larger. Military expenditure had dropped to 4.9% of GDP in 1979 but increased to 6.1% in 1983. The ratio of the federal government deficit to GDP had reached 4.3% in 1976, dropped to 1.6% in 1979, but again increased to 6.1% in 1983 under the first Reagan administration.[24] As the central bank that pursued a restrictive monetary policy did not underwrite the public bond, it had to be bought in the city and it caused the so-called crowding-out and interest rise, thus deepening the depression. On the other hand, this high interest rate absorbed foreign money, which appreciated the dollar and weakened the competitiveness of American exports, enlarging the trade deficit.

The good result of the first administration was in controlling inflation. The rate of consumer price rises was kept as low as 2 to 3% after 1983 and throughout the Reagan administrations. The unemployment rate, which was around 5% in the 1960s and 1970s, and still was over 7% in 1980 and 1981 after the oil shocks, rose further to over 9% in 1982 and 1983. This held down the demand for wage increases and contributed to the control of inflation.

The accumulation of the deficit in the international balance of payments made the debt of the US the world's largest in 1985. To meet this problem and the hollowing out of industry, it was deemed important to strengthen its

---

[24] Department of the Treasury and Office of Management and Budget.

international competitiveness. Although 'downsizing' on the firms' side was already going on, a quick remedy was necessary until its competitiveness would catch up. Thus it was necessary to depreciate the dollar further. The 1985 Plaza Agreement was the confirmation to help maintain the trust by other countries in the world's key currency.

The Second Half of the 1980s to the 1990s – Recovery of the Economy

In 1985 the Gramm-Rudman-Hollings Act (the Budget Balancing act) was enacted, which enabled an automatic budget cut. It was followed by similar Acts in 1987, 1990, 1993 and 1997. Under this Act, in the following years, except for 1990, 1991, and 1992 when the budget deficit grew again under depression, the ratio of deficit to GDP kept decreasing and finally turned surplus in 1998. The trade deficit grew until 1987 and then started decreasing. From 1991 to 1999 it has shown a somewhat upward trend but is about 1% of GDP compared to 3% in the 1980s.

Partly helped by the decline of competitiveness of foreign competitors such as Japan and Germany in the 1990s as the result of their long depression or, in Germany's case, the large burden of reunion of the divided countries, such traditional manufacturing industries as automobiles and aircraft have regained their competitiveness since the second half of the 1980s. On the other hand, industries such as transport, communications, information, and finance have grown under the deregulation that started under the Reagan administration. Combined together, they generated a rising trend of stock prices, leading to a consumer boom. This then led to the growth of tertiary industry, which increased jobs although at lower wages.

The rising trend of stock prices has supported the prosperity of the US by encouraging larger consumption in the 1990s. Stock prices have tripled on the average from 1990 to 1999. The number of households benefiting from this price rise has increased from 32% in 1989 to 41% in 1995 (*Newsweek*, July 5, 1999, p. 48). In the end of the 1990s people are supposed to be spending their income from stocks on consumption, which now expands firms' sales, thus raising the stock prices again (*Nikkei*, March 22, 1999).

We might then be able to assume such a linkage as that the firms first obtained the money from the stock market when they needed it for investment, and then obtained consumers when they needed larger purchasing power. But with half of households investing in stocks, the US economy has in a sense become very sensitive to the fluctuation of stock prices, a richer but a more risky society. If the stock market collapses, the damage would be huge. Japan may have been an example of this in the early 1990s. Japanese stock prices, after having risen four to five times in the 1980s, lost their value by 30 to 40% compared to 1994 level after the burst of the bubbles (PHP, 1995, p. 170), which resulted in the decade-long depression.

Effects of the Policies

Economy

In the anti-inflationary policies in 1980-82, the unemployment rate rose from 5.8% to 9.7% and 9.6% in 1982-83. Through this determined economic downturn and high unemployment period, the inflationary pressure was held down. It had risen from 7.6% in 1978 to 11.3%, 13.5%, 10.3% in 1979-81, but dropped to 6.1% in 1982 and 3.2% in 1983. It never rose over 6% in the following years until 1997.[25] On the other hand, the high interest rate resulting from tight monetary policy absorbed foreign money, which appreciated the dollar but, on the other hand, weakened the competitiveness of American exporting industries. Current account balance turned deficit since 1982 and grew from 0.4% of GDP in 1982 to 2 to 3% in 1984-88, whereas the massive inflow of foreign money supported the growth of internal demand. Thus success in stable prices and dissolution of budgetary deficit, but continuous current balance deficit are the results of the policies in the 1980s and 1990s.

Figure 3.12 US: economic performance; GDP, inflation, unemployment, 1971-97

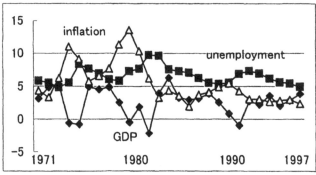

Source: Statistical table of the US (Appendix).

---

[25] Deregulation and accompanying 'downsizing' seems to have been another cause to hold down the inflationary pressures from labour's side. Serious anxiety about losing jobs in an economic downturn must have changed the workers' attitude.

Figure 3.13 US: government deficit, 1970-98

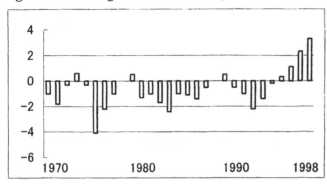

Source: Statistical table of the US (Appendix).

Figure 3.14 US: current account, 1973-97

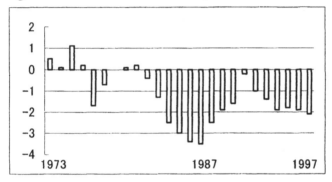

Source: Statistical table of the US (Appendix).

Welfare

The significant characteristic is that public social protection expenditure has remained relatively stable even in the neo-liberal years of the 1980s; 14.2% of GDP in 1980 to 14.8% in 1990. For 1982-83, it was 15.1% and 15.5%, when GDP fell sharply (OECD, 1996, *Economies at a Glance*, p. 107). The ratio of pension benefit to GDP in the US scored a little higher than Japan, but one half of that of Sweden: 5.9% in the US, 11.9% in Sweden in 1990, 8.3% in the UK, and 5.0% in Japan. Public expenditure for health has constantly increased from 3.9% in 1980 to 6.1% in 1993. Non public health expenditure has also increased from 5.4% in 1980 to 7.8% in 1993 (ibid., 109). Public expenditure for the aged has remained almost the same, 5.8% to 5.9%, except for 1982-83 (ibid., p. 107). One unique characteristic about health care in the US is that although the ratio of public health spending is

90

similar among the four countries at around 5 to 6%, private spending is as high as 7.8% compared to 1 to 2% in the other three. But the unemployment benefit replacement rates (for a single 40-year-old with an unbroken employment record) decreased from around 60% in the 1970s to around 50% in the 1980s and 1990s (Lazar and Stoyko, 1998, p. 20).

Income Difference

The problem of income difference looms particularly large in the welfare problems in the US. The Gini index (by market income) had risen a little in the 1970s, from 35.3 in 1970 to 36.5 in 1979, and then rose sharply in the 1980s and 1990s to 42.5 in 1996 (Miringoff, 1999, p. 201). In the mid-1980s, the inequality was the highest in the US, marking 34.1 for 1986, compared to 31.7 in Japan for 1989, 30.4 in the UK for 1986, and 22.0 in Sweden for 1987 (OECD 1996, *OECD Economies at a Glance*, p. 15). We can look at this trend from various angles. The income inequality measured by the ratio of the income of the top to the bottom decile was 5.78 in the US in 1991, compared to 4.67 in the UK in 1990, 4.17 in Japan in 1992 and 2.75 in Sweden in 1992 (Sweeding, 1997, cited in Navarro, 1998, p. 645). The gains and losses by quintile in the mid-1980s to 1990s were: the middle three lost, the highest gained most, and the lowest gained a little in the US (OECD, 1999, p. 69). Wages increased little during this period, and only among the top group. The rate of annual growth of wages for men in the top, median, and bottom deciles was 0.4%, –0.6%, and –1.4% for 1970-90. The same figure for Great Britain was higher at 3.4%, 2.2% and 1.2% (Navarro, 1998, p. 641). Poverty ratio increased in the 1980s and in the early 1990s in the US as well as in the UK as shown below (Smeeding 1997, cited in Navarro, 1998, p. 648).

US		UK		Sweden	
1979	16.6	1979	9.2	1981	5.4
1994	19.1	1994	14.6	1992	6.7

One of the reasons for this increasing income difference lies in the low growth of wages. Unlike the UK's case, the US shows a clear difference between the two indices, productivity increase (real value added in manufacturing) and wage increase (hourly earnings). For most of the years after the 1980s until 1993, the former surpassed the latter, thus containing the employees' incomes (OECD, *Hist. Stat.* 1992, 1996). Low-paid employment (wages of less than two thirds of median full-time workers') in the US increased by a few percentage points to a little over 25% during the 1980s to the mid-1990s, while the UK also increased by a few percentage points to around 20%, and Japan decreased by a few percentage points to around 15% (OECD, 1999, p. 24). This growth of the low wage group is a major cause of the poverty problem (ibid., p. 77).

Low wages are related to the changes in the industrial structure. In the US it was the sales and service workers whose number has increased most during 1981-96, with clerical and related workers second. In Japan it was professionals and technicians, and in Sweden, clerical and related workers. This kind of workforce shift is universal in 20 countries that were examined. The only country that had the highest growth in production and related workers was the Philippines (ILO, 1999, *World Employment 1998-99*, p. 34).

Alan Greenspan of Federal Reserve Board explains this stagnated wage increase by the anxiety of the workers about job losses even under prosperity. He testified in the Congress that an exceptional constraint on the increase of the reward for labour had been clear for several years, which seemed to have stemmed from growing anxiety among the workers. He pointed out that the increase in the number of those who worried about being unemployed in big companies rose from 25% in 1991 to 46% in 1996, the decrease of the number of workers who would change jobs, and that the workers themselves were demanding that labour agreements be lengthened from three years to five to six years, all of which showed that they regarded job security more important than wage rises. According to the research of the Department of Labour of October 1996, the number of workers who lost jobs in the middle of the 1990s, from January 1993 to December 1995, was 9.4 million, 4.2 million of who had worked more than three years. Of these 4.2 million people, 81% found full-time jobs again but those whose salary rose by more than 20% was 370,000, much smaller than those whose salary decreased by more than 20%, 610,000 (Otsuka, 1998, pp. 25, 30).

The reform of the tax system is another major factor for the income difference. The highest personal income tax rate was lowered from 54% in 1980 to 42% in 1984, and 28% in 1988. The rate, which included state and local taxes, became 40%, which was followed by the Clinton administration, too. The highest tax rate for unearned income was lowered from 70% to 50% in 1981. Tax rate for capital gains was also lowered from 28% to 20% (Mishra, 1991, p. 31). It is estimated that for the years 1983-85, households with incomes above 80,000 dollars gained 35 billion dollars, those under 20,000 dollars lost 20 billion dollars, and those under 10,000 dollars lost 1,100 dollars a year on the average (ibid).[26]

The income transfer was favourable for the upper middle group and unfavourable for the lowest in the first half of the 1980s. Between 1979 and 1986, the bottom fifth income group's share declined from 29.7% to 29.2%. That of the second from the top increased conspicuously from 14.7% to

---

[26] Against the argument that the Reagan tax cuts were effective because the wealthiest people paid a larger part of the total personal income tax after the rate was reduced, we have to examine if the ratio of their tax to their total wealth declined or not.

17.5%, and the second from the bottom remained almost the same, 21.1% to 21.2%. The middle fifth's decreased from 17.4% to 17.1%, while the top group's decreased from 17.1% to 15.1% (Japan Keizai Kikakucho Keizai Kenkyujo, 1998, p. 30). Up to the mid-1990s the income difference remained large in the US, as we also saw in the case of Japan – Gini coefficient after redistribution at 34.1 (1986) and 34.4 (1995).

Unlike the European trend, American workers now work longer hours. According to the ILO, they worked nearly 2000 hours in 1997, 83 hours more than in 1980. The report of the ILO even warned that the US worker might be in danger of burning out. The lower growth of hourly wages might be forcing them to work longer. At the same time, however, those who are satisfied with their jobs have increased for 1989-99. Those who are somewhat satisfied decreased from 61% to 47%, and those completely satisfied increased from 28% to 39% (Gallup Poll, CNN.com September. 6, 1999).

Evaluating the above changes in the welfare field, the then Secretary of the Department of Labour, Robert Reich, argued that as a result of the decrease of workers' wages in spite of prosperity, American society was being divided between the 'haves' and 'have-nots'. He understood that the tacit social contract in American society – namely the three agreements of first, to give everyone the opportunity of education, secondly, that workers also benefit, when the firms flourish, and thirdly, to lend hands to the needy – was falling down. Thus he suggested the danger of the collapse of the whole social structure, not just a cyclical hardship of the employees or the lower income group (Reich, 1994 farewell speech).

Like the UK, the US has followed the anti-inflationary and anti-public deficit path, which was anti-labour, anti-welfare but pro-profit at the same time. The results have been similar: higher economic performance in terms of growth, employment and low inflation, but increasing income difference. How we should evaluate this shift from the viewpoint of social balance will be discussed in the following chapters.

2.3 ANALYSIS 2 – relations between policies, growth, and welfare

2.3.1 Cost Reduction and Firms' Performance

In Section 2.1 we posed the theoretical relationship between economic growth and welfare, and then in Section 2.2 we looked at the changing processes of growth and welfare in the four countries. The intentions and policies for these changes were mainly to promote economic growth by reducing firms' burdens such as wages, taxes and social contributions. The focus in this section is to examine this relationship closely. We will see there the general trend of the economy and firms' investment accompanying the

93

changing government policies. But how we should evaluate the significance of the economic recovery achieved in this way by the broader criterion of social balance will be discussed in the following chapters.

SWEDEN

Movement of Firms' Burdens – Labour Costs, Taxes and Social Contributions

Lower labour cost: labour cost measured by the growth of real hourly earnings in manufacturing industries remained low, –4.3% in 1977 and 1980, –1.7% in 1983, but recovering to 3.0% in 1986, 2.2% in 1987, 2.1% in 1988, 3.3% in 1989. It decreased sharply to –1.0% in 1990, –3.5% in 1991, then recovered to 2.3% in 1992, and fell again to –1.3% in 1993 (OECD, *Hist. Stat.* 1992, p. 94, 1996, p. 98).[27]

Lower tax rate: corporate income tax rate decreased to 28% through the reforms of the beginning of the 1990s, which figure is the lowest among the EU countries (January 1, 1998). If exemption for losses is added, the effective rate will be around 26% (ISA, *Facts & Figures 1998*).

Higher tax and social security burden: the ratio of the total tax and social contribution to GDP was around 5% to 6% in the 1960s, kept increasing in the 1970s, reached around 14% to 16% in the 1980s, and then slightly decreased to 15.2%, and 15.5% in 1994 and 1995.

Movement of Profit Rate, Productivity and Competitiveness

Steady profit rate   The realized profit rate for Swedish firms was kept around the 30% level in the 1980s (measured by gross operating surplus as a percentage of gross value added in manufacturing) except for 1980, 1981, and 1982. This level was the second highest in the four countries after Japan's figure of above 40%. The same figure for industry plus transport and communication was around 30% to 35%[28] (OECD, *Hist. Stat.* 1992, pp. 78-9).

Recovering productivity   Swedish economy lagged behind eleven competitors between the second half of the 1970s and the first half of the 1990s in the productivity growth in manufacturing industries. It showed that the active labour market policy unique for Sweden was not enough to sustain the competitiveness necessary for the Welfare State (SAF, *Facts about the Swedish Economy*, website, and Masumura, 1998, p. 282). However, after

---

[27] Corporatist policies to trade wage rises with full employment was a part of the background of this wages movement.

[28] The difference between gross and net figures is mostly through tax and social contributions, and interest payments.

the structural reform of its economy at the beginning of the 1990s, its productivity recovered fast from the middle of the 1990s. The improvement in the current account in this period could be explained by the increased productivity that accompanied the liberalized international capital movement and intensified competition. The productivity compared to the US (100) in 1987 was 82.0 for Sweden, 59.4 for the UK, and 66.5 for Japan. It grew to 91.8 for Sweden, 64.1 for the UK, and 76.6 for Japan in 1993. Among the nine countries (the US, Japan, Germany, France, the UK, Canada, Australia, the Netherlands, and Sweden) Sweden came top in productivity only in paper products and printing, and metal products in 1987, but it came top in four industries in 1993, adding basic metal products and electrical machinery to the former two (measured by value added per hour worked, OECD, 1996, pp. 112-13). Competitiveness measured by current deficit declined in the first half of the 1980s, recovered in the second half, declined again around 1990 and has been recovering quickly from the middle of the 1990s.

UK

Movement of Firms' Burdens – Labour Costs, Taxes, and Social Contributions

Equal labour cost The growth rate of real hourly earnings in manufacturing alternated, rose and fell from 1977 to 1980 and then rose steadily from 1982 at 2.4% until 1988, at 3.4%. After a recession, it went up again to over 2% in 1991-93 (OECD, *Hist. Stat.* 1996).
　　Lower tax rate Corporate income tax rate was cut to 33% in March 1997 and to 30% in April 1999. That figure was 40% for the US, 41.66% for France, and 56.6% for Germany in April 1998.
　　Equal tax burden The ratio of corporate income tax and social contribution paid by firms to GDP rose from 4.5% in 1965 to 5.9% and 6.1% in 1970 and 1971 and reached 8.1% in 1985. It then decreased from 7.5% in 1990 to 6.3% in 1992 and 6.7% in 1995. This was mostly because of the fluctuation of tax revenue and social security burden on the firms remained stable at around 3.5% of GDP from the 1970s to the present.

Movement of Profit Rate, Productivity, and Competitiveness

Recovering profit rate The profit rate in the UK manufacturing industries was not particularly low compared to other countries in the 1950s and 1960s. But it decreased significantly under the stagflation caused by the oil shocks in the 1970s (Oughton, in Hughes (ed.), 1993, p. 50; George and Wilding, 1984, p. 159; Martin, 1981). Net operating surplus of the net value added in manufacturing was 20.8% for 1960-67, 17.9% for 1968-73, and 11.8% for 1974-79. It fell to 8.5% in 1980 and 6.1% in 1981. It then started to recover, growing from 10.0% in 1982 to 19.3% in 1986, and then 21.0% in 1989. In the worldwide depression it declined to 13.3% and 14.7% in 1991 and 1992 but recovered again to 17.4% and 20.9% in 1993 and 1994 (OECD, *Hist. Stat.* 1992, p. 78, 1996, p. 82).

Higher investment   Investment has followed the movement of profitability by one to two years (Oughton, in Hughes (ed.), 1993, p. 60). The overall productivity growth of the UK in the 1980s and up to the mid-1990s has remained relatively high and constant (Table 3.14).

Table 3.14 Productivity growth; real GDP per person employed (%)

	1960-79	1979-89	1989-94
UK	2.8	1.9	1.9
US	1.9	0.8	1.2
Sweden	3.5	1.4	2.4
Japan	8.1	2.8	1.0

Source: OECD, *Hist. Stat.* 1996, p. 53.

It is argued by Oughton (1993) that labour costs put a heavy burden on UK manufacturing industry and reduced its profit rate. He asked which factor influenced the profit rate more, the profit share in the net value added which largely reflects labour cost, or the output-capital ratio, which is the result of the operating rate. Oughton finds that profit share explains two to three times as much as output-capital ratio in the periods 1954-81 and 1981-91 (ibid., p. 67). This relationship is shown in the contrasting moves of net profit rate and unit labour costs in UK manufacturing, too (ibid., p. 64). The rising trend of real wages continued in the 1990s until at least 1994, showing a sharp contrast to that of the US. The rate of wage increase from 1990 to 1995 for the UK by 32.3% was larger than in Italy, 31.8%, the US, 18.0%, France, 18.8%, Canada, 17.3%, and Japan, 21.2% (Japan Keizai Kikakucho Chosakyoku, 1998, p. 248).

Recovering current balance   Current balance, a measure of competitiveness, turned surplus at the end of the 1970s and remained so until the mid-1980s. It turned into deficit and grew rapidly from 1987 to the mid-1990s. Although the trade deficit continued from 1997 to 1998, the current balance turned surplus in the same period, which shows that service revenues offset the trade deficit (OECD, website, *Main Economic Indicators*, 1999).

Capital inflow   One characteristic of the UK economy is the positive influence of the influx of foreign capital. The UK's receipts from foreign firms inside the country accounted for one-seventh to one-eighth of GDP in 1990 while that of the US was one-fortieth (OECD, *Hist. Stat.*, 1992, p. 10).

Almost the same amount is contributed by UK firms operating in foreign countries.

JAPAN

Movement of Firms' Burdens – Labour Costs, Taxes, and Social Contributions

Lower labour cost   The growth rate of real hourly earnings in manufacturing were volatile in the second half of the 1970s, but then remained over 1% in most of the 1980s, and reached 4.0% in 1988, and 3.5% in 1989. After the bubble burst, it fell to 0.2% in 1991, – 0.7% in 1992 and – 1.1% in 1993 (ibid.).

Lower tax rate   The corporate tax rate decreased from the 1950s to 1960s to promote the growth of firms, from 42% in 1952 to 35% in 1966. In the 1970s, in order to finance the personal income tax cut and to realize financial reconstruction, it was increased from 36.8% in 1970 to 43.3% in 1984 but then followed a long downward trend in the 1990s from 42% in 1987 to 30% in 1999. At the same time a consumption tax was introduced in 1989 and its rate was soon raised in 1997.

Higher tax and social security burden   The ratio of corporate income tax and social security burden to GDP on firms rose from over 5% in the 1960s to over 10% in the 1980s, but decreased to over 9% in the 1990s. This has been the result of the increasing social security burden and reduced income tax in the depression. This burden is likely to decrease.

Movement of Profit Rate, Productivity, and Competitiveness

High profit rate   The gross profit rate of manufacturing industries in Japan has been much higher than in the other three countries, 50% in the 1960s compared to that of over 20% for the UK and the US. This reflects the lower income share of the employees. As for the fluctuation of this figure, from 1970 to 1979, the figure for the US remained the same, while that of the UK dropped by about 4% points compared to before the oil shock period. The Japanese figure dropped by about 10% points to over 40%, which level continued throughout the 1980s (OECD, *Hist. Stat.*, 1992, p. 78). Since it plunged into recession in the 1990s, it went down slightly to 41% in 1992, and 38% in 1993 (ibid., 1996, p. 82).

High competitiveness   Current account balance has shown constant surplus since the 1980s. It showed a somewhat decreasing trend in the middle of the 1990s, but increased again in the recession because of lower imports in 1998 and 1999. In all, its competitiveness as a whole remained intact in the 1990s, judged by this continuous surplus. As a result of the high rate of return, the ratio of gross investment to GDP was very high in Japan at around 30% in the 1980s when the other three countries' figures were mostly less than 20%. It then achieved much higher productivity growth than the others from the middle of the 1970s to 1980s while it fell to the lowest among the four in the 1990s depression.

US

Movement of Firms' Burdens – Labour Costs, Taxes and Social Contributions

Lower labour cost The growth rate of real hourly earnings in manufacturing fell sharply in 1979-81, i.e., –2.5%, –4.3%, and –0.5%. It then remained around 0%, and fell to –1.8% in 1987 and –0.4% in 1993 (OECD, *Hist. Stat.*, 1992, 1996).

Low tax and social contribution burden The total ratio of tax and social security burden to GDP remained over 5% to 6% throughout the years from the 1960s until the mid-1990s.

Movement of Profit Rate, Productivity, and Competitiveness

Higher profit rate The ratio of net operating surplus to net value added in manufacturing increased from 13% to 14% in the early-1980s to 17% to 18% in the mid-1980s, and then further to 23.8% in 1989. In the years 1990-93, it reached between 21% and 23%. This represented recovery of the high profit levels of 1960-73, whose average was 21.5% (OECD, *Hist. Stat.*, 1992, p. 78, 1996, p. 82).

Recovering productivity: current balance continued to be in deficit in the 1990s, too. Productivity growth measured by real GDP per person employed increased from 1.1% in 1981 to 2.3% and 2.5% in 1983 and 1984. It then declined from 1986 to less than 1% until 1994, except for 1988 and 1992, when it was 1.7% and 1.9%. The average figure for 1989-94 was 1.2% in the US, 1.0% in Japan, 1.9% in the UK, and 2.4% in Sweden (ibid. 1996, p. 53).

From the four cases above we can observe a general movement toward lower labour and tax cost and at the same time recovering economies except for Japan. This downward movement was especially conspicuous in corporate tax rate in recent years, which seems to show the common determination of the governments to provide advantageous environments for their firms. We will now look at this question more closely.

2.3.2 Comparing the Firms' Burdens of the Four Countries

Recent policies for smaller government and social welfare provisions are not only directed to reallocating the resources to the firms but are also accelerated by the considerations of competitiveness with foreign firms. In this sense it is useful to compare the burden in the four countries, namely the tax rates and social contribution rates.

A: Tax, social security contribution, and wages as burdens for firms Table 3.15 below shows the ratios of profit, corporate income tax, social security contribution, and wages to GDP in 1993.

Table 3.15 Ratio of three factors to GDP (%) (1993)

	Sweden	UK	Japan	US
tax	2.2	2.4	14.9	2.2
social security	12.8	3.5	5.1	3.6
payroll[*1]	59.4	56.2	57.2	60.1
payrise by 10%	5.9	5.6	5.7	6.1

[*1]: Employees' payrolls.
Sources: Statistical tables in the Appendix page and Zaidan Hojin Yano Kotaro Kinenkai, 1997.

The burden of tax and social security contribution on firms was heavier in Sweden and Japan and lighter in the UK and the US. The effects of wage increases are large. If wages increase significantly in a period such as today when the competitive pressures both from the international and internal markets are strong, it will have strong effect on profit rate. Between tax and social security burdens, we should note that although tax fluctuates with the firms' income and business cycles, social security contributions remain more stable, related to more stable payrolls.

B: Total burden of tax and social security contribution Below is shown a rough comparison of tax and social security contribution burdens actually levied in 1994 and 1996 among the four countries (Table 3.16). This also shows that the total burden of firms is heavier in Japan and Sweden.

IMD also shows similar figures for these four countries as follows for 1988 and 1996 (Table 3.17). The UK is conspicuous in these four, reducing the figures from about 9% to 7% while others more or less increased theirs.

Table 3.16 Tax and social security burden on firms: 1994, 1996

		corporate income tax		social security contribution (employers')		total
Sweden	of TTR*(%) 1994	5.4		24.6		30.0
	1996	5.6		24.9		30.5
	m.t.r, p.t.r**		28.0		29.9	
UK	of TTR (%) 1994	8.0		10.0		18.0
	1996	10.5		9.6		20.1
	m.t.r, p.t.r		30.0		10.0	
Japan	of TTR (%) 1994	14.8		18.0		32.8
	1996	16.4		18.6		35.0
	m.t.r, p.t.r		34.5		11.4	
US	of TTR (%) 1994	8.9		13.3		22.2
	1996	9.6		12.9		22.5
	m.t.r, p.t.r		40.0		10.5	

*: total tax receipts. **: maximum tax rate and payroll tax rate, 1999.
Source: OECD website and *OECD in Figures*, 1997, 1999.

Table 3.17 Tax and social security contribution by firms as % of GDP

	1988		1996	
	tax	ssc	tax	ssc
Sweden	2.1	12.2	2.9	12.8
UK	6.0	3.4	3.3	3.4
Japan	4.5	4.0	4.4	5.3
US	1.5	3.8	2.6	3.6

tax: taxes on corporate income, profits and capital gains.
ssc: social security contribution.
Source: IMD, 1990, 1998.

C: Common trend: to lower corporate income tax rate We have seen above the downward trend of corporate income tax in the four countries. Most recently, the corporate income tax rate in Sweden was 28% for 1999, in the UK 31% for 1999, in Japan 48% in 1998. The effective corporate income tax rate for Japan was 37.5% in 1998 and was 34.5% for 1999. In the US the corporate tax rate was roughly 40% for 1999, which includes federal tax rate of 35% and state and local income tax rates between 1% and 12%. The effective rate is approximately 40%[29] (KPMG website, International Tax and

---

[29] Countries are eager to invite firms from abroad today. ISA in Sweden advertises that it has the lowest corporate tax rate compared to the eight countries investigated, Germany, USA, Japan, Ireland, France, Netherlands, UK in 1997. It goes on to argue that it has the lowest relative business costs for 1997, winning even over the US and the UK (from the website). But

Legal Centre, Amsterdam, 1999).

But this trend is not restricted to these countries alone. It has been generally common in many countries in the second half of the 1990s. Its process is explained by the UNDP's report as follows: 'The fiscal resource base ... is being squeezed in four ways'. The first is by trade liberalization, reducing import taxes; the second is by globalization of the tax base, the traditional tax system finding it hard to catch up with it; the third is by tax competition; and the fourth, by the growth of the black economy. We have focused on the third, the tax reduction competition, in this book. It describes it as, 'With capital tending to prefer low-tax situations, countries compete in lowering their corporate and capital gains taxes, reducing tax receipts. Of 35 Commonwealth countries that had an individual income tax before 1990, 29 reduced their rates by 1990, and none increased them' (UN, 1999, pp. 92-3). '... globalization makes some tax bases more mobile and less easy to tax. Furthermore, the burden of labour taxes will fall more heavily on workers if globalization erodes the economic rents previously earned by capital' (OECD, 1999, p. 137). 'There is little prospect of increasing taxes: the capital tax base is at risk of erosion through globalization, and increased labour taxes may harm employment, especially of low-skilled workers' (ibid., p. 37).

Thus the rankings of not only companies but also 'countries' as below have taken on significance today for the entrepreneurs and political leaders in the ever-more globalizing world market economy. For a country to be ranked high in such a table, governments cannot but compete in tax cutting and other business-friendly policies.

Table 3.18 Country ranking in competitiveness: 1997, 1998, 1999

	1997. Sept.	points	1998. Sept.	points	1999. Mar.	points
1	Switzerland	92.1	Switzerland	93.4	Switzerland	92.7
2	USA	92.1	Germany	92.9	Germany	92.5
3	Japan	91.5	Netherlands	91.9	US	92.2
4	Germany	91.3	US	91.2	Netherlands	91.7

Source: IMD, 1990, 1998.

Tax rates among these countries have been falling constantly for several years. *The KPMG Corporate Tax Rate Survey* of January 1999 noted, over 'the past four years the average corporate tax rate among OECD countries has dropped by almost three percentage points at January 1999'. Among the

---

it should be noted that social security contributions must be included in the final comparison of pro-firm conditions. At present such a pro-firm tendency seems to prevail over the need to strengthen the safety net for unstable jobs under economic globalization.

OECD member countries, the average rate was over 37% in 1995 but dropped to a little less than 35% in 1999. Among the EU countries the rate was a little higher than this, at 39% in 1996, but dropped to 36% in 1999. 'The trend toward lower tax rates is due in part to the increasing globalization of business and the rapidly evolving new technologies that are making it possible. As business and capital become more mobile, developed countries are under more pressure to keep their corporate tax rates competitive or risk seeking businesses migrate their activities and profits to lower tax jurisdictions.' The report also shows that in January 1999 'less developed regions of the world levy lower tax rates compared to the more developed nations. The developed countries in the OECD have an average corporate income tax rate of about 34.8%. The comparatively less developed nations in the Asia Pacific that were surveyed have an average rate of 31.7%. At 28.6% the average rate among Latin American countries is even lower.'

D: Social security burdens The amount and composition of social security contributions is quite different among the countries. Compulsory social security contributions by employees and employers shown as a percentage of wages (employees) or gross payrolls (employers) for the four countries for 1997 are as follows in Tables 3.19.1 and 3.19.2. The figures are the maximum figures (which actually cover a larger majority of workers), and therefore are subject to change under specific conditions. It clearly shows the highest burden for the firms in Sweden, with the other three almost at the

Table 3.19.1 Social security contributions by employees and employers

	Sweden		UK	
	Employee*	Employer*	Employee*	Employer*
Old age and survivors insurance	0	19.06	10.00 *[1]	10.00
Health/maternity insurance	4.95	4.04	included in old age insur.	
Unemployment insurance	33-100kr/mo	5.42	included in old age insur.	
Disability insurance	included in old age insur.		included in old age insur.	
Prof'l accident/health insurance	1.40	1.38	included in old age insur.	
Family allowances	by taxation		by taxation	
total	6.35	29.9	10.00	10.00

*: Employee – of wages; Employer – of payrolls. Even if not specified as 'by taxation', some amount is possibly financed from government such as administration costs, etc.
[1] rounded.

Source: US Social Security Administration, website.

102

Table 3.19.2 Social security contributions by employees and employers (continued)

	Japan		US	
	Employee	Employer	Employee	Employer
Old age and survivors insurance	8.675	8.675	6.2	6.2
Health/maternity insurance	4.3	4.3	1.45 [*2]	1.45
Unemployment insurance	0.4	0.75	0	0.8
Disability insurance	included in old age insur.		included in old age insur.	
Prof'l accident/health insurance	0	0.6-(14.4)	0 [*3]	2.05 [*4]
Family allowances	0	0.11	by taxation	
total	13.375	14.435	7.65	10.50

[*2] for hospitalisation.

[*3] nominal in a few states.

[*4] average costs, whole costs in most states.

Source: US Social Security Administration, website.

same level, about one third of Sweden's.[30]

E: Firms' share in social security finances As we have seen above, firms' burdens and their relative compositions are quite different between countries. Here we will compare the firms' burdens with the social protection expendi-

Figure 3.15 Firms' burden (left, 1995) and social security expenditure (right, 1990), % of GDP

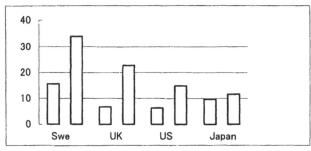

Source: Appendix table and OECD (1996a) p. 107.

---

[30] Policies to reduce employers' social contributions for low-wage groups have been carried out in Belgium, France, and the Netherlands recently (OECD, 1999, p. 98).

tures and see how much of it is financed by firms' contributions. Figure 3.15 compares social security expenditures with firms' total burden, Figure 3.16 with social security burden, and Figure 3.17 with firms' tax burden. Because of the availability of figures, the ratio of the firms' burden is for 1995 and the ratio of social security expenditure is for 1990 (1985 for UK). Both are in terms of ratio to GDP. The ratio of social security expenditures was 33.9% in Sweden, 22.6% in the UK, 14.8% in the US, and 11.6% in Japan. The ratio of firms' burden was 15.5% in Sweden, 6.7% in the UK, 6.2% in the US, and 9.5% in Japan. Thus the firms' share of burden of social security expenditures differs significantly, ranging from roughly three-tenths (UK) to eight-tenths (Japan) of total social security expenditures, reflecting the cultural difference. The difference is paid by employees' contributions and personal income tax.

Figure 3.16 Firms' social security contribution (left, 1995) and social security expenditures (right, 1990), % of GDP

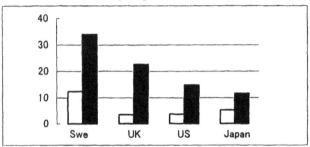

Source: Appendix tables.

Figure 3.17   Firms' income tax (left, 1995) and social security expenditures (right, 1990), % of GDP

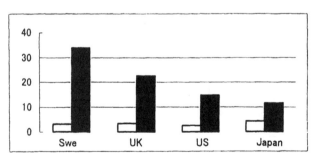

Source: Appendix table.

These figures show that a higher level of welfare provisions does not necessarily correspond to higher firms' social security burdens. Figure 3.15 shows that in Sweden, the UK, and the US, the large difference between the two figures is largely covered by the relatively larger burden borne by citizens. Countries that largely finance social welfare provisions by a larger share of corporate income tax, such as Japan, tend to lose their funds in depressions when firms' income drops significantly. It might suggest the desirability of financing such constant expenditures as social welfare provisions by other more stable revenue resources as employees' contributions, personal income tax, or general consumption taxes.

F: Different revenue sources and social security expenditures As an indication of the possibilities for increasing other resources for social security expenditures, we will compare the ratio of social protection expenditures and various revenue resources of governments for 1990 (Figures 3.18.1 to 3.18.4). In Sweden, employees' contribution is zero, and employers' contribution covers about half of the social protection expenditures, which means the other half is financed by personal income taxes. Personal income tax finances more in the UK, two thirds of social security expenditure, and in the US more than half. Japan finances an exceptionally large part, almost all of it, by employees' and employers' contributions. Although this kind of difference in financing may reflect some traditional cultural attitudes, it also suggests the possibility for a different way of financing the social security expenditures.

Figure 3.18 Social protection expenditures – 1 (1990) and revenue sources – 2 (1993), % of GDP

Figure 3.18.1 Sweden

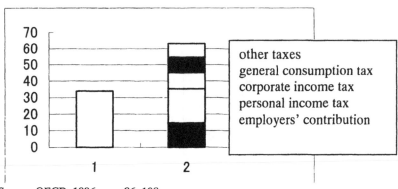

Source: OECD, 1996a, pp. 96, 108.

105

Figure 3.18.2 UK

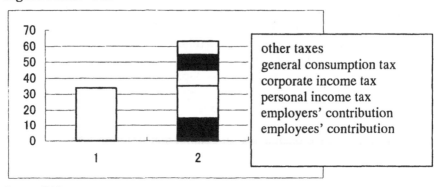

Figure 3.18.3 Japan

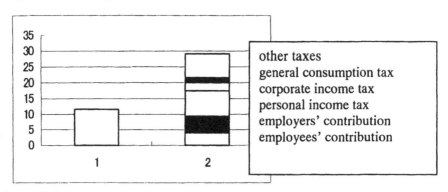

Figure 3.18.4 US

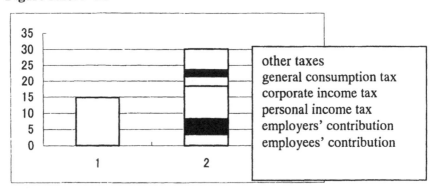

2.3.3 Some Arguments on Growth and Welfare

We have seen the policy developments and some of their relations with social welfare provisions. Drawing on the findings obtained above, we will examine the two arguments closely related to the above framework of the Welfare State since the 1980s. The first argument about big government implied the necessity to reduce welfare provisions and the second argument about high wages implied the necessity for anti-labour policies.

Argument 1: 'Big government raises the unemployment rate' The negative effect of big government has long been noted. (Here we restrict our argument to the effect of the scale of government spending. We do not deal with the effect of regulations.) For example, Vedder and Gallaway argue that 'Longer term levels in unemployment ... are influenced by structural and institutional factors, including the size of governmental involvement; the bigger the relative size of government, the higher the natural rate of unemployment', 'If high-taxed European and other nations were to lower their tax burden as a percentage of output by 10 points ..., it is predicted that this would lower the natural rate of unemployment by 3 percentage points', and 'The American success in maintaining relatively low unemployment is at least in part due to ... the smaller size of the U.S. Welfare State' (Vedder and Gallaway, 1999). Gwartney et al. also argued along the same lines, and emphasized the crowding-out effect of government spending, either by taxation or deficit financing (Gwartney et al., 1998).

But as Taylor-Gooby argues, the data do not necessarily show the close relationship between them (Taylor-Gooby, 1996, pp. 202-3). He shows that for the period 1984-94, low spending and tax rates and a successful economic record appeared in the US, but also high spending and tax rates and successful performance were clearly observed in the Netherlands. The data with other countries, too, indicate that the link between spending and prosperity is not simple.

Among the four countries, Sweden, the UK, Japan, and the US, the relationship between tax and social security burden and the unemployment rate was not clear, either. As was seen above, too, a higher spending country like Sweden performed fairly well in the 1980s. As Vedder and Gallaway themselves show, the fact that we can draw a regression line among the sample countries does not necessarily show the existence of a rigid relationship between them. And in dealing with this kind of comprehensive question, what matters is the difference in many spheres of a society. For example, people's or firms' attitudes or preference for more equal or unequal income distribution, or of more stable or unstable incomes, would have important influences on firms' or people's behaviours under the same level of government spending or tax rate. By going through these different 'filters', the same level of welfare spending is likely to generate different economic performances. In this sense the overall relationship between the scale of government and unemployment rate is not fully proved yet. These two factors are to be understood only as the start and goal of a long chain of relationships.

And what is important is that 'higher growth' is not necessarily a higher priority in every society. As we noted before, what counts is the overall satisfaction of the society. We will consider this question fully in Chapter 5. From this point of view, the kind of argument of Vedder and Gallaway's is far too simple and needs to be discussed further.

Argument 2: 'Higher wages reduce employment' As shown before, the Welfare State works to support and raise wages through labour laws and welfare provisions. For this reason, this function of the Welfare State has also been under attack.

'Economic theory suggests that unemployment and real unit labor cost move in concert. As real unit labor cost rises (falls), unemployment increases (decreases).' 'While the United States data are persuasive (for 1959 through 1996) ... information for some 24 different countries' shows a 'powerful confirmation' of this relationship, too[31] (Vedder and Gallaway, op. cit.). Trade union power is an important factor there. Andrew Henry argues 'Equilibrium occurs at a level of output [and unemployment] where unemployment is sufficiently high to equate trade unions' real wage aspirations with firms' ability to pay' (Henry, 1990, p. 78). As an application of this understanding he attributes unemployment in the 1970s' and early 1980s' to great trade union power.

This 'high wage, high unemployment' argument is simpler than the previous one. As the market mechanism never functions without high enough profit rates, excess wage burden surely reduces entrepreneurship. But even in this simple sense, there again can exist unique relationships in each country. As for the four countries, the growth rate of real wages was generally higher in the UK and Japan and lower in Sweden and the US in 1971-95. But for the two higher wage countries, the unemployment rate was higher in the UK and lower in Japan, and for the low wage countries, it was higher in the US and lower in Sweden (Keizai Kikakucho Kokumin Seikatsukyoku, 1996).

But even if we could observe a close correlation between lower wages and higher growth, we also know that if it is the result of the market

---

[31] Real unit labour cost is the wage cost divided by the number of goods produced (and sold). This means it is affected by the operating rate of the firm. In depression the operating rate drops and it raises unit overhead costs and unit labour costs. This suggests that real unit labour costs could possibly be the affected factor, not the causing factor, depending on the given situations.

mechanism alone, it could be an unsound result of the excessive exercise of the superior power of the employers. The question thus becomes how much wage increase (or decrease) is equitable or appropriate. As discussed before, wage-profit distribution must use the equity criterion according to the notion of contribution. With this condition fully realized, we should then proceed to the question of actual appropriate distribution of resources between production and consumption at this stage. As the whole mechanism of market society itself rests on the consent and welfare of the social members overall, the criterion applied here is appropriateness, not 'necessity'. From this perspective, George refers to the question of the fair level of wages in relation to productivity and seems to suggest the proportional growth of wages to productivity growth as desirable. 'Since 1980, however, it has been wage levels rather than profits that have suffered. In all EU countries as well as in the US, wages adjusted for inflation have risen by less than productivity and profits have taken a greater share of value-added' (George and Taylor-Gooby, 1999, p. 9).

Whether wages should grow with productivity is itself a question to be solved from the more comprehensive perspective of the overall welfare of the society. As profit and wages are the different expressions of investment and consumption, it becomes the question of growth rate and redistribution, as has been contested about the Welfare State since the 1980s. It should also be noted that the real question seems to be that it has often not actually been contested but is being forced on the peoples and governments by the overwhelming power of the 'competitiveness' ethics of market mechanism, which used to be, and should be, a tool for the people.[32]

The conclusion of this chapter: After having grown until the 1970s the Welfare States have entered a stagnant, setback era. The reasons have been the neo-liberal 'welfare vs. growth' reaction and policies to the 1970s economic problems and the increasing pressure of economic globalization, 'welfare vs. global competition'. In these movements, profit, the nucleus of market mechanism, has been paid more attention and the 'unfavourable' effects of 'excess' wage increases and social welfare provisions, together with tax and social contribution burdens on firms, have been addressed and restrained, creating wide income difference and more insecure societies.

---

[32]The adequacy of the restrictive policy for the four countries has also to be answered. The analyses in Section 2 seem to suggest the difference in the problems to be addressed between the four countries. Compared to Sweden, the UK, and US, Japan seems to be in a quite different condition with its tendency to secure high profit rate. The continuous surplus problem of current balance and the bubble boom of the late 1980s both seem to suggest the problem of weak consumption rather than shortage of investment. This difference may be interpreted to suggest the greater desirability for social welfare growth in Japan. This question will be further discussed in Chapter 4.

4 Arguments on the Future Welfare State

This chapter questions whether the setback trend will continue.

In this chapter we will deal with the arguments on the future of the Welfare State. We have seen in Chapter 2 that the Welfare State has been devised to meet the defects of the market mechanism, in Chapter 3 that it grew large in the post-war period up to the 1970s and that it has been in a process of change in the 1980s and 1990s. We have also seen that the major forces for this change have been the profit-recovery motive against wage and labour and profit-increase motive in the globalization movement. We have thus seen that the welfare containment process is the reality and shaping the present Welfare States in the industrialized nations. Thus far is the fact. Next we have to evaluate this process – if this process will or should continue – in order to judge our direction in the future.

To approach this goal, we have two important materials, the arguments of government leaders and the general opinions of the peoples. As already discussed in Chapter 1, we know that the question facing us today is a complicated choice between economic growth and social welfare growth, or the most desirable mixture of them that maximizes people's satisfaction overall. Thus our argument will be largely focused on this balance. As referred to above, considering a balance is an extremely difficult question in social sciences because it has to take into account several factors including criteria problems. But we believe that the ultimate criterion rests on the total human satisfaction in a society or a nation. As such, the final decision is shown by the people's will in elections. Based on such a perspective, it will be helpful for us to understand the arguments of the influential leaders both in and outside politics (Sections 1 and 2), and conscious and unconscious attitudes and reactions of the people themselves (in the next chapter).

Although some of the influential arguments at present seem to be seeking for even somewhat different types of society other than traditional type Welfare States, the present state of countries is still largely in the realm of the Welfare State and this framework will not drastically change in the near future. So in this chapter we will consider the questions under the title of 'future Welfare State' instead of a neutral one of 'future state'.

We first look at the views of government leaders. These are important in that these people are given the power to lead the society and directly affect our daily lives. There we will be able to see their 'determined' attitude to continue and even reinforce the present pursuit of higher competitiveness and survival of the economies of their countries. Second, we deal with the views of influential writers outside governments. But, of course, ordinary people are the most influential in that they have the power to choose government leaders. In this sense, the views of people are studied to foresee the longer-run prospect of society in the next chapter.

As it is understood that the three countries – the UK, Japan, and the US – that are more deeply committed to the neo-liberal and pro-competitiveness path than Sweden, are beginning to experience more serious problems concerning the overall social condition, the discussion in this chapter and the following will concentrate more on these countries.

1 GOVERNMENT LEADERS

SWEDEN

The views of SAP – Swedish Social Democratic Party –, which has been in power for most of the time since the 1930s except from 1976 to 1982 and from 1991 to 1993, the centre-right coalition government, should be viewed as the deepest fundamental layer for the Swedish Welfare State. It is widely known that the unique social democratic view that significantly values security of life is not only that of SAP but also of a broader stratum of Swedish society, forming the core of its common social ideal. Its former leader Per Albin Hansson coined the phrase, 'the People's Home'. He said, 'The basis of the home is togetherness and common feeling. The good home does not consider anyone as privileged or unappreciated; it knows no special favourites and no stepchildren. There no one looks down upon anyone else, there no one tries to gain advantage at another's expense, and the stronger do not suppress and plunder the weaker. In the good home equality, consideration, co-operation, and helpfulness prevail' (Tilton, 1991, p. 127). Such a concept of a secure society has long been the keynote of the SAP. The former prime minister Erlander, whose idea was passed on to Palme and Carlsson, emphasized the core of this idea, the security of life, stating that they were living in an anxious society, and stability, particularly of employment, was always the most important value (Okazawa, 1991, p. 91). The fact that even the latter-day Swedish conservatives have invoked this conception to criticize the SAP's policies in the 1980s shows how prevalent this idea has become in Sweden's society (Tilton, op. cit.).

This spirit of solidarity and security for all has been the basis of the Swedish Welfare State development in the post-war years. Stability in economic growth and employment, and solidarity in income distribution, meaning pay differentials being minimized as much as possible, were given

111

the first priorities in society's goals. This sense of solidarity was supported by its belief in its compatibility with efficiency. Mr and Mrs Myrdal were the most influential in settling this idea among the people: 'Preventive social policy, far from being a drain upon social resources, would be productive; a large part of the state's expenditures for the health and education of the young and the working generation, and for the welfare of families generally, increased not only the population's enjoyment of life but also its quality and its productivity' (Tilton, 1991, p. 176). This understanding that 'Justice paid. Equality promoted efficiency. Social welfare policy generated returns much higher than many alternative investments' (ibid., p. 164) provided a strong support for the development of the Swedish Welfare State. An active labour market policy was also a major characteristic of this society with the role of combining efficiency and justice (Heclo and Madsen, 1987, p. 49).

But with the newly emerging conditions both inside and outside the country, the Swedish Welfare State faced new challenges after the 1960s. Some new ideological challenges appeared from the left wing, demanding more attention to the excluded people in the 1960s and 1970s and more economic democracy in the workplace in the 1980s (Ginsburg, 1992, pp. 32-3). Another challenge came from the right wing, calling for a smaller government and the more competitive market society in the 1970s and 1990s. The latter has become the major challenge to shape the policies in the following decades. It came from the background of an unsettled export environment, both internal and external. Within its Welfare State regime, inflationary pressure was threatening in 1969 to 1970. The major impact soon came from outside, first by the instability of the currency system and next by the oil price shock. With the flotation of the dollar in 1973, 'the international economy's price signals took on a volatile quality that was unfamiliar to the post-war generation of economic managers. For Sweden, this less predictable international environment meant that it became much more difficult to calibrate central wage negotiations – and thus economic policy – according to price and productivity trends in the sectors of the Swedish economy exposed to foreign competition and prices'. This external pressure caused difficulty in adjusting major distributive shares on the one hand, and the internal changes such as the drying up of the workforce shift from the rural areas or lower productivity industries on the other worsened the export environment (ibid., pp. 54-5).

It challenged the traditional consensus about the social goal, security or stability, and whether its measures would survive in the new conditions of post oil-shock years. In meeting this tumultuous period, Sweden first experimented with generous spending. It was pursued by the SAP and then by centre-right governments in the mid-1970s till early-1980s. But the conditions worsened. 'Exports lagged, production and investment remained weak, and borrowing to cover deficits was reaching record levels that made interest on the national debt the largest category of state spending' (ibid., p. 62). State spending, and also welfare provisions, came under political examination.

The two consecutive elections in which the SAP lost became the major turning point for post-war Swedish economic and social policies. Faced by the economic difficulties, rethinking was proposed even from inside the party, too. In the 1981 election 'within the labour movement a vigorous discussion broke out between proponents of the expansionist policies the party had advocated in opposition and advocates of a pruning of the public budget. From the consideration of foreign experience and the need to preserve harmony within the movement there emerged a gradual coalescing around the vague slogan of a "third way" whereby Sweden would both "work and save" its way out of the crisis, but the central document embodying this "crisis programme"... avoided specifying the mix of policies to be applied' (Tilton, 1991, p. 236). Prominent young economists associated with the Social Democrats sent an open letter to a leading newspaper in February 1981. They argued that the problems of the Swedish economy stemmed from too much consumption, both private and public. 'Our total consumption ... is too large in relation in our production, which is seen partly in the balance of payments deficit, partly in the state budget. It is now a question of forcing production up and forcing consumption down. ... This can only occur if the Swedish production costs rise more slowly than those of the rest of the world' (Heclo and Madsen, 1987, p. 85). As consumption is determined by wages and redistribution, containing total demand meant either restraining wage increases or reducing redistributed expenditures.

For this purpose, the most powerful policy measure was to tighten government spending and redistribution. Reduced demand for labour meant smaller allowance for wage increases, too. Thus, what was necessary were 'measures that ... cut back on the public sector's expansion'. It also meant shifting the income share to the profit. Increasing profit and thus investment raises Sweden's competitiveness: '... investments and future employment, such a profits increase is highly desirable at present ... investments are urgently needed now and profits must be allowed to rise as soon as possible!' This is necessary because retaining expansion would make the situation worse. 'The current problem is that Social Democracy must break with many of its traditional means, such as promoting the public sector, in order to maintain the traditional aims of full employment and equal distribution of the welfare. ... The alternative is England's situation with a set of Thatcherian policies enforced in Sweden during the 1980s' (ibid., pp. 84-7). Reflecting such a course of argument, the 1983-4 budget statement explained that the government would reduce the balance of payments deficit through devaluation and also reduce the public deficit by a tighter budget. The trade-off between short-term and long-term welfare was aimed at and declared. It would mean, 'short run sacrifices ... in the form of decreased real income and lowered living standards' for the long-term benefit. But it also did not forget to add that the sacrifices would be borne by 'every group' in the country (ibid., pp. 98-106).

The strong leadership of SAP thus embarked on a cutback of government spending. And it was further pursued by the conservative parties. Pushed further toward budget restraint by the demands of joining the EU, the ideology of promoting competition gained a strong hold over the Swedish politics. The increasingly export-oriented Swedish industry supported this trend strongly. They became 'markedly less interested in a compromise with domestic labour'. Their main concerns became centred on access to foreign markets, lower wage costs, and less competition for labour from the public sector (Stephens, 1996, p. 50). In the worldwide depression of the early-1990s, Sweden's GDP dropped sharply and the unemployment rate exceeded 8%. But having experienced the difficulty of countering downturn by budget expansion, which had always been met by reduced competitiveness in the long run and larger deficits, this exceptionally high rate of unemployment was allowed to develop under the centre-right government: '... its double-digit level in 1993 indicated that full employment was not a top priority for the conservative coalition government' (Olsen, 1996, p. 8).

But we should take note that the 'retreat' then was largely confined to the employment sphere. The income replacement level was reduced from 90% in the mid-1980s to 80% under the conservative government in the early 1990s, and then 75% under SAP in 1995 (ibid., pp. 7, 8, 16). But these modifications were 'relatively minor when compared with the dramatic restructuring that has occurred in other nations such as the UK' (ibid., p. 9). Means tests were not introduced and universality was maintained. Although modified in some aspects, the fundamental structure of the Swedish welfare provisions with its universality has been left largely intact, and so have the 'basic Social Democratic values – equality, democracy, freedom, solidarity, efficiency, work, and security' (Tilton, 1991, p. 280). With such a national consensus still alive at its basis, Sweden will be unlikely to directly follow the road to intensifying competition with the same speed and depth as the champions of neo-liberal countries such as the US. It seems that the most probable prospect at present for the future of Swedish welfare society would be, if it had to change further to adjust to globalization, still a gradual and reluctant change, based on a much stronger national consensus on security and solidarity, following other countries from behind and keeping its welfare system at a relatively higher level than the others. This prospect seems to be further supported by the change of the attitude of middle class people after the experience of the hardships in the early 1990s. Most of all, the fear of unemployment created there may have added to their support for the traditional Swedish Welfare State (Svallfors and Taylor-Gooby (eds), 1999).

UK

The Conservative Policies of the 1980s to the mid-1990s

The major change in the policies on the Welfare State in the UK after the 1980s, in the years of the both Conservative and Labour governments, would be the emphasis of the necessity of strengthening its competitiveness. The influence of this line of argument became apparent in the mid-1970s from Bacon and Eltis's argument of declining competitiveness (1976). It argued that the increase of social services and the growth of the power of trades unions led to higher taxes and higher wages, thereby reducing investment and competitiveness in exports. It also argued that the equilibrium of trades unions' and firms' powers led to continuous price rises and inflation (ibid., pp. 28, 110-11, 163). In a word, they argued, purchasing power had been shifted from the wealth-making to wealth-consuming sector (civil servants, social workers, pensioners, etc.). And when workers and management resist losing their shares, inflation occurs and it disturbs the economy, creating slump and unemployment; this was their diagnosis.[1] This view has regulated and dominated the basic trend of economic and social policies in the UK in the years since.

A similar view was expressed in the political sphere in 1975 by Margaret Thatcher. She argued in the general meeting of the Conservative Party that the Party should go back to its spirit that existed at its establishment. Too many things were regulated by the state, governments spent too much money based on its own judgement, and taxpayers could keep little money (Mitsuhashi, 1989, p. 44). Smaller government is what is required. It is what revives the society again. This was her understanding. She told the people that by getting rid of too much dependence on unions and social welfare, a new society of people's capitalism would be realized. This new type of society was supposed to be a middle class society, everyone owning stocks and their own houses, not a society of a small minority of capitalists and a large majority of workers. A part of this middle class ideal is glimpsed in the profit-related wages system designed for the administration in the spring of 1986 by the Chancellor of Exchequer. It had such ideas as: 1) dividing wages into basic part and profit related part (20% of the total wages); 2) the latter changes with the profit; 3) half of this part is exempted from tax; and 4) the system is reviewed every three years. It was pointed out by the unions that

---

[1] For useful comments on this view, see George and Wilding, 1984, pp. 152-6.

the fluctuation of wages would be too large, and that public employees were excluded (ibid., pp. 183-4).

Two alternative goals, reviving the industry and the value of currency, were set by neo-conservatism. The decline in industry and its competitiveness in the UK in the latter half of the 1970s was a common understanding of politicians both in and outside the government. The index for this weakening competitiveness was the trade deficit and depreciating pound. It was argued that state payments to help the poor and weak were too generous, undermining the incentive to find work and making them benefit-dependent on the one hand and cutting down profit and investment on the other. The Labour Party had tried to improve the situation by making an agreement with the workers to refrain from excessive wage increases, but it did not succeed in the tumultuous years of the 1970s.

This restrictive policy led to a serious depression, which, as has been seen before, mostly affected the power relations between labour and management. Anti-labour policy, weaker position of workers, and the resulting relatively lower wages attracted foreign capital into the UK. Finance and assembly industries grew in this environment. But productivity in manufacturing has not recovered enough, as has been shown in the continuous trade deficit. Under the worldwide depression at the beginning of the 1990s, the trade deficit grew large and the pound was depreciated. Too much anti-welfarism by the Thatcher administration caused unrest in society in her final years. Although the economy had been recovering again, the serious depression in the following years under John Major's administration and the anti-welfarism in the Conservative Party led to the return of political power to the Labour Party in 1997.

Labour Party and Competitiveness Policy

Unlike the pre-Thatcher years, the 'new' Labour Party in the late-1990s continued most of the Conservatives' policies, especially the aim of reviving the country's competitiveness, and thus also the two major policies of controlling the unions' power and restricting welfare spending. In doing so, the Blair administration has accepted the major part of its predecessors' macro-economic policies: priority of budget balancing and anti-inflationary monetary policy. And the biggest change made by the predecessor, the lower tax regime, seems to have been accepted and continued by the Labour Party and also by the majority of people at present. Thus the major change of shifting the weight of economic life from the public to the private sphere has been continued. In emphasizing the competitiveness of the UK industries not only in manufacturing but also in new information and communication industries the Blair administration appears even more eager to do so than its predecessors. Under these smaller government policies it is difficult to increase its welfare provisions. While it is also eager to refurbish its health care, transportation, and most of all its education system, the administration has not succeeded in this for its first term. In meeting the dissatisfaction or anxieties of the people under globalization (as will be seen in the next chapter), the administration does not seem to have succeeded yet in ensuring them the security they had hoped for.

The Labour government's emphasis on the UK's competitiveness is well shown in the following debates in which Labour MP Jim Cousins took part in 1993. In this meeting low productivity growth was addressed: '... productivity growth (was) only 2.2 per cent between 1970 and 1980'. Two reasons were 'oil shocks in 1973 and 1979' and 'considerable industrial relations difficulties' (Cousins, in Hughes (ed.) 1993, p.158). Two more causes, the high exchange rates because of the newly found oil-currency status and high interest rates, raised manufacturing costs higher. As a result, output fell by 17% between 1979 and the low point in 1981. But recovery in competitiveness followed after 1981 with major strides. Output rose by 22 % and productivity 58% between 1981 and 1991, business expenditure on R & D rose by 6% a year (in the same period), the industrial relations climate changed into much greater participation by employees, and the quality of products improved. The increased competitiveness of a country and therefore its ability to attract foreign capital was also reflected in that 40% of all the US and Japanese investment into Europe in the 1980s came to the UK (ibid., pp. 158-9).

But it was argued that the UK was still not internationally competitive: '... in the long-term a much higher rate of investment will be required to rebuild manufacturing capacity'. The exception was in the financial centre: 'massive growth in the international flows of money and capital, of which London took full advantage ... followed [by] the deregulation of financial services in 1985 ... gave building societies broader lending power and unleashed the credit boom of the late 1980s.' UK competitiveness in Europe was improving. UK exports to EC countries was at 33% in 1970 but increased to 46% in 1980 and 57% in 1992. But 'the Dollar-based areas (North America and Asia/Pacific) will represent the major challenge in the 1990s'. 'Europe has become a high labour cost low-productivity production area relative to North America and Japan. This mainly reflects a high proportion of non-wage labour costs, such as social security payments. These elements account for almost 50 per cent of total labour costs in Germany, France and Italy.' 'It is against this background that industry, government and the City need to operate within an accepted framework which has the long-term competitiveness of UK industry as its key determinant factor' (ibid., pp. 159-60).

Based on this understanding, reinforcing the competitiveness through a suitable industrial strategy was understood to be a major policy issue.

Macro-economic policy was one of the measures. To avoid boom/bust cycles (ibid., p. 161), it was said to be necessary to do away with the twin deficits: £ 11 billion in the balance of payments in 1992 during the depths of the recession, and £ 37 billion anticipated public sector borrowing requirement in 1992/3. Their very scale implied immediate constraints on economic policy. It was argued that it was necessary for the trade deficit, along with the budget deficit, to be reduced because it left little room for macro-economic manipulation. To improve the trade deficit, low interest rates and export-tradable investment based on retained profits were regarded as important (ibid., p. 166). Low inflation was deemed critical and education to improve workforce skills was also emphasized.[2]

Cousins also argued for the necessity to change the attitude of the business world. In March 1993, the President of the Board of Trade had said that 'the deep-seated short-term attitudes are prevalent ... this is why we as a nation have performed less well', seeking profit 'by acquisition and financial engineering'; '... a small group of fund managers, market-makers, and those exercising financial brokerage functions on the fees ... from the turnover in stock, the setting up of deals, the creation of weak targets and the promotion of acquisitions'. In line with this, Cousins argued that government spending and procurement to promote British innovation and competitiveness were necessary. A strong sense of fear of being left behind in the world market was the background of this argument. He went on to say that the world did not owe Britain a living, and the government must in all its activities assist British wealth-creating capacity and achievements (ibid., pp. 167-70). Such understanding was in the Labour Party just as there was in SAP in the early 1980s in Sweden. This pro-competitiveness attitude grew and flourished in the Party in the mid-1990s. Tony Blair's 'New Britain' vision presents the image of the UK society the new Labour Party has come to pursue.

Tony Blair and his Social Image

Based on this competitive-society image, Tony Blair describes the present and future of the UK (Blair, 1996). We will start with his understanding of British economic conditions. First, he points out the importance of the coordination of monetary and fiscal policies. By 1976, inflation and external balance of payments were critical, and the Callaghan government took a new turn, with the phrase 'option no longer exists'. From 1976 to 1979 a tight budgetary regime was adopted with monetary targets. Since 1979 Thatcher

---

[2] Social cohesion was also addressed. Cousins argued that policies were necessary for the two million people who had lost jobs in the past two years: 'In previous periods of mass unemployment occupational identities endured. Too many of today's young people have never experienced it', and 'the creation of underclass lowers the potential of society as a whole, increases long-run social costs' (ibid. p. 167).

focused on more medium-term targets. But her failure was that she 'confined to monetary policies'. Fiscal policy had to be coordinated, too. 'In the late 1980s fiscal policy was being relaxed, with tax-cutting budgets in 1988, 1989 and 1990 at a time when interest rates were being kept high to curb inflationary pressure. That meant interest rates had to be pushed that much higher to slow down the economy and curb inflationary pressure' (p. 81). Thatcherism failed and unemployment doubled. 'In 1979 Mrs. Thatcher came to power promising to cut unemployment and reduce welfare dependency, but after the fifteen years since then, the numbers on income support trebled and more people became dependent on benefit than in the whole of the period 1945 to 1979. This is despite all the changes to the benefit rules'; 'The Tories in Britain, like the new Right elsewhere, have failed' (p. 141). Thus Blair criticized the previous administrations in order to emphasize the importance of tight budget policy to contain boom and inflation.

Second, he addresses the UK industries' competitiveness in the world market. Meeting the globalization trend in the world, or equalizing its competitive power with the rest of the world becomes the first priority in his agenda: '... the increasing globalization of the world economy means that the required levels of education and skills are now being set by international standards, and we continue to be left behind' (pp. 78-9). 'Since it is inconceivable that the UK would want to withdraw unilaterally from this global market-place, we must instead adjust our policies to its existence' (p. 86). Although this choice to stay in or not is a question for a nation as a whole, for him meeting globalization is a must, not a choice. If, as he says, we have only the choice to win or lose, his answer is right. And so, like Thatcher, he tries to enthuse the people for this way. If what Thatcher did was to re-establish the work ethic in the UK, Blair's may be more ambitious, that of keeping up with other countries and excel them, which is a relative competition and has no absolute limit. 'Britain must be a leading player in Europe' (p. 128). Competition thus urges modern people to win the race, which often threatens to break the balance between economy and society. Blair's emphasis on competitiveness leaves some anxiety at this point, to which problem we will come back soon.

Investment was thought to be the key factor for promoting competitiveness: '... investment is vital', which is 'supply side investment including education and infrastructure' (p. 82). Asian countries are the good examples. Asian Tigers 'have spent massively on education and on investment in infrastructure'. And for investment, savings are necessary. Again the Asian countries: 'They save more' (p. 110). And, securing profit is of course necessary: 'Companies will not invest without decent profits'. Stimulating work incentive is another factor for higher competitiveness. A lower tax regime is confirmed from this viewpoint: 'Penal rates of taxation do not make economic or political sense. I want a tax regime where, through their hard work, risk-taking and success, people can become wealthy.' 'Britain needs successful people in business who can become rich by their success' (p. 112). So his view is not that of labour's or the management's side anymore, but that of a coordinator between management and labour.

He emphasizes the importance of containing inflation. Under the growth rate of 3% on the average and low unemployment rate in the 1950s and 1960s, two eroding factors were emerging, which people did not pay much attention to: inflation and catching-up by other countries through post-war reconstruction. He says, for an economy 'the control of inflation ... [is] important' because 'Temporary failures over inflation have permanent adverse effects on the real economy' (p. 85). This is the problem he particularly pays attention to, just as his Conservative predecessors did. This posture of anti-inflation, the attitude to give it a higher priority than temporary financial generosity, seems to have become deeply rooted in the political attitude of every government since the 1980s. It means that when inflation is suspected, governments will not hesitate to solve it by all means, even with higher unemployment.

The capital-labour relationship is expected to change to the benefit of higher competitiveness: '... deeper seated reasons for the deterioration in the underlying performance of the British economy' were 'the polarized hostility between management and unions', and 'fault on both sides' (p. 78). Thus, truce is necessary: '... a cooperative attitude between workers and management [is] vital' (p. 85). Both were in the wrong but probably more so on the labour's side. 'Industrial action was frequent, crippling to industrial efficiency' that led to the lack of high-quality investment (p. 78). So, here he will walk in the footprints of Thatcher: 'the key elements of the 1980s legislation affecting trade unions will be retained' (p. 82). It was rather the unions who should change: 'The union excesses of the 1970s were wrong' (p. 85). He proves himself to be a pragmatist here. He does not refer to the contradictory relationship between the two any more. His criteria for all the policies became the UK's recovery and competitiveness.

But this posture may dangerously emphasize the efficiency criterion too much, leaving equity and human fellowship behind. This danger, however, is not for him alone. This kind of pragmatism is probably prevalent in the British or in any market society in general today. We saw poor economic performance in the 1970s. If we cannot produce, we cannot redistribute. It is a simple causation. Let's forget about the class concept, if only we could get back to the prosperity or the world's top table again. This reaction is natural when people cannot find other practical measures.

Concerning this question, greater progress will be made in management-labour relations when we find out how to measure the contributions or 'right' shares of social members in a market mechanism.[3] Today, it is only decided by the plain 'demand and supply' mechanism, which is largely influenced by the inequalities in the positions of social members. Keeping such an imperfection of our economic system in our mind, we should be very careful in pursuing the policies for higher efficiency to their fullest.

As was seen in Chapter 2 and will be seen in Chapter 5, our society is supported both by material goods and by human relationships. And the market mechanism has a tendency to prioritise the former and undervalue the latter. The idea of 'without goods we cannot do anything' contains a possible danger for this efficiency-first direction. In thinking of this question of social balance, it would be ideal if we could always have the clear image of a society that allocates the present resources in the best manner so that the society can obtain maximum satisfaction from the allocated resources to growth-purpose and welfare-purpose. But such an image is often difficult to obtain, and the question of human relationships is particularly difficult to deal with by clear indices. That is why it is difficult at this point to judge if Blair's policies are right or not. And so we have to be careful in assessing it, and his ideas and the proceedings of his government should be continuously monitored and given careful considerations.

Economy and Social Cohesion

As above, in Blair's strategy for economic growth there is some latent danger for social imbalance. His idea of coordinating management and labour will probably work well when the economy is good. When bad, his policy will be challenged seriously because his is basically a policy of efficiency, not of equity or human fellowship. In a period of economic hardship, is he prepared to rescue the most deprived, whose number would increase considerably, and if he is, how can he do it without jeopardising the interest of the firms that he currently values so much? With such a reservation about these questions we will go on to look at how his ideas about workers and disadvantaged people are described.

For the workers, he supports the minimum wage policy. He stresses that the UK does not follow a cheap labour route like the US: 'While we clearly cannot ignore the recent employment record of the US, we should be aware of drawing simplistic conclusions. The benefits of deregulated labour markets have not been qualified, and increased flexibility has not been won without costs.' 'The best of our international competitors ... accept ... a responsibility to nurture and improve the skills of their workforce.' 'Britain cannot take the "cheap labour" route. We will never be as cheap as the

---

[3] Cf. Tsukada, 1998, Chapter 5.

low-wage countries' (p. 92). He argues for the merit of the minimum wage. 'This minimum wage is a good policy ... It's wrong that employers pay people in many cases below their marginal product and that the tax system spends hundreds of millions of pounds subsidizing employers'. But at the same time he is careful not to frighten the management. He tells business that it will not mean an anti-business, or anti-competitive, level, and they will set up a Low Pay Commission 'with business representations'. The European Social Charter 'is a set of principles ... A Labour government will not pursue such a course [= import of inefficient practices to Britain]' (pp. 107-8). He also opposes the unstable employment conditions expected in the globalizing pressures: 'if deregulation leads to a large increase in part-time or contract labour, with little mutual commitment between firms and employees, companies may well be less able or willing to finance training or apprenticeships' (p. 92). This insecurity of jobs is particularly threatening when globalization pressures push firms toward downsizing or constantly adjusting the workforce. Here again we must keep questioning how effectively this posture can be maintained when it is based at least partially on the competitiveness target.

He addresses the problem of social disintegration. He emphasizes the two fundamental elements of society, fairness and efficiency: 'I believe ... a fair society and a more efficient one go hand in hand' and 'the stronger and more cohesive society' (p. 97). He points to the divided UK society in front of him: 'There is nothing more destructive or corrosive in Britain today than the tearing of the social fabric and the rupture of social cohesion.' 'We live in a society increasingly scarred by... social disintegration.' 'Drug abuse and the crime associated with drugs have risen dramatically.' Crimes more than doubled since 1979, violent crime increased by more than 130%, robberies by 300%, and the cost of criminal justice doubled since 1979 (p. 245).

He refers to the insecurity and poverty of the people. The people he has in mind are not only the excluded, long-term unemployed people but also those presently at work, too. He calls his approach 'the second generation welfare'. The long-term unemployed must be addressed to. We have to 'help a forgotten generation of 600,000 under 25s' (p. 117). 'Even with a semblance of recovery in the economy there are a large number of people afraid for their jobs, working with much less secure conditions, wondering whether their children will have the same start in life as they had ... a crisis of opportunity which extends far beyond what some call the underclass'. Thus, 'second-generation welfare' attacks the 'insecurity of middle-income Britain and the poverty of low-income people'. He also refers to the changing patterns of family life: 'Second-generation welfare adapts to the changing patterns of family life, where work and parenting are shared, and where retirement can last twenty or thirty years' (pp. 141-3).

Problems are thus listed, both in economy and society. The fundamental cause and cure for them are argued: '... in the face of the social breakdown detailed above there has been a recognition that unfettered liberalism will produce an atomised, uncaring, rootless society'. '... the crude individualism of the Tories' governing philosophy ... should be replaced ... [by] a strong civic society' (pp. 244-6). Then how? We have to remember here that his economic strategy didn't seem very far from the Tory course. How can he cope with the social problems that he attributes to crude individualism or conservatism when he has adopted a similar strategy to theirs? Wouldn't it bring about the same results?

He believes that there is a good economic growth, which does not promote crude individualism. He believes he can realize it by changing the ways government spends the money, and most importantly by not raising taxes, which might harm competitiveness. He believes in the necessity to hold down taxes for higher competitiveness, and believes that 'Social justice can be extended within existing levels of spending' (p. 150). Both welfare and economy, but the former should not harm the latter; this is after all his final answer. Wouldn't there be a case today for larger expenditure to create larger social justice? He does not believe so. If this is his basic answer, then the only policies allowed must be to find more efficient ways to spend for social welfare.[4]

Several expenditures, however, are to be given more resources. Education is one of the most important. It raises productivity and also reduces the under-class problem: '... this new era ... must not divide our societies – a relatively secure and prosperous top part and an unskilled, under-educated bottom part ... What is striking about the way Japan has educated its people is not just its commitment to basic numeracy and literacy, and the huge numbers that go on to advanced education, but also its success in pulling up the lower-achievers, raising standards for all' (p. 127). Reform for higher education to increase college graduates is also addressed. '... middle-class parents have to pay thousands of pounds to support their children at university'. Increasing students' loans deters poorer students[5] (p. 149). Positive unemployment policy ('workfare') is necessary, too: '... training as well as unemployment benefit' is effective (p. 143). To afford the money necessary, he goes on to propose a certain rationalization of welfare provision, such as of child benefit, asking should 'everyone, irrespective of income ... receive the same level of financial support for their children?' (p. 146).

---

[4] The cornerstones of British social security reform that contribute to this purpose thus became such principles as 'From welfare to work', 'Preparing people for jobs', 'Making work pay', 'Supporting the working poor', 'More services getting the unemployed back to work', etc (Hyde et al. 1999, pp. 73-4).
[5] But since he set up his government, this very deterring policy has been introduced in 1998.

Bearing in mind all of these ideas, how can we evaluate his prospective social image of the UK today? As far as he puts the first priority for this society on the recovery of competitiveness, we will probably not be able to discard the fear of some imbalance between growth and welfare being generated under the surface. The most serious problem is, or will be, the very 'insecurity of the middle income Britain', which Blair hopes to address. Although he is well aware of it, it remains to be seen if his administration can really cope with it with such a competitiveness-first social view. As this problem of 'insecurity' is intractable, it is feared that its seriousness will be only felt after it has deeply affected the society.

Thus, whether the social phenomena he himself described as 'social disintegration' are too serious already and whether the competitive atmosphere he is trying to create in the UK society will aggravate it or not are the major questions today. We will consider these questions in depth in Chapter 5, Section 2, by focusing on pathological social phenomena that are commonly observed in several countries. 'Children are affected by families, families by local communities, and communities in turn by the ethos and policy of society as a whole' (p. 247). Whether his policy as a whole is effective enough to create such kind of communities is the key question today, and a question to be addressed in the coming years, too.

After two years in his cabinet, although confronted with traditional Labour members with such demands as rethinking the abolition of housing benefit, the restoration of the pensions' link to earnings, benefits for 16- and 17-year-olds, the safeguarding of child benefit, to rethink the treatment of disability benefit claimants, and to give state support to people such as carers who are unable to make national insurance contributions (*The Times*, May 22, July 5, 1999), he confirmed his basic position (ibid., June 3, 1999): 'We govern for all the people'. 'I will never again have Britain forced to choose between a Labour Party that ignored the importance of business and ambition and a right-wing Conservative Party, which ignored the need for justice and compassion.' He is determined to pursue his basic strategy, and from what we have seen above, the prospect is not very encouraging yet, threatening the growth of those problems he himself once sought to contain.[6]

JAPAN

Recent Japanese political leaders have set the maintenance or reinforcing of economic competitiveness as the prominent goal for their society today, just

---

[6] This policy was also expressed by the Chancellor, Gordon Brown, in his speech to the Confederation of British Industry's annual conference in October 1999. 'I want Britain to be ... (an) enterprising economy', 'The new economy will need more competition, more entrepreneurship, more flexibility', and 'Businesses, indeed countries, which fail to adapt, reform and lead the way will simply be left behind' (BBC on the website, Nov. 1, 1999).

like the UK or the US. The background motive for this argument in the 1970s, when it was first introduced, was the fear of 'the sickness of the advanced nations' observed in the UK or other European and American countries. The sickness was the stagnation of the economy and weaker competitiveness under large or pro-welfare governments. But since experiencing the 1990s' depressive years and rapidly developing globalization movement in the world, the main cause has been changed into catching up with the globalization-friendly countries such as the UK or the US, whose new economic structures have been succeeding in attracting foreign capital and realizing higher economic growth in the recent years.

At the same time, as we shall see below, the goal of 'real affluence with relaxed way of life' has not been officially discarded. This goal was introduced after the 1980s in the transition period toward a 'lower growth economy'. It was set by the Conservative government as the next goal after having caught up with European and American advanced nations. It was thought that productive capacities had been sufficiently accumulated, and the next goal was to utilize them for easing people's lives, by higher consumption. Such an understanding was behind the 'truly affluent society' argument. But it was rather the competitive and anti-social welfare philosophy that actually came to dominate the following decades of the 1980s and 1990s.

After the booming 1980s and depressive 1990s, there is more anxiety and dissatisfaction in the people's eyes than in the 1970s. This social atmosphere has even coined the phrase of 'dead end society' in the mid-1990s. Although the economy is low, the anxiety and dissatisfaction seems to be disproportionately high. Successive pathological social incidents even seem to warn of the breaking point of the society itself. Here again, together with the task of joining the worldwide globalization movement, the difficult question of balancing between competition and cohesion, or efficiency and equity and human fellowship, seems to loom large in society.

Just as in the UK, Sweden, or the US, Japan is also facing the competition challenge in a globalizing world, and is struggling to harmonize this goal with social cohesion as in the other countries. As was seen in the previous section, finding the best mix of economic growth and welfare distribution is the fundamental question. How Japanese political leaders are trying to meet this problem at present is vividly observed in the various discussions convened by the Prime Minister. The following three discussions show us the three views existing side by side in the government about the competitiveness path: doubt, admission and promotion. First we will see the discussion of the Prime Minister's Commission on Japan's Goals in the 21st Century (21st Century Commission) that was convened by the Prime Minister, Keizo Obuchi, in 1999 (based on the publication on the website).

Doubt on Competitiveness: The Prime Minister's Commission on Japan's Goals in the 21st Century

We can find the first attempt of this kind of Commission on Japan's Goals almost two decades ago when the ex-Prime Minister, Masayoshi Ohira, convened a research group on policies. Under nine specific themes, 200 people took part in it and argued about the common theme, 'the age of culture'. The chairman of this 21st Century Commission, Hayao Kawai, was one of the members then. The intention of this study was similar but the atmosphere seemed more optimistic then, describing the problem as how to realize the age of culture after the economy matured. With the death of Ohira and the coming of the bubble years the argument died out. After a decade, in 1991, the Prime Minister, Miyazawa, promoted the slogan 'high living standard nation' and 'true affluence'. But then, under the crash of the bubble economy and soaring globalization, the competitiveness-first ethos affected the whole Japanese society. Meanwhile, under the deteriorating economic situation, anxieties about employment and declining social security became the main issues for Japan. After having been unsuccessfully addressed by two administrations, the underlying problem seems to have worsened furthermore.

At the beginning of 1999, Prime Minister Obuchi declared the administration's most important task as: 'to realize the true affluence' on the basis of 'five kinds of stability' – economic recovery, securing employment, protecting environment, realizing secure older years, and secure child care and education (*Nikkei*, Jan. 1, 1999). He explained his intention in more detail at his policy speech in the January Congress, that Japanese people had pursued affluence for the post-war years and succeeded in it to a certain extent, but lacked virtue or noble will, or kindness to other people: 'Although our wish to become affluent has been realized to an extent, it is not deniable that we have been apt to forget the most important thing for human beings, the spiritual content'. 'Since I took office, I have often referred to "wealth and virtue". Sound capitalism cannot be maintained by pursuit of profit alone. This is asserted by world famous philosophers such as the German sociologist, Max Weber. A nation without "virtue", or "noble will", cannot continue to be affluent, and it will be distrusted by the world.' 'I believe that it is necessary to construct a society in which we can be "kind to others and feel naturally what is beautiful as beautiful", and a society in which neighbours can associate gently with each other' (*Nikkei*, Jan. 20, 1999). Such reference to the mental conditions of the people by the political leader eloquently shows the very keenness of this question in Japanese society today. At the first meeting of the 21st Century Commission, he referred to his intention, citing Eiichi Shibusawa, a successful Japanese entrepreneur and his words 'the co-existence of the Analects of Confucius and abacus', or human morality and profiteering. Obuchi said that we had to keep a balance between selfishness and altruism, and identified with the words of Amartya Sen that we would become 'rational fools' when we lost 'sympathy and commitment to other people'.

However, what should be noted here is that such an instinctive sense of crisis of his is quite apt to be overwhelmed by his recognition of another urgent issue for Japan, namely the necessity of reinforcing its competitiveness – although this very invasion by economic goals of spiritual ones was the very subject of Weber's warnings. As we shall see, Obuchi's posture leaning much toward competitiveness is quite likely to betray his own anxiety about Japanese society. The reason for this prospective failure to address the problem properly probably stems from his inability to synthesize the two facets of a society, namely 'economic Japan' and 'social Japan'. We have already seen a similar difficulty to address and answer this question in the argument about the UK. The serious situation in Japan has at least led the Prime Minister to convene a conference. Although it may not succeed in dealing with the problem in sufficient depth and breadth, the argument itself should be taken as a warning to the people today. The arguments there are divided into three: questions on the present competitive society, the necessity for competition and profit, and they way to synthesize growth and stability.

The problems concerning competitive society, focused rather on its negative effects, are addressed and discussed by some members. (Opinions are exchanged freely in the meeting, so speakers' names are not referred to in most of the quotations below.)

First, at the beginning, the main question is introduced again by Prime Minister Obuchi: '... although modern Japan has realized a highly advanced industrial society, from now on we have to aim at a socio-economy, where every single citizen can actually feel the affluence and happiness ... maintaining the vigorous economy at the same time' (Subcommittee 2, May 28, 1999). But the sense of a turning point from growth to welfare has been long felt but not addressed fully for the past two decades, always returning to the growth-first route either by budgetary or globalization pressures. Having been understood as an export-dependent country, technological competitiveness still occupies a significant place in the argument about Japan's future: 'In the reality, scientific technology is being pursued in a world of survival, ruled by money and competition. It is hard to compose a social ideal of scientific technology-based nation together with high dignity. It is quite important to treat scientific technology properly from a higher standard of perspective' (General meeting, April 21, 1999). This confession of the difficulty to pursue an ideal in the world market may be the very origin of the whole problem generating in Japan and other countries discussed later in this book.

The fundamental treatment of the possible imbalance would begin with the recognition of the seriousness of the problems generated by this competitive lifestyle today. Probably reflecting the general subconscious anxiety of Japanese society today, the loss of self-respect is referred to as one of the serious problems. 'The self-respect enables him/her to recognize oneself as being worthwhile and significant. The ultimate anxiety in the modern society may be that we are losing this sense of dignity' (Subcommittee 3, Tasteful and Stable Life, June 18, 1999).

The fear of 'high-speed society' in Japan is pointed out as a problem: 'In a society where torrents of information are appearing everyday and everything changes as fashions, people seem to have the fear of being left out and isolated' (Subcommittee 3, June 18, 1999). The most significant example of this fear would be in the workplace. Evolution of technology at the workplace is itself a positive facet. But when it emerges as something threatening to humans, and if it is implemented without due care to those who are affected, it means the lack of responsibility of the society for the less able. And as discussed before, this is the problem that is easily generated and repeated in a market mechanism, where 'individual responsibilities' without proper and enough equity and human fellowship are unduly emphasized.

The weakening support from the traditional lifestyle is pointed out as a cause of this insecurity: 'The anxiety for most of the people today is brought about by that the traditional stability and ease which they used to have by belonging to larger entities is now being disturbed' (Subcommittee 3, June 22, 1999). One of the most significant traditional security factors in Japan has been the firms' attitude to maintaining lifetime employment. But recent gradual abandonment of this tradition, sometimes appearing in a large number of dismissals of workers, has added to the insecure feelings. Behind this concern is the hidden sharper conflict between the fit and less fit for the intensified market competition.

As a cause and remedy for the deeper anxiety, religious mentality and the question of possible difference between Japan and Western nations are also referred to: 'People tend to obtain peace of mind by relating to entities which transcend them. In Western societies, it is the case that even if people change companies, their belonging to Christianity does not change. As for Japan where this is missing, the disturbance of the ease that they used to have by belonging to firms becomes a much more fundamental problem' (Subcommittee, June 22, 1999). Spiritual strength in this sense may explain a part of the greater anxiety -- if such is the case -- prevailing in Japan.

The problem of children in an unduly competitive society is referred to as 'the loss of childhood' in modernized and urbanized societies (Subcommittee 3, June 18, 1999). This problem has been talked of often, but it is also true that busy adults quite easily neglect the problem with the excuse that it is an inevitable by-product of the modern age. But its effects may be more serious than we usually think today. To understand it, it may be useful for adults to look back to one's own childhood days. Although they may have had poverty problems, many of them will also recognize how better off they were with natural and human environment. Of course the natural sciences were not as developed as today, and people didn't live as long, but instead they were endowed abundantly with the most important factors for growing up, nature and people, or human relationships. Which would be happier: to live fifty years of fulfilled days or seventy years of dissatisfaction? That is a question.

It may probably be because they had experienced the merits of these blessings that Obuchi could have a sense of social illness and other members could sympathize with him. If we had asked children today if they felt the same problem, they would be unable to point out the existence of the problem itself. They would surely express some kind of anxiety and dissatisfaction, but would be unable to describe it as clearly as the older generation, who know what it was in the past and can compare with it today. It suggests that it is an urgent matter to address and change the harmful trend that is eroding children's environment, while the older generations are alive.

Humans may be the lords of all the animals, but they are susceptible to whatever changes take place in the environment. Between nature and human relationships, the latter is a more influential environment for children's growth. Even under harsh geographical and natural conditions, children would develop well as members of society if only the human relationships around them are firmly established. The nucleus of this relationship is the existence of those who think and take care of them, not only parents but teachers at school and neighbours around, and, when they grow up, colleagues at the workplace.[7]

To go no further in seeking for the root cause of these anxieties in the society, the necessity of profit, hence competition as its promoter, is addressed: 'Many argue that the purpose of enterprise is not the maximization of profit, but a certain amount of profit' is necessary (Subcommittee 2, June 7, 1999). It is true that it is not the purpose but it is necessary. But when it becomes the most necessary in a company's goals, it becomes the purpose. And the most profound question in the argument about social balance lies here, too. Humans have progressed from the feudal age to the civil age. We chose the latter as better than the former. But, 'Certain profit is necessary.' It is true. How much profit is necessary, and how much competition? And how can we measure this necessity? The question is dealt

---

[7] College students are not the exceptions: '... college students today ... are saturated with material affluence and cannot find out values to replace it' (Subcommittee 2, May 28). This kind of opinion is often heard today, but the real question is if they are really given what they need. It would be social cohesion and sense of solidarity that could give them motivation and courage in their adolescent years.

with in the balance between market mechanism and state. Until we find the answer to it, we will remain half-civilized and while we are unable to answer it, market power tends to prevail. Profit often becomes not a secondary, but the first 'purpose'. It is obtained by winning market competition. Success in the market competition tends to outgrow any other social virtues. 'We need competition, but we also need kindness.' Saying so without having any criterion to arbitrate their conflict helps us little.

But this question of balance is not pursued further. While the last report from this 21st Century Commission is not issued yet, we can tell from the discussions above that the critical questions revealed are not addressed in any depth. As Obuchi posed the question again in August that 'I believe that the minimum safety net is necessary', but 'too strong a net reduces the challenging incentive' and '... where to take the balance is a difficult question', this question remains unanswered, which suggests a danger of Japanese society tilting further toward the competitiveness-first answer.

Admission to Competitiveness: The Economic Council

Although the question of the overall balance of the society has just started to be addressed in Japan, one of the two contestants, the competitiveness argument, is winning the battle by default in the practical spheres. The argument, by the Economic Council at the Economic Planning Agency, is positioned between the above argument, which at least shows the need to question the proper balance in society, and the third one, which shows a clear positive stance on the competitive policies. It seems to present the majority view, a reluctant admission of a competitive society, of Japanese leaders when they face the social balance and economic competitiveness problem. While the 21st Century Commission deals with the 21st century, this report addresses the years until 2010, and the next pro-competitiveness argument by the Economic Strategy Council the next several years. (Based on the publication on the website unless otherwise noted.)

In this report of the Economic Council, 'the Future Socio-Economy and Policy Planning for the Renewal of the Economy', July 5, 1999, the development and difficulties that post-war Japanese society faces today are described. It argues that the national consensus existent in the post Second World War period was to fully engage in economic development with the West, develop industries in a cooperative relationship between the government and people, and to create an acquiescent and cooperative workforce suitable for mass production and long term employment. This policy has been successful so far, and of per capita income reached the highest of all of the countries with a population over ten million in 1987. But this course also reached the limit then. The mass production type industries had expanded to their limit in the second half of the 1980s and they found nothing to invest in except speculation. The surplus money was directed to foreign finance and investment, and internal land and stocks. Thus, the old style Japanese growth course 'became outmoded from the major current of human civilization'. 'What is needed now is ... a new way of thinking for the whole society.'

Defining present Japan as being at a turning point, it tries to 'show clearly the figure of how the socio-economy in 2010 should be' in Japan. The report answers and characterizes this new society as a 'society of wisdom'. Japan is 'at the turning point transcending a modern industrialized society toward one with diverse new wisdom.' This new society is one where 'the major means of production are human knowledge, experiences, and sensibility' (Section 5-2). This is largely true not only for Japan but also all over the world today. In order to survive in this type of world, it is necessary to take in information from the world and to have an easy access to dispatching it. For creating knowledge, it is necessary to promote 'uniqueness and creativity', which needs adequate 'social dispositions'. These dispositions are to be nurtured through childcare, education, employment customs, and so forth. Attracting people and firms is also necessary in the borderless world. Reforming the organizational structures is also necessary: 'In functional organizations, prompt decision makings are needed.' 'The old collectivity in decision making, from bottom up' takes too much time. In this new condition, long-term employment becomes impossible too.

And the report stresses the importance of 'freedom'. It argues that the nature of the people itself will change under this condition. A new fundamental virtue, 'freedom', which is meant to be the freedom of choice and innovation through incessant competition, will be supported and added to the traditional three virtues: efficiency, equality and safety. Thus the new socio-economy is one with an 'economic structure and disposition that pursues prosperity and joy through self-help and competition'. If not, 'Japan will not be able to stay as the major player in the world economy.' (How similar this phrase is to that of Tony Blair!) 'A country like Japan, who does not become a big military power, has to remain as a major player in the socio-economy in the world in order to stay in a position to secure safety in the world.' Thus, the report shows a clear emphasis on the economy, which, by their reasoning, is an inevitable weapon for survival in the world today. This is, whether right or wrong, an answer to the question posed about the social balance in Japan. Such a strong word as 'survival' is given the ultimate importance as the basic criterion in this question. If it is really a matter of survival, no one can resist to it. Weaker competitiveness, reduced imports and reduced salaries are of course a matter of 'survival' in a sense. But don't the Japanese people need a higher criterion to arbitrate economy and society today? Wasn't it the original intention of the 21st Century

Commission? The argument here seems to have leaned much toward 'survival' and competition as a matter of fact.

It does foresee negative effects accompanying such a new society and says that an increase in losers and the weak becomes a serious problem: '... in a competitive society like this, not a few losers and weak people exist. In the socio-economy that should come, everyone's human right must be protected completely and the opportunities for challenge for success and dignity of humans must be secured.' In the first place, there are two kinds of equalities, of opportunities and of results: 'That kind of social structure which presupposes "equality in results" proved unsuccessful.' 'The should-be socio-economy becomes the composition of "equality of opportunities" and an ex post facto adjustment ... the latter corrects the economic difference and establishes a system [safety net] for everyone to fare.' But the safety net must be one not to generate 'serious discontent' 'on the side of those who bear the burden'. Reinforcing the safety net to meet the growth of insecurity, but with the agreement of those who bear the burden, is their conclusion to the economic growth vs. insecurity problem there. The main points here are three: first, saturation of demand for mass production goods, second, the necessity of adjustment to a new worldwide competition, the major weapon for which is knowledge, and third, reinforcing the safety net to the extent which those who pay do not complain.

We can further understand what these lines mean by looking at the subcommittee report of the Council. The report of the subcommittee of the Economic Council (the joint report of the subcommittee on the Socio-Economic Prospect and the subcommittee on the Economic Subjects, June 1998) speaks more clearly of the priority of the path of economic growth or competition over that of welfare (publicized by the Bureau of General Planning). The necessity for this report is the need to answer the ambiguity of the future socio-economy, which is generating anxieties among the people[8] (The Report, Chapter 1, 1-(4)). It is argued that the containment of social welfare and government is inevitable today because of the difficulty of corporate taxation in the globalizing economic activities (Globalization Working Group Report, Chapter 3 Globalization and Adjustment of System, Section (3) Globalization and Internal System – Can the Internal System be Autonomous? Sub-section (2) Globalization and Taxation). 'Globalization is positively related to the tendency toward larger personal taxes', and 'with globalization the tax burden has come to be more supported by less mobile citizens rather than highly mobile corporations.' 'This shift makes the tax source more vulnerable and makes it difficult to sustain a large government.'

---

[8] Most of the members are from the financial and industrial world. Working group members consist mostly of scholars. The effect of globalization on the Japanese economy is studied in detail in the Globalization Working Group.

'Also, taxation both on capital trade and corporate income becomes less autonomous with firms becoming more multi-nationalized, and with institutional adjustment of those nations to whom Japan is closely connected in economy.' 'After all, globalization necessitates the government to be more efficient so that it will not raise the per capita burden. In order to hold down this burden under the larger weight on personal tax, realizing an efficient government by reforming social security system and slimming down administrative works are necessary.' Thus, their conclusion is smaller government and a smaller Welfare State from the competitiveness viewpoint.

The report ('The Future Socio-Economy...') was supposed to provide one of the major scenarios for Japanese society. A few questions are pointed out immediately. First, as to the assumption that the people had agreed to the education of a mass production-oriented workforce, it should be understood that it was the political leaders who were most conscious of this 'necessity' and actually leading them to it, and the people in general were only unconsciously following the path or this framework given to them. If we understand this point in this way, what is necessary becomes the formation of the true consensus of the people. Secondly, about the saturation of mass productive goods thesis, we should recognize that there remains the possibility that the low internal demand for manufactured goods is not necessarily the outcome of saturation but because of unstable income. Low consumption is conspicuous in the 1990s, which suggests that recovery of income – and probably confidence – may well increase such demand again.

The most important is their policies toward the weak, namely the strength of the safety net. This was also one of the major questions that led the Prime Minister to convene the 21st Century Commission. The report proposed the creation of 'a safety net to protect human rights and human dignity', but it is conditioned by the phrase 'within the agreement of those who pay', which is again at the centre of the problem today in many countries. A major part of it is actually paid by firms, their income tax and social security contributions. As shown in Chapter 3, the former is being reduced in many countries so as to survive international competition. At what level or what balance should we harmonize the principles of human rights and human dignity on the one hand and the principle of 'survival' in competition on the other is the key question to be addressed in this rapidly globalizing world. As shown above, the report's stance is that of leaving it to the attitudes of those 'who pay'. Thus, it speaks of the importance of protection, but avoids making the case for it, leaving it to 'the people' who pay. It may be that the 'elected' few people are finding it too difficult to decide such a critical balance in society. What we should learn from their report is that the people themselves must take up the task to choose this balance of society. This issue does have considerable importance. Without being supported by sufficient arguments among the people, leaders will feel themselves incompetent and fail to represent the people's will. In a democratic society, how the people judge or how they choose in this balance of economic growth and social protection, will determine the future path. Recognizing that the present government's proposal has not tackled this core question sufficiently, we have to be serious about addressing it ourselves.

Promotion of Competitiveness: The Economic Strategy Council, and The Industrial Competitiveness Council

We will see now more positive arguments for competitiveness, which seem to determine most strongly today Japan's future path. Before we examine the arguments of the late 1990s, we need to look at their origins in the early 1980s. The report of Rinji Gyosei Chosakai (Rincho), the Temporary Administrative Investigation Committee, which was to determine the major course of Japanese politics and economy in the following years, claimed that Japanese welfare policies had grown too large and created too big a government (1983): 'As a result of the necessity of the government to meet the problems in the 1970s (environmental destruction, pollution, social welfare needs, and oil shocks) the government was demanded to play a larger role than ever, and the enlargement of government and finance with a huge public deficit have been brought forth.' 'If this trend is untouched, Japanese socio-economy will suffer the "advanced nations' sickness" without fail.' 'Reconstruction of this enlarged, stiffened finance is an urgent task' (p. 18). 'The new role of government should be to secure the truly necessary policies for the welfare of the people, and to secure sufficient freedom for the private sector.' Also, 'To contribute to the stability and prosperity in the international society' is an important and inescapable task. These two became the 'two major goals' in Japan in the 1980s and 1990s (pp. 25-6).

Although it referred to those issues of 'advanced countries' sickness' or 'proper government size', it did not explain in detail what the sickness was or what the right size was. What was only clear for them was their belief that 'too much social welfare deteriorates the society'. Although it lacked detailed argument, it appeared powerful alongside the accumulated government deficit. With the tumultuous experiences in the 1970s, this argument gained enough force to brake the progress of the Welfare State in Japan.

After setting the basic direction toward slimming down the government and generating a larger private sector, the argument was then directed to which expenditures to reduce. The report of subcommittee 2 On Budget Planning, Administration, Government Investment and Lending (Jan. 1983) argued that 'As for the causes of the structural imbalance of finance, ... the introduction of social security, cultural and educational institutions, and their levelling up ... have become a major cause for the financial expansion. Another cause was the lack of the sufficient reviews of the existing institutions and policies'. 'As the easy thought that new spending would be possible without larger burdens, which was born in the high growth period, settled down among the people', 'the debates in the Congress tended to become those to realize sectarian interests rather than restricting and reducing spending' (ibid. p. 324). 'If various partial interests are to be reflected to budget planning, spending will keep increasing, and those small groups of people who are solidly united will obtain government's favor unilaterally' (ibid. p. 332). Although the argument about pressure groups is generally true, the real question to be answered was what kind of expenditure was unnecessary and what was necessary; which should have meant tackling the very problem of what kind of society they should pursue between economic growth or competitiveness on the one hand and welfare provisions and securities on the other. Such an argument should have been answered by addressing the nation, which has not been carried out yet. This temporary committee was regarded as the only authoritative representative of the people, and their stance was turned into the basic national strategy for the next decades.

Two important committees for strengthening Japanese firms' competitiveness were established by the cabinet in 1998-99: the Economic Strategy Council, 1998 and the Industrial Competitiveness Council, 1999. The former had two goals, to generate the economic recovery from the present depression of the 1990s and at the same time connect it to the higher-competitiveness path, and the latter focused mainly on competitiveness itself.

The Economic Strategy Council

In its first report the Council addressed the recovery and recommended such measures as financial expansion, investment of public money into the ailing banks, smaller government, lower personal income tax and higher indirect tax, employment policies, and private pensions. Its major report on Feb. 26, 1999, 'Strategy for the Recovery of Japanese Economy', focused on strengthening Japan's competitiveness. It argued the necessity to change Japan from an 'equity and equality' to 'efficiency and fairness' society. It points out that past policies have been too protective for firms and people. The past Japanese social system had thought too much of equality and equity, and 'if that kind of situation, in which "the reward does not change much whether you work hard or not", called the "convoy system", continues, the so called "moral hazard" will inevitably prevail in the society and keep down economic vitality. One of the causes of the depression of Japanese economy should be understood to be this moral hazard.' It has enlarged the public sector, which will not be maintained any more, it argues. It also criticizes the traditional way of financial management of Japanese firms. Management, based on the latent values in the assets, that avoids risk-taking and depends on finance by land-secured-loans, was attacked.

The alternative way they suggest is smaller government. At this point, they highly praise the US experience. They argue that the US-type deregulation and deficit reduction are effective for economic recovery: 'The reasons why the US, who had suffered from twin deficits until the 1980s, could succeed in vitalizing the economy and balancing its government finance at the same time, are that the deregulation has vitalized economy and realized higher growth, and that it resolutely carried out budget deficit reduction thoroughly by the Omnibus Budget Reconciliation Act of 1993.' The US 'has recovered well in the 1990s. It is only recently that the demerits of the Anglo-American economic system have been conspicuous.' Japanese society must reform itself from too much equity and equality to 'efficiency and fairness'; '... what is inevitable ... is to challenge positively ... without fear of pain from reforms.'

But, it adds that this procedure should not lead to a chaotic or destructively competitive society. It says, 'a society is where people compete with each other but also a place for mutual help when in need'. Therefore, 'so that the major principle for such a new system functions effectively ... constructing the safety nets to secure ease and make possible the consolation matches' are necessary. For this purpose, 'to raise the ability of the workers so they can shift to different jobs and to make pension, health, and elderly care systems that will assure people security are necessary'. Unfortunately, this reference to security seems less passionate compared to their emphasis on competitiveness. They even recommend subsidizing particular higher growth industries through national projects, which are said to be commonly observed in advanced countries today. Although this is a violation of the smaller government principle, it is justified as: 'When we look at major advanced countries abroad, the development of these fields is helped by national projects and their outcomes have become substantial cause of their economic powers'. 'We are urged to be the top runner in the world'.

What kind of society will Japanese people have by following this path? As for a concrete model, it says, 'different from Anglo-American or European models, Japan should pursue its own "third way"'. Third way is such a popular word today in industrialized nations, but what would it be like in Japan? The argument of the Economic Council suggested it would be one between the US type and European type, with government and social welfare larger than that of the US, and smaller than that of Europe. But to the extent that they prioritise the goal of maintaining their competitiveness, Japan or any other country would be very likely to follow the front runner country toward the less secure but more competitive society. Probably being conscious of this impotence of politics today in the face of economic forces, and believing it to be the only way left, it urges the people to win the race first, and then they can taste the fruit, the social welfare: '... a competitive society is often connected with a struggle for survival or disposing of the weak. But it should be interpreted as a measure to enrich the society as its result. If we are afraid of competition and get away from it, the society as a whole will stop growing and relief of the weak will be impossible.'

The Industrial Competitiveness Council (All the Ministers and Major Members of the Industrial World)

The awareness of the necessity for stronger competitiveness is much keener in this committee. In the arguments of this committee were expressed such a sense of crisis as 'If nothing is done, we will lose the competition with the US', and 'we will never win the global mega-competition'. Demands for newer policies and legislation to strengthen competitiveness were piled up by the private industrial world. Requests for the reform of corporate laws and labour market laws, support for particular industries, and strengthening the partnership between industry and universities were made.

On the other hand, resistance to this new trend was given by a few, such as the Minister of Labour, who asked the firms to avoid dismissals and to train the workers inside firms. He said, 'I believe that firms have two obligations, profit seeking and maintenance of employment. It is a problem that the sort of management who asserts the latter is discredited, and the weight is being shifted to profit-seeking alone. Different from the US criterion, those who pursue these two responsibilities should be credited.' Although such a comment was met by some favourable words, the actual labour market has been characterized by increasing dismissals under restructuring, thus creating a fundamental change in the employment culture.

Firms' Views on Competitiveness – Keidanren (The Federation of Economic Organizations)

Lastly, we will look at the views on this issue of Keidanren, a group with considerable influence on the government, which will help us understand the policy development. Together with downsizing and huge dismissals of the workforce, firms are eager to reduce their public burden. Keidanren, the most influential financial and industrial group in Japan, has been asking for corporate tax cuts. It kept proposing a corporate income tax cut in 1997 and 1998. It asserted that Japan was still 'too much dependent on income tax with high progressive rate', which raised production cost, impelled the firms to move headquarters to lower tax countries and hindered the influx of foreign firms (based on the publication on the website). As evidence for the necessity of tax reductions, they pointed out the disadvantageous competition conditions compared with other advanced nations, and the declining effective tax rate of other advanced countries from the beginning of the 1980s. It was also argued that although that rate for Japan decreased in the tax reform of 1998, it was still relatively high. Following these requests, corporate income tax rate was reduced to 34.5% in 1998 and again in 1999 to 30%.

In the chairman's message at the first annual meeting of Keidanren in May 1999, Chairman Imai called for the dissolution of excess capacity, including excess workforce, and increased productivity. He also argued that (although having been largely lowered) the present corporate laws and tax system were not suited to a 'global standard', and needed to be improved soon and called for an emergency employment policy to meet the unemployment that was inevitable by firms' restructuring. As for the social security system, he emphasized that taxation and social security contribution were both recognized as important issues for the Japanese people. From the competitiveness view of the firms, it may possibly suggest their hope for the redistribution of social security contributions between firms and citizens.

US

President Clinton, who was in office for the most part of the US's years of recovery since 1992, described his views on the US economy and society in 1996, after having completed his first term. It should be noted that he also shares two main views in common as a politician with Blair or Obuchi: the urge to higher competitiveness and concerns or anxieties over the balance in the society (Clinton, 1996).

First about the economy, he addressed the government deficit, asserting the importance of lowering interest rates by reducing government deficit (p. 23). He also stated that downsizing was a success and created more new jobs. Compared to the low-wage jobs of several years ago, two thirds of the new full-time jobs were paid more than the median wage for the last two years and average wages were finally beginning to rise again (p. 27). He spoke of globalization positively. He was straightforward in admitting that his 'strategy … has been to help Americans take maximum advantage of global trade growth', and this strategy has succeeded. Although 'Open markets mean products come into America that are made by people who work for wages Americans can't live on', 'overall, trade has brought vast benefits to most Americans.' He stressed the competitiveness of US industries: 'Hundreds of thousands of good American jobs are being created by the export of our airplanes, telecommunications equipment, food products, movies, and cars. And jobs in exporting companies on average pay considerably higher wages than jobs in companies that sell only within the United States' (pp. 33-4). '... fair trade among free markets does much more than simply enrich America, it enriches all partners to each transaction', and 'That's why we have worked so hard to help build free-market institutions' (p. 36). Thus it was the strategy of the US, to promote economic globalization. And in such a growth period, he emphasized that we should ensure that 'all Americans have the chance to seize the opportunities that growth creates' (p. 21).

This, so far is the growing, positive side of America. He was quite sure and proud of it. But, he also had to address the other side, too. The economy as a whole grew but was prosperity really shared by every American citizen? Did everyone really seize the opportunities given by this growth? About the social welfare of the state, he expressed his fundamental stance of 'workfare' policy, to move people from dependence to work (p. 173). He also added that he had made only small cuts in Medicare, Medicaid, education and environment (p. 25), suggesting that he had not meant to be cruel to the needy by his policies. Was it really a success? We have already seen that this growth has also accompanied unfavourable results such as an expanding income difference. Here we can consider this problem through Clinton's own analysis of American society. Like Blair, Clinton addressed the problems of disintegrating society, too. He admitted that in spite of economic growth, America had a serious problem in the community or in the sphere of human relationship, which is the very basis of a society and without which no 'efficient' economy can continue to exist for a long time. We 'must ... provide people opportunities, demand ... responsibility for their own futures, [and] ... strengthen the community' (p. 21). We 'can, each of us, be responsible first in our individual, family, and work lives, and then as citizens who do what they can to make our communities and nation strong' (p. 61).

As discussed in this book, the most important question is the relation between market economy and society, coping with the former's negative effect on the latter. As for this connection, he admits the intrinsic vulnerability of market economy: 'In the absence of responsibility, for example, free-market capitalism veers off into consumer fraud, insider trading, and abuse of employees ... In the absence of responsibility, individual liberty is just selfishness.' 'America is about more than individuals exercising their rights.' 'In the Preamble to our Constitution they (our Founding Fathers) said our objectives were not just to "secure the blessings of liberty to ourselves," but also ... they said it was our job to "promote the general welfare"' (pp. 62-3). His quote from one citizen's words at a flooded village is symbolic. He refers to this episode: a damaged resident said, 'You know, as awful as this is, people have come in here to help us and they've been here everyday since the flood happened. Don't you just wish we could behave this way all the time?' This is introduced as 'the most sweeping lesson' for him. Unification, not division among people, is thought much of there. He concludes, 'when we are divided, we defeat ourselves' (p. 114). It seems that such a view was not just a casual idea. He refers to Robert Putnam, a political scientist who 'found troubling trends that suggested a deterioration of the networks of common interest ... I had the same feeling in 1991. I wanted to help re-inspire a sense of common purpose, to help rebuild those citizen networks, and the trust ... That was one of the most important reasons I sought the presidency' (p. 114).

He elaborates this assertion in various ways. He refers to a penny that has the word liberty on one side, and *E Pluribus Unum*, on the other, which means out of many, one. 'That humble penny is an explicit declaration – America is about both individual liberty and community obligation. These two commitments – to protect personal freedom and seek common ground – are the coin of our realm, the measure of our worth.' They 'must balance their private interests with the public interest, their own welfare with the general welfare of the community and the nation.' 'In short, America is not just about independence, but also about interdependence.' 'The lesson of America's history is that the good life is about more than individual liberty and material well-being; it's about cultivating community relationships and attending to public concerns.' And his hometowns, Hope and Hot Springs, in his boyhood in Arkansas are quoted. They were 'tight-knit communities' and 'that's still what we want' (pp. 117-19). He concludes that 'One vision foresees an "every man for himself," "you're on your own" America. This vision pays lip service to the importance of individual effort and strong families without assuring individuals and families the tools they need to succeed. This vision divides rather than unites us. ... in America we must go forward together, and we don't want to have a single person to waste' (p. 172). The measure of our worth is in the unity of freedom and community. He cherishes this idea; re-establishing a sense of common purpose.

It surely appeals to our heart, but painfully. It is because we still see the difficult situation of the US society today: income difference and insufficient social welfare. We will see other social problems that seem to be connected to this growth-first society later in Chapter 5. In his words above we can again confirm the very similar postures of the leaders of the countries: sense of mission for both competitiveness and social cohesion. Both problems seem to be pressing, and in every case the leaders seem to be drawn toward the former, which is no exception for the American President, either.

Conclusion for this Section

After having been through the opinions of political leaders, what we notice is the difficulty of fully recognizing and properly tackling the problems, finding and realizing the balance between economy and society. What we have seen in their opinions, particularly in the three countries above, the UK, Japan and the US, is their recognition of this problem but inadequacy in addressing it. The overriding force at present seems to be the trend toward higher competitiveness in these societies. Today, we, as nations, are thus being overwhelmed by a huge, gigantic idea of 'survival', especially in the globalizing economic competition. According to the political leaders' understandings and determinations, pushed hard by the industrial and financial world, the social balance may well be tilted toward limitless economic competition. Market power seems to be prevailing over any other powers today.

The Welfare States up to the 1970s were permitted to grow in favourable conditions of economic growth. But after these two decades, we are now challenged by the question of how to maintain the Welfare State in unfavourable conditions. Facing two major challenges – low economic growth and higher competitive urge – keeping the balance between growth and welfare will be the key question for discussion. We are challenged to answer the question of how to design the best possible Welfare State in these new conditions. This has become a more difficult question since the 1970s. What is most necessary today will be the new determination of the peoples themselves to take up this new question. It is more so because it concerns the basic framework of a society that the very will of the people alone can decide.[9] In approaching this task, we will look at related arguments by non-governmental writers in the next section. We will then look in Chapter 5 at people's will as expressed either explicitly or inexplicitly. With these observations and considerations taken together we will then proceed in Chapter 6 to our alternative idea of the Welfare State that best answers the social balance question today.

2 ARGUMENTS BY NON-GOVERNMENT WRITERS

We will now examine the non-government writers' arguments about the relationship between economy and welfare or how to locate welfare and economy properly in the social framework. First, we'll see arguments in general and then arguments about the four countries. Please note that if and how the Welfare States have changed have been already introduced in Chapter 1, Section 4. We'll focus our attention here on the arguments about if such a change should continue or not.

---

[9] That Prime Minister Obuchi called for the Japanese people to express their opinions on the report by the 21st Century Commission might show his recognition of this aspect of the problem.

Arguments in General

Worries and Warnings about Enlarging the Economic Sphere in a Society

From the standpoint of social welfare, the general condition today in the globalizing world seems unfavourable. A UN Human Development Program's report featured 'Globalization with a Human Face', describing the present situation as being ever more serious: 'People everywhere are more vulnerable. Changing labour markets are making people insecure in their jobs and livelihoods.' It comments that the trend is now threatening to the achievement of the Welfare State: 'The erosion of the Welfare State removes safety nets'. Particularly about workers' conditions, 'The structure and composition of labour markets in both developing and developed countries are changing rapidly. Some are moving towards jobs that are highly skilled and highly productive. But there are also pressures to be more flexible ... and that can mean throwing out the protection of workers' incomes, rights, and working conditions' (UN, 1999, p. 90).

This concern about the bad-effect of globalization on overall social welfare is also directed at the politically fundamental question of national sovereignty. The calls for financial supervision after the financial crises in 1997 are often only about symptoms, but the concern today seems to be directed toward the core of the problem, the social balance between the economy and society. A then financial commissioner of the Ministry of Finance in Japan, Sakakibara, said, 'political repulsion is occurring against the dominance of economy and market', and Daniel Yagin argued that the criteria for social ideals are the security of employment, social justice, identities of each nation, etc, and how people's ideas about them would change would be of significant importance from now on (*Nikkei*, Nov. 29. 1998). Although such a view has only just started to be made, it will inevitably become a critical question as the imbalance of economy and society grows.

As the arguments ripen, the question will probably converge on who should play the key role, market or the people. In major economic or political questions the main issue that will decide the people's will will be their judgement of the social balance between economic growth and social security: 'It is the balance and the right mix of social and economic policies that is the crux of the matter for a vigorous Welfare State' (George and Taylor-Gooby 1999, p. ix). It concerns the possibilities of material and spiritual welfare under various mixes of production and consumption or growth and welfare. What kind of society or social balance should be realized becomes the major issue for the industrialized countries. People will be asked more and more to answer this question of how to strike a balance between them.

Arguments on the Criteria of Our Judgement – How Should we Judge the Balance?

As for the criterion for our judgement of the balance, several arguments have been presented. It has been pointed out that it is important to pay attention to human nature in approaching this question. If we can observe what kind of inclination humans have in terms of redistribution, it will help us decide the social balance problem. George and Wilding (1993) suggest to seriously consider the human inclination toward equality. They understand that the New Right's view of the fundamental realities of human nature is self- and family-centred, but this statement is not a proven one (p. 36). Concerning this question, George and Howards argue that 'poverty in such affluent societies as the US and Britain is morally indefensible'. 'The justification that poverty is necessary in order to encourage economic growth is not only morally unacceptable but also not sustainable by empirical evidence' (George and Howards, 1991, p. iii). Tsukada regards humans as having basic fellowship feeling and asks how much of an egalitarian character people have because of this. From his inference, obtained by general observations, he understands it not to be a completely egalitarian nature, but one in which people cannot tolerate too much hardship for one's fellow human beings. It is also inferred that this feeling is often unduly suppressed when insecurity and pressures caused by market mechanism are allowed to grow excessively. But as with similar statements, this inference is not proved true until people's behaviours do converge into this direction.[10] Although difficult, this question of human nature must not be left aside, because it is the very basis on which various social ideas and policies are actually constructed.[11]

If we could really adopt one criterion to evaluate social conditions concerning the trade-off question of economy and society, it would be very helpful. Longevity may be argued as a simple, single, and possible criterion for judging social balance. Longevity is surely a criterion, something like the greatest common measure, which shows the human welfare. It has empirically been roughly in proportion with economic growth and thus it might be argued that policies that keep higher economic growth are desirable. But one problem is its precision. It can only relate to the gross economic growth in macro terms. It can be useful when we compare societies roughly but not when we have to find the differential effectiveness between similar Welfare States whose peoples' longevity are more or less close to each other

---

[10] Tsukada (1998). As George and Wilding (1994, p. ix) say, being confronted with the unfavourable years and the ensuing years of social democratic parties' recovery in European countries, the matters are much more complicated today than up to the 1970s, and 'the defenders of the welfare state need hard thinking'.

[11] As more data are accumulated from an increasing number of countries, it may become possible to obtain some kind of consensus of the inclination of humans on this question.

such as today. Longevity is useful, but only as a rough measure for significantly different societies.

No clear, single criterion for judging the best society and best balance between economic growth and distribution is to be found in this book. Although complex, it is assured that social members measure and judge it by the aggregated satisfactions they feel from various aspects of their lives. In practice, people have to measure it somehow, especially when they are confronted with the question at election times. And particularly in a time such as today when the social environment is rapidly changing and prospective social images are not very clear among the political leaders themselves, the voters must more positively create such social views for themselves. The core question asked there concerns the balance between growth and welfare. Their judgement is formed and influenced by the opinion leaders of the times on the one hand and also by their own experiences of the various experiments of different governments (Robson, 1980).

The argument that social welfare grew too large before the 1970s and hindered economic growth appeared in the late 1970s. This linkage was particularly argued in the US and the UK with their declining competitiveness (as introduced and discussed in Chapters 1 and 3). In addition to this argument from a resource-related point of view, Hayek and Friedman argued that social welfare should be restricted in order to protect the fundamental virtue of modern society, freedom, and to maintain work incentives. Based on these two reasons, social and economic, the neo-liberal governments and opinion leaders attacked the Welfare State.

But what made their stand complicated was their attitude toward the needy. Attacking the 'overgrown' Welfare State on the one hand, they referred to the necessity for a minimum level of social welfare: 'In a free society, there is no reason that the government must not provide security for too much a loss in order to support the minimum income or minimum level under which no one should not drop ... The problems we consider here happens only when the impersonal mechanism that gives directions to individuals as to their effort are thus stopped to work' (Hayek, 1976, p. 87). The impersonal mechanism referred to here is the market mechanism. Here he intends to establish the consistency of his argument by defining 'excessive welfare provision' as when it hinders individual effort.

This is too broad a definition and almost impossible to be applied to the actual policies. This difficulty is enhanced by his definition of market mechanism as an impersonal one. It is not impersonal but a very personal mechanism. The impersonality appears most clearly in price mechanism, where no single person, either producer or consumer, can influence the market among numerous competitors. This mechanism has come to be often undermined by larger sellers or buyers today, but even if we assume the prevalence of free competition, it still is a very personal mechanism. Most of all, this mechanism is at the mercy of the decision of the entrepreneurs to invest or not. And their determination depends on the prospective rate of profit. It would not influence the market much if only a few investors lose their confidence, but it would if many do so, which will lead to a huge disruption in economy as we often see. So because of the ambiguity of his assumption and incorrect characterization of the 'impersonality' of the market mechanism, his argument unnecessarily deals a heavy blow to welfare provisions. Because of the abstract character of their argument, they cannot show this level of minimum security in practical words. But when we hear M. Friedman say that 'Life is not equal', we learn that we cannot expect much from their stance on the minimum welfare level (Friedman and Friedman, 1979, pp. 136-7).

Today's consumption lowers tomorrow's production. But we will starve to death if we keep producing productive goods alone. We have to strike a balance somewhere in between. They regarded the limit to be at the extent up to which social welfare would not obstruct production. But this is not so simple. As was discussed, lower production and higher redistribution could bring greater satisfaction. We cannot depend on the market mechanism for choosing this balance. If all assets were in the employers' hands, and they could produce goods with their automated machine alone, they would find no need to employ anyone, and so no wages would be paid and there would be no consumption demand in the market. They'll only produce goods that are, and can be, demanded, the productive goods. It works but only according to the unevenly allocated purchasing power among the social members. Under such a condition, the government or the society as a whole must decide the social balance politically. Thus it must make a decision, for example, how much to reduce investment and how much to increase consumption or welfare provision. It may harm some people's incentives for investment but it might be better for the overall welfare of society. This understanding seems to be missing from their argument. For them the government is something additional. Of course, any social member would oppose making the welfare provisions so large that the total economy shrank heavily. But other than that, how much and how fast the gross economy should grow, and how much the redistribution should be realized are questions to be answered by the whole society, not through the market mechanism alone. When this social balance is determined, market mechanism is allowed to perform freely in this framework. Accordingly, Hayek needed to show how much disincentive or how much anti-productivity effect should be allowed. Without this, his idea remains only a simplistic accusation of the Welfare State.

Concerning this issue, M. Feldstein examined a relationship between welfare and the economy, or that between public pensions and savings on the one hand and economic growth on the other. He asserted that social security would reduce savings, hence it would lead to reduced investment and lower economic growth (Feldstein, 1974). This and similar studies are useful contributions. But the real question here is not to find welfare provisions that do *not* reduce the economic growth rate, but to maximize the sum of the satisfactions from reduced or increased growth and increased or reduced welfare provisions.

William A. Niskanen examined the relationship between welfare and dependency and argued that there was a close relationship between an increase in benefit and an increase in dependency (1996). This is also a useful contribution to thinking about the balance in concrete terms, but again we should be careful about its implications. He quotes F. D. Roosevelt's words that 'continued dependency on relief induces a spiritual moral disintegration'. But this does not necessarily mean that people by nature prefer to live on benefit. As argued before, humans in general are never happy without participating in the social fabric, working together with other people. Work gives one a strong feeling of attachment, which is a major support to one's self-esteem. There may be an individual case where being idle takes on a self-perpetuating character. It is when these people are treated as being born idle. People, to a great extent, try to respond to others' expectations.[12] They form their aspirations conforming to their surroundings and expectations. If nothing is expected of them and they are treated as being born idle, and ironically this is just what the neo-liberals' argument seems to mean, they would respond to this 'expectation' by becoming genuinely idle. Although this contradicts their original disposition, the sense of loss of self-respect inflicted by others overrides it. In natural science there is said to be an occasion that the observer affects the observed object. The same might hold true here. Unintentionally, the observer might well aggravate the problem, thus making a vicious circle between expectations and reactions.[13] Thus, if people are claimed to be satisfied with their position of being on benefit, it may suggest a deeper cause in the society, a cause that may well be

---

[12] Mcleod (1995), in observing the children as a social worker in city slums, explains how the underclass people create their aspirations, conforming to their environment and the expectations of surrounding people.

[13] Rawls' difference principle is referred to as supporting liberal thoughts. But it should be noted that neo-liberalism could reach the same conclusion with the difference principle in some cases. If the statement 'if the present profit rate does not rise, firms will not invest. For this rate to rise, the income of the upper level people must increase' holds true, the policy to widen the income difference will be adopted by Rawlsians. Difference principle is the one that approves this wide difference, if it raises the amount of the allocation given to the least advantaged, in this case the lowest income group (Rawls tries to escape this conclusion by his assumption of benevolence in human nature, but this argument seems unsuccessful. See Tsukada 1998).

connected with discouragement by indifference or unfairness in the society.

Concerning this point, however, we should bear in mind that there is a different kind of deep-seated problem in the market mechanism that causes lower work incentive in general. It is the loss of the sense of being the master of one's own life. This loss is related to the transition of society from the feudal age to the civil one and caused by the division of labour, which seems inevitable for higher productivity. Although serfs were under the control of the landlords, they had the control of their own works at their workplaces. In production and consumption they did not have to depend on the invisible social complexity or the market mechanism. Their work and life were transparent. The relationship of their work and reward was clear, although a larger part was taken from them by the landowners. Although in a restricted sense, as they were the masters of their own works, they were able to decide most of the aspects of their lives on their own, as what to plant, when and how to work, etc. In the workplaces they could enjoy larger freedom than many of the modern workers, who are now unable to control their own work, what to produce or how to work. This sense of loss lowers their work incentives. We should keep in mind that civil society has developed this fundamental problem and not solved it yet. When we forget this, we often make the mistake of seeing human nature as an extremely work-hating one and having a natural tendency to be lazy. From this point of view, the solution for work incentives might well end up in heavier pressure on workers rather than realizing greater autonomy in the workplaces.

We should address one more point concerning the views of Hayek and Friedman. We have argued that the choice of the social balance by the people themselves is important today. This issue is related to another fundamental question. It concerns the freedom of choice, which even such champions of 'freedom of choice' as Hayek or Friedman do not refer to. It is not the choice of balance between economic growth and welfare but the choice of the market mechanism society itself. Most of us usually choose to stay in one country for all of our lives, but this does not necessarily mean that we are deeply loyal to the country we are born in. It is often because the cost of moving is so huge that we choose to stay in the mother country. Even if we get enough money to move, when most of people in the world live in a market mechanism society, we are in a sense compelled to accept this system. In order that this choice of our country and economic system should become the result of the true 'freedom of choice', we have to determine first the best possible shape of this kind of society.

In thinking about the social balance between economy and society, the harmful effects of economic globalization were addressed in the 1990s. Economic globalization itself has been the inevitable outcome of the market economy. It is being promoted today by innocent entrepreneurs, optimistic economists and reluctant politicians. Optimistic economists are those who believe fundamentally in the invisible hand of the market mechanism on the world scale. Opposing views have been posed, focusing on the necessity for controlling its harmful effects on public welfare.

Arguments on the harmful effects of globalization intensified when the world economy met the turmoil of financial crisis in 1997. The argument centred mainly on the financial field, but it raised the question even among the supporters of this trend. The need to reaffirm the purpose of economic activity and globalization was addressed by those concerned. For an example, in convening the 1999 conference of the World Economic Forum (Davos Conference), whose theme was 'Globalization with Responsibility', the founder of this forum Klouz Schwab of Geneva University, confirmed their basic position that 'free market and economic affluence produced by entrepreneurship is the ground of our prosperity', but he also emphasized, 'the reason why they are important is that they serve the public welfare of the world', and 'if a larger number of people do not receive its benefit, except for just a small group of people, globalization is not a success' (*Nikkei*, Jan. 27, 1999).

A leading capitalist, George Soros, has warned of the threat of capitalist economy. According to him, it has had three spurious beliefs: laissez-faire economics, Social Darwinism and geopolitics. After the demise of Communism in many countries, geopolitics in the sense of the cold war era is losing its power but he is afraid that the other two are gaining more power than ever. He argues a society is not just made of competition but also of cooperation, which is being driven out today: 'guided by the principle of the survival of the fittest, states are increasingly preoccupied with their competitiveness and unwilling to make any sacrifices for the common good' (Soros, 1997). His warning that financial markets were particularly unstable and needed regulation became true in the Asian financial crisis. Through this experience he argues, 'Once it fully grips its power, the power of market could cause, if we talk in purely economic and financial spheres, disturbances and even the collapse of the global capitalist system eventually.' 'It is not true that financial market always works for equilibrium, but it swings between countries as a huge iron ball to destroy buildings, and has knocked down the weak countries'[14] (*Nikkei*, Jan. 7, 1999).

Lawrence Klein also criticized the harmful effects of present globalization on international finance by its lack of proper information. He asked if the market could give the optimal answer to international finance,

---

[14] His ex-partner, Jim Rogers, said, 'what is right is the long term investment' (TV documentary, NHK, Nov. 1998). He explains the reasons as: long term investment creates a community that shares the fate of the invested, it is done on one's own responsibility not exploiting or outmanoeuvring the mass movement and needs a serious decision, but short term investment only needs the ability to grasp the current of money at the moment and does not need to feel any concern for the fate of the invested.

and said that the real world was too complicated for every member in the market to obtain the information and for the economic hypothesis of perfectly free competition to hold, and that unstable markets would expose even nations to risks. He asserted that in order to cope with this problem, it was particularly necessary to secure transparency, and the investors should be required to report their transactions frequently wherever they were located. He argued that as the instability of the market grew with the increase of supranational corporations, governments would have to strengthen their regulation. At present, market capitalism faces instability and deteriorating profitability by having pursued economic rationality too much. Liberalism seemed to have been driven recklessly, indifferent to improving the relief system of the weak or public welfare. He went on to say that in order to ameliorate the effects of market failure we needed to keep the balance between market principles and regulation by the government and that we had come to the point when we should increase the level of equity in distribution (Nikkei, March 20, 1999). In the cases of Soros and Klein, they agree with the necessity for global political governance of globalizing economic activities, with the latter suggesting larger equity in distribution.

Based on his experiences as a lawyer dealing with Karoshi (overwork to death) in Japan, Kawahito warns of the harmful effects on working conditions. He argues that globalization generates limitless competition: 'Economic globalization will bring forth limitless cut-throat competition in the worldwide dimension, if it is not controlled by human reason. The deterioration of labour conditions in one country will prevail in the world if it is understood to be advantageous for competition. The law of the jungle, increase in inequality and unemployment, will be seen all over the world.' He introduces the view of the ICFTU, the united organization of many labour unions in the world (124 million members, 137 countries, Nov. 1997) that warned that economic globalization became the same word as under-employment, unemployment, and increased inequality. He evaluates this comment as genuinely true, based on his own numerous cases (Kawahito, 1998, p. 185).

In coping with these new problems, self-regulation on the part of entrepreneurs doesn't seem effective. Although people like Soros utter warnings once in a while, the behavioural principle for them is reduced to profit maximization. It has been and will still be so tomorrow. An example from Henry Ford may be illustrative. Workers were exhausted by the mass production system Ford had launched. A wife of a worker appealed to Ford in a letter that her husband was so exhausted at the factory that he was unable to hold his baby when he came back home. Following this episode the words of Ford are quoted: 'I do not know if all that I have done is right or wrong', 'but human beings are already advancing the way which they cannot return'. From these words we learn that we can expect from them technological

149

progress and material abundance, but not proper distribution of its merits.[15] It is the task of the whole of society and thus the people's. Such worries or fears by some giant entrepreneurs are repeated on a larger scale today. How to harmonize the merit and demerit by minimizing the latter remains the fundamental question with the ever-growing market economy, which today exercises its power as a globalizing economic force.[16]

Drawing on these opinions, to find the answer to the question of balance in the growth – welfare trade-off and the new conditions of globalization and to make it be reflected in the policies of the government are the tasks of the people today. As referred to before, when the problem concerns the very difficult, delicate choice of this kind of social balance, it is often too much a burden for the representatives to decide. Support from the people or the thought-out choice on the people's side is necessary.[17]

Arguments on the Conditions of the Four Welfare States

The following arguments about the experiences of the four countries concerning the social balance question provide some useful materials and suggestions.

SWEDEN

As shown before, Sweden has achieved the two goals of welfare and growth up to the 1980s, but has experienced serious downturn in the early 1990s.

According to Pfaller et al. (1991), the Swedish Welfare State model until the 1970s was characterized as one that reduced the firms' burden as much as possible to increase their competitiveness in exports and was supported by the internal redistribution among the citizens. 'The country has for a long time relied heavily on the taxation of households to finance its expensive Welfare State while capital has been taxed rather modestly in international comparison. Thus by its very design, Swedish welfare statism has entailed less redistribution from capital to labour and more "solidarity" among wage earners than it has been the case in other countries. The proposed tax reform,

---

[15] From a TV documentary, NHK, *Over the Century*, Jan. 23, 1999.

[16] Arthur Schlesinger emphasizes the importance of government. He says that the market economy always wants innovations and thus disturbs society and becomes a cause of instability, but there are many problems the market cannot solve: education, social welfare, infrastructure, crime prevention, etc., and so government must stabilize society, and protect the people (Nikkei, July 25, 1998). Such used to be the common understanding. Today, when such a view is being overwhelmed by market forces, we need to emphasize it.

[17] For this purpose the information from the government is essential of course. The most important is this participation of the peoples. We are in a period of a great social transformation.

which intends to shift the burden radically from direct to indirect taxes, would even go one step further towards securing the non-interference of Welfare State solidarity with economic efficiency.' And 'Sweden was able to carry out a drastic competitive devaluation and make it stick in real terms.' '... the Swedish population ... had to accept the loss in real income which was the necessary consequence of higher import prices ... they had to abstain from compensating for this loss through higher wages ... Swedish business, in turn, benefited from higher profit margins on the markets which are exposed to international competition' (Pfaller et al., 1991, p. 286). From this experience, we can see the possibility of supporting the large-scale Welfare State by an increase in the citizens' burden.

They also point out the importance of the types of political regime to meet economic problems. They argue that knowing how to form social consent makes a great difference, and argue for the advantage of corporatist societies on economic performances. They point out the two ways to challenge economic problems in the Welfare States, consensual and compulsive: 'The decisive issue ... is whether consensual discipline in the absence of economic sanctions can match the discipline which is enforced by economic compulsion' (ibid. p. 295); '... nowhere did the analysis of these problems point to the rigidities which some critics associate with excessive welfare statism. On the contrary, it appeared that the most complete Welfare States in our sample, that is Sweden and West Germany, were most thoroughly successful in orientating the national economy to high-productivity and high-quality production ... Purely contractual relations between the buyer (the enterprise) and the seller of labour services (the employee) were largely recognized as an inferior means of achieving maximum collective performance with regard to productivity, quality and innovation.' This had been true until the 1980s, but it was also true that it was reaching its limit in some sense then. A high rate of unemployment, which Swedish economy had long avoided, was prevalent in the early 1990s. Although the economy has been recovering since then, how much this consensual process would be effective in the new environment should be studied further.

Concerning the possibility of wage restraint in a corporatist type consensus society, the rethinking of the once-abolished Employee Investment Fund may be worth attention (Maruo, 1986). Maruo argues for this because of the shortage of bargaining materials to restrain wage increases in the 1990s, and pays attention to assets redistribution or transferring a part of profit to labour. An Employee Investment Fund was proposed in 1975 by Rudolf Meidner, an economist of the Federation of Swedish Labour Unions (LO). Esping-Andersen also supported it then as an idea acceptable to the people in a liberal democratic parliamentary system. This idea was that the ownership of a part of the profit invested into a firm was to be transferred from the original owners to communal ownership of the employees. The ratio was to be determined by the employees. The firm would issue stocks equivalent to that amount which would be given to the Fund. Thus it was a barter of wage restraint with a part of the resulting profit, which was to be reinvested under the employees' ownership (Pierson, 1991). Esping-Andersen regarded it as highly feasible as it would not generate direct depreciation of stockowners' assets. But because of a strong resistance from the firms' side, this policy was abolished after having been tried for a short period in 1990. Although once abolished, a rethink of this plan may be relevant in the new economic conditions for Sweden or the harsher competition and the stronger necessity to hold down inflation. The experiment is probably worth attention in other countries, too.

The tight budget policy for four years by the Social Democratic Party in the mid-1990s, which accompanied a high unemployment rate and setback of social welfare, cut their seats in the 1998 election, barely keeping them in power by a narrow margin. The Left Wing party, which advocated increased social welfare provisions, doubled theirs. The Moderate Party, which advocated deregulation, an open market policy, privatisation and joining NATO, won 82 seats. The Scandinavian countries that embarked on welfare reform in the 1990s are thus met by opposition of the people and pressure to change. But such a change then again would meet opposition from the firms' side, too. There is also worry that a highly talented workforce would leave the country to escape the high income tax rate. This may add a new threat to the traditional mechanism of large-scale Welfare State by the people's burden. In the harsher competitive environment, the Swedish economy seems to face the difficult question of how high a level of welfare provision it can maintain, which depends largely on the people's willingness to pay and to consent to wage restraint.[18] This is a problem for the Swedish society but also a problem only the highly advanced Welfare State is going to suffer from. In this sense, to reach this state may be the first choice to be faced by the other three countries today.

UK

Friedman characterizes that the 'drive for equality in Britain failed' because it went against a basic human instinct (1979, p. 144). Mitsuhashi points out that the core of the thoughts of the Conservative Party was provided by

---

[18] Okazawa even argues, 'to stop the hollowing out, and the firms moving to lower wage countries, labour cost must be lowered, even if it accompanied lowering social welfare level to a certain extent' (Okazawa, 1991, p. 200). Stephens refers to the firm posture of 'all political actors' who believe that the economic situation is critical and thus warrants cuts in entitlements, and the widespread conviction that Sweden will not be able to return to the 2% unemployment rate (Stephens, 1996, p. 45).

so-called 'wets', or the guilt feeling of the upper class, the thought of dominance, and sympathy for the weak (Mitsuhashi, 1989, p. 45). But if this sympathy from above or paternalistic attitude had supported the post-war Welfare State of the UK, it was also this attitude that decreased with the decline of the British economy. Lindbrom (1977) argued in the late 1970s the fragility of this consensus, that it was originally based on the impossible harmonization of firms' demands and the demand of workers for social welfare. He wrote 'It is now a possibility that the market-oriented polyarchies cannot much longer reconcile the necessary privileged demands of business with the demands of strong unions and the Welfare State. Indeed, lagging economic performance in Britain is enough to convince any observers that at least one nation has already succumbed to a fundamental problem in irreconcilable demands.'[19] Based on this 'irreconcilable' view neo-conservatism took power. Mishra understood the 1988 tax cut of the highest personal income tax rate to 40% to show the death of the post-war social consensus. These changes represented 'the final disappearance of the last vestiges of the post-war consensus', and 'the concepts of equity and justice reflected in the tax system lost its last trace of "the pretended aspiration" of the Conservative Party' ('Budget for the Rich', *Manchester Guardian Weekly*, May 27, 1988, cited in Mishra, 1990, p. 31).

This new track, or loss of post-war consensus, has been pursued further in the 1990s and in the main by the Labour Party after 1997. Thus the change of social consensus is more conspicuous in the UK. As this change was rather an emergency measure for the chaotic economy of the 1970s, the problem for the UK is that it has not yet established a new social consensus today. Above all, such a consensus must be one to ensure hope and security for all the people. But the neo-liberal slogans such as self-help, hard work, and less dependency do not seem to have provided enough of these for society yet, and it seems to be the same with Tony Blair's 'new Labour' policies. This difficult condition of the absence of a new social consensus seems to be reinforced by the new pressures of globalization, which further promote the retrenchment of the Welfare State. 'In some ways fears of taxation [for] work disincentives are the issue of yesterday. What worries governments more these days ... is the possibility of capital flight ... to [countries] with low capital taxes and low labour costs' (George and Taylor-Gooby, 1996, p. 18).

One argument prompting consideration of the possible alternative rather than just adjust to the given trend of anti-welfarism is that of the increasing

---

[19] He also applied this view to Sweden; '... these observers would explain Sweden's escape from the problem as an only temporary respite in a period in which Swedish business has been able to profit from unusual resources of timber and minerals and other vanishing special opportunities in international trade' (Lindbrom, 1977, p. 351).

welfare demand. George and Miller et al. (1994) and George and Taylor-Gooby (1996) discuss the strong tendency for the welfare demand to increase in the UK. As for the reasons for this increase, 'The factors that make for more demand for social service provision are many and varied: unemployment, the growth in the size of the elderly population, the rise in the number of lone parent families, rising public expectations for better services, technological medicine, recognition of disability as a public issue, and so on'[20] (George and Taylor-Gooby, 1999, p. 10). About rising expectations, it is argued that if we anticipate the 'diminishing return on welfare spending' (Bonoli et al, 2000, p. 76), more spending might be necessary to get the same satisfaction from social welfare provision. And we also have the possibility of increasing aspiration level, newer generations taking higher welfare spending for granted (op. cit. pp. 76-7). We may also be able to add that an increased anxiety in society necessitates larger welfare spending to strengthen the safety net.[21] Such are the underlying trends possibly expected from a longer-term perspective. And these trends are in turn often affected by the short-term effect of business cycles with fluctuating unemployment provisions.[22] Newer welfare demand is pointed out to be necessary for compensating the damage incurred by globalization. As Euzeby argues, such demand will surely be augmented by the increased

---

[20] An OECD study points out the factors 'which are requiring a new approach to social and health policies'; that people are living longer and dependency ratios will rise, the increase in elderly people living alone raises the demand for care services, the proportion of children in lone-parent families has risen, the increase in dual-earner households caused by increased female labour force participation makes child care and parental leave policies more important for the well-being of the families, low-skilled workers have a higher risk of unemployment, other forms of non-employment or low wages insufficient to support their families, etc (OECD 1999, *A Caring World*, p. 13). The ratio of lone parent families increased in the UK, Japan, and the US:

Sweden		UK		Japan		US	
1980	19.0	1981	17.8	1980	8.9	1986	22.7
1995	18.0	1991	20.7	1995	12.8	1996	27.1

(The number of lone-parent families as a percentage of all families with dependent children: ibid. p. 18.) We should also take notice of the favourable effect of welfare provisions. In a comparison between 1930 and 1960, the relationship between fertility and female labour force participation seems to have changed between those born in 1930 and 1960. The rate of fertility used to become lower with labour participation, but the relationship seems to have reversed (ibid. p. 17).

[21] Giddens sees this anxiety in a more general perspective, as being born from the reflexive nature of modern society, and as something we have to face with a positive attitude (Giddens, 1998).

[22] Of course these long-term factors are also susceptible to change according to the changing attitudes of the peoples.

harshness of such problems as growing unemployment and reduced job security, widening pay differentials and a decline in the position of self-employed workers (Euzeby, 1998).

To tackle the problem of the social fund for meeting these welfare demands, George and Miller et al. consider the three possibilities for maintaining or increasing social welfare spending (1994, pp. 215-17). The three possibilities are the minimum wage, progressive tax rate, and artificial consumption urge. They argue for introducing a minimum wage by showing that those countries that have it do not show the economic difficulties predicted by opponents. They argue for a progressive rate of direct taxation, claiming that the OECD already showed in the middle of the 1970s that a high tax rate did not lower work incentives. And they argue that the present resistance to income tax rate is largely due to the deliberately produced consumerism. The first argument is persuasive and is further supported by the fact that after it was actually implemented in the UK in April 1999 business maintained its recovery. The third argument is difficult to prove or refute. It appeals to our common sense, but needs to be studied further. The second point, higher income tax is rarely referred to in politics today but this also needs to be studied further, too.

The issue of raising income tax is discussed with the phrase of 'citizens' Welfare State'. Based on the understanding that demand for social welfare has a strong tendency to increase, they suggest paying for it with higher tax for the citizens, thus realizing the citizens' Welfare State. It features 'high rates of direct or indirect taxes'. They argue that it is necessary as 'an alternative to residualism' 'to preserve the welfare entitlements of citizenship'. But they also are aware that 'its viability is so highly dependent on the will of the people'. And here they expect the possibility that 'governments can exert [influence] on shaping public opinion' and the emergent necessity for this type of government. They believe that 'There is a strong democratic case for giving the public the choice between a residual Welfare State with low taxes and a citizens' Welfare State at a higher tax cost before the former wins out by default on the assumption that it is the only way of squaring the welfare circle' (pp. 223-5).

As we have seen before, the present conditions for policy options seem very unfavourable for maintaining the traditional Welfare State. But the same conditions are what make the maintenance and strengthening of the Welfare State the more necessary, too. As was observed in Chapter 3, the severe condition of increasing competitiveness increases its necessity both in absolute and relative terms. It produces more insecure jobs and expands the income difference. It reduces the welfare fund by corporate tax cuts when it is becoming more necessary. The competitive lifestyle, a major spiritual by-product of this movement, necessitates the provision of a stronger safety net, such as higher and longer unemployment benefit, adequate health care, or adequate old age pension. Demographic or social trends increase its necessity still more, with an increasing ageing population and more lone parents. But the same competitive conditions strongly exclude higher corporate income tax today. This seems to lead us to the choice of higher personal income tax or indirect tax to maintain the Welfare State. In regard of these conditions, the citizens' Welfare State seems to be an effective, feasible, and inevitable alternative today.

In a sense, it might seem a concession to the management from the labour's side. But it may well be accepted by the people as an emergency measure. If the consumerism that they argue about were so strong, then it would need strong effort by the government or opinion leaders to persuade the electorate to realize this path. But if this is what ensures necessary security for the welfare of the people, their effort will eventually succeed. And how much the choice of maintaining the security of the people is needed today will be discussed in Chapter 5.

Fuller recognition of the positive effects of welfare provisions will help maintain the Welfare State. As even the IMD study admitted, there are factors that are related to the Welfare State that will add to the competitiveness of a society. Political stability or higher work incentives are the first examples. An OECD study argues that when the social welfare system is fully working, 'Because the elderly need not fear serious deprivation, their adult children are freed to work, raise their children, and to take advantage of opportunities and to make contribution to society that might otherwise be denied them; the unemployed are provided with income not only for survival, but also to permit time to search for a job appropriate to their skills, or to acquire new skills; public intervention in education and support for children is an investment in tomorrow's resources, and in everyone's future; provisions for health care are an investment in the productive capacity of human resources. Together, these and other benefits of social policies contribute to a more efficient and a more just society' (OECD, 1994, *New Orientations for Social Policy*, p. 10). These positive effects are not necessarily self-evident and may vary between countries. But still such positive viewpoints should also be taken into account fully in evaluating the effects of the Welfare States. These merits may also be re-enforced by increasing efficiency in the welfare provisions. The transparency of social service provision, 'clear accounts of public expenditure', and 'a more participatory and user-friendly Welfare State' would increase support for higher welfare provisions (George and Taylor-Gooby, 1996, p. 24).

One negative factor is the so-called 'culture of contentment' of the middle class and upper class people. Joined with consumerism and the competitive urge, when people contain themselves within the contentment culture of themselves and stop paying attention to the lower income people, the will to maintain the Welfare State will be weakened (Galbraith, 1988, p.10 and 1993, p. 26). How strongly this culture exists is itself a question but the increasing competitiveness in the society will without doubt promote this atmosphere. This problem should be addressed and this culture of contentment should ultimately be ameliorated by governmental and citizens' efforts. But we should also bear in mind that its possible negative effect may well obstruct Welfare State maintenance at first.

When the people firmly convince themselves of the necessity and feasibility of maintaining the Welfare State, the government will be able to act accordingly. But probably with the lack of this strong support from the people, present governments are rather less confident of doing so today. For this reason, 'All in all ... the differences between the parties' economic and social policies are contained within the common paradigm of the affordable Welfare State' (George and Miller, 1994, p. 218). The British people once rejected higher taxes and a higher Welfare State in the 1992 election: 'If anything, the agonizing of the Labour Party was further stimulated by the result of the 1992 General Election, in which the voters appeared to reject the modest increases in taxation which the party proposed, despite popular criticisms of the Conservatives' handling of the welfare services. Labour have to establish whether this apparent public unwillingness to pay higher taxes is indeed real, and so firmly embedded in British society that there is no point in persevering with any such policy; or whether, with new leadership and better presentation of policy, enough of the electorate can be won over' (ibid. pp. 220-1). But in 1997, the 'new' Labour Party did not propose higher taxes any more. It criticized the anti-welfare attitude of the Conservatives but only within a similar tax regime.

JAPAN

Japanese society is credited for its success in keeping the balance of growth and welfare until the 1970s, if we put aside the serious pollution problems in the 1960s. It was praised for its low spending and relatively high welfare level. It was even said that with far less state intervention than in Europe, Japan matched American and European standards of health, education, and security in old age (Rose and Shiratori, ed., 1986): 'By conventional material measures, Japanese citizens today enjoy a very high level of welfare. The current life expectancy of a Japanese person is 77 years' (p. 4). 'If Scandinavia is a model of what the state can do to provide welfare ... then Japan is a counter-example of how a society can do without high levels of public provision, yet have a population that is educated, healthy, and secure in old age' (p. 11). 'Job security is high ... pension arrangements guarantee security in old age. ... family solidarity remains high ... Notwithstanding the tensions that a very competitive education system creates for young people, juvenile crime rates ... are far below those of Europe or the United States' (p. 4). Such accomplishments had been realized under the Liberal Democratic Party, which pursued economic growth first and also 'greatly increased expenditure on welfare during their thirty years in office' (p. 9).[23]

But the situation has changed drastically from the 1980s to 1990s. The 1980s were when growing demand for pensions and medical spending was at the same time confronted with a growing government deficit. The mounting fear about the shrinking Welfare State under the tight budget policy was aggravated by the 1990s depression. Anxieties about employment mounted. When the newly developed modern style social security system faced a difficulty, the argument for social balance tilted toward growth and investment rather than welfare and consumption, as shown in the previous section. Various views concerning the negative effects of this competitive path have been put forward.

From a long-term perspective of the competitiveness-oriented society, Sawa warns of the possible social unrest resulting from the inevitable large income differences. He characterizes this type of society as a winner-takes-all society. According to him, today we are living in an information society where larger scale leads to higher productivity. It is a society where large corporations grow ever more larger by mergers and affiliations, thus leading to a 'winner-takes-all' society. Under this condition income differences will grow larger and conflict among social members will be harsher. In order to prevent it, a new economic regime that can establish both efficiency and equity becomes necessary (Nikkei, Jan. 6, 1999). Actually, world-scale mergers and affiliations have been growing in the globalizing world market. And when we look into the Japanese society, this warning of social unrest under such growing 'winner-loser' culture does seem justified. We will consider this question in the Chapter 5.

Ito (1999) argues against the competitive path from the viewpoint of the solidarity culture of Japanese people. He argues that the human relations expressed in the income distribution in Japan are based on the Japanese spiritual climate, which is more common in Europe, and it does not suit the US-type business culture: 'When we reflect on the post-war history and managerial climate in Japan, even if the leaders of Keidanren (the Federation of Economic Organizations) and Doyukai (the Japan Association of Corporate Executives) should head for American managerial climate as the global standard, it would not be established in the [Japanese] society. It's because there is a tradition in Japan in which the huge reward, which is incomparable with the employees', will make the entrepreneurs feel some guilt, and there is a sense of dislike to competitiveness-first, efficiency-first

---

[23] The level of old age pension is not high for every pensioner in Japan. In particular, quite a few of the self-employed population only receive a much smaller public pension.

way of living, taste for less unequal income distribution, and feelings for others' (p. 205). Such characteristics do seem to be embedded in Japanese society. How long and to what extent they will remain in the harsher competitive environment is an open question and has to be studied in order to examine the adaptability of Japanese society to the emerging competitive conditions in the world.

Kawahito (1998) criticizes the competitive course from the viewpoint of its serious effect on working conditions in Japan. He claims that the present competitive situation in Japan has reached the point where it has severely affected the labour intensity and work hours of individual employees, thus generating Karoshi (overwork to death) that is the worst and ultimate negation of the workers' welfare. Based on this understanding, he opposes the more-competitiveness track and calls for an alternative way. His grasp of the situation in Japanese economy and society, based on his involvement as a lawyer, is keen and convincing. He summarizes the problems of the past decade as follows. Today in Japan 'when large corporations and banking facilities go bankrupt one after another, and the unemployment reaches its record high level, the word "Japan as the economic giant" is hardly heard. Not only firms but also the overall society feel anxious about the economic prospect and are uneasy.' But 'the proposition to change work- and life-style of Japanese people, which was actively discussed from the second half of the 1980s to the beginning of the 90s was not necessarily based on the presumption of economic affluence. The significance of the question seems to have lain in the reconsideration of the system and consciousness that produced material wealth.' 'But ... as expressed in the words "labour hours suitable for Japanese economic power" (by the Research Bureau of the Japan Federation of Employers' Association), there were those who thought relaxed life should be realized within the limit of strong economic power.' And in reality this thought on the employers' side often became the dominating one. 'While the argument about economic power and relaxation had not matured, economic situations changed. With the crisis of firms, and Japanese economy being brought to the fore of the argument, workers came to pay attention not to be victimized by restructuring than to shorter working hours or relaxed way of living' (p. 202).

Thus the word 'survival' occupies people's mind in Japan today: 'Now has become the goal of Japanese people the survival of Japan in international competition, of firms in competition and themselves in competition.' 'I do fear that such goals will aggravate the social illness of modern Japan in which workers lose more time and relaxation of mind, are deprived of happiness, and overwork to death prevails' (p. 206). At present in Japan 'the thought of almighty market radicalism' casts a spell on people's mind. 'But 'market' is not a benevolent God ... Surely it selects out cheaper and more convenient goods', 'but it is a brutal monster which may destroy not only humans but also the earth itself, if not controlled with might by human beings' (p. 207). This warning and accusation of the excessive competitive urge and the danger of its being accelerated are forthright and powerful with ample evidence of hundreds of victims to back them up.

Concerning this tragic phenomenon, Kawahito urges us to pay attention to the seriousness of the fear of unemployment: 'In the background of fear of unemployment of Japanese people lies the economic difficulties caused by unemployment. Although they can get an extent of security from unemployment benefit, when they have loans, unemployment could mean self-bankrupt. For elder people, the present pension level is not at all sufficient for their retirement years.' Thus he argues that in a very difficult situation like today, the security net must become stronger so that they can obtain secure feelings in the swiftly changing, or deteriorating, conditions: 'It is now urgently needed to fully equip a social system so that the unemployed don't have to meet hardship, by reducing the economic difference between those who stay at work and leave, or by promoting occupational training by public institutions and so forth. It has come to be heard recently that in a competitive society strengthening safety net is inevitable. Safety net is necessary for all the workers, for it provides ease in mind' (pp. 183-4). As this fear of unemployment in Japan is caused by the rapidly changing job environment and less secure welfare provisions, this tragedy can be said to be one of the genuine outcomes of the competitive track on which Japanese society has started to proceed. No one would deny the necessity to provide the kind of safety net that can save the most affected from the worst conditions. And his argument suggests that the problem has spread further into ordinary employed workers, too. The strength of the safety net should be judged by the outcome, if it could save both kinds of the weaker people, the unemployed and the poor. Kawahito's arguments eloquently show that by this criterion the Japanese security system may well be insufficient.

Uchihashi (1998) criticizes the 'more-competitiveness' argument for the reason that it fails to recognize the real cause of the present economic depression, namely the income distribution imbalance, which is the grave structural defect in Japanese society.[24] He points out that the imbalance lies between the production sector and the 'livelihood' sector and this structural defect is argued to be the real cause of the 1990s decade-long depression. He argues that the 'incessant income transfer from home sector to producers sector' (p. vii), or from household = consumer = citizen sector to industry = firm = producer sector, accelerated capital accumulation on the firms' side,

---

[24] He is also one of the few who foresaw the prolonged depression of the 1990s soon after the collapse of the bubble economy in 1991. This judgement seems to have been possible based on his unique viewpoint of 'discrepancy between two sectors' as shown in the text.

delayed citizens' assets formation and also weakened the consumption market (p. 22). He argues that the real cause of the 1990s depression lies in this excess investment in the bubble period because of this large income transferred into the producers sector (p. 12). He also argues that the consumption boom in the latter half of the 1980s was largely based on consumer loans, not on the genuine income of the workers.[25]

This excess accumulation and resulting bubble economy is explained as follows: 'Most of the large Japanese corporations, as in automobile, electronics and machine tool industries, had already finished the investment into, and renewal of, productive equipment in the bubble period.' 'Most of the fund necessary was provided by equity finance ... and they could gather huge amount of money with almost no cost'. 'The total amount of money that firms obtained in the five bubble years (1985 to 1990) reached as high as 68% of GDP.' 'The security for this fund was the unrealized value of stocks, which was three times as much as this.' 'The ratio of private investment in factory and equipment to GDP rose to 20%, which was almost twice as much as that of other advanced capitalist nations' (pp. 30-1). The fund thus raised was directed to financial investment, too. From this viewpoint, he also criticizes the attitude of the present business world, which was not a responsible one in this period. He argues that it is actually an evasion of managerial responsibilities to explain the necessity for restructuring only by the need to strengthen competitiveness while at the same time ignoring this corporate behaviour (p. 12).

According to him, such a 'transfer of income' is not a coincidental outcome in the late 1980s but had been internalized in the structure of Japanese society, supported by various economic policies. The low rate of public interest rate that has continued in the 1990s is referred to as a significant example. It is argued that it must have been clear to the financial and monetary authorities that such a low interest policy would not lead to recovery, given the accumulated excess capacity, and it must have been clear that such a policy would only work as an income transfer from depositors to banking facilities to rescue the latter (p. 32).[26] Thus, he argues that an important task in re-establishing the balance between efficiency and equity is

---

[25] He points out that consumer loans except for housing increased rapidly from 27.4 trillion yen at the end of 1985 to 63 trillion yen by the end of 1990 (p. 40). 'The balance of consumer credit to disposable income ... had reached 21% in the end of 1990, which was more than that of the US', 20% (p. 42).

[26] He also points out another transfer problem, which is within the firms themselves, from the workers to the employers through 'the difficulty of getting the equitable reward to the employees' work' (p. 292). This issue is more universal, common in every market mechanism society, and needs to be analysed further in depth both theoretically and empirically. A preliminary consideration on the principle of this issue is shown in Tsukada, 1998, Chapter 5.

to reform the traditional pro-business policies that constantly worked as an income transfer siphon. In all, his argument suggests that, if we leave such volatile behaviour and responsibilities of the firms and the supporting structure intact, the same hardship will be repeated, and what is really necessary today is to focus on the proper balance of income distribution or the balance of investment and consumption.

Similar arguments to those in the UK society about the favourable effects of social welfare on economic growth have come to be pointed out recently in Japan, too. Okamoto (1990, 1996) for example compared the social welfare systems between Denmark and the US, and argued that social welfare contributed to economic growth by creating jobs in the welfare field and promoting larger entry of women into the workforce. Precise comparison of the effects of expenditures on economic growth is also addressed by Jichitai Kenkyujo (the Research Institute of Local Government) (1998). It compared the effects of public works and social welfare expenditures on economic growth, concluding that the effects of the latter were no less than the former. But in thinking about this question, we also need to address the balance between export and import to sustain a certain level of economic circulation. Even if we could produce the same amount of income by welfare industries, if we could not export them, it would mean a lower level of living standard for the country as a whole. In this sense, we have to be careful in comparing the effects of them. At present, Japanese society takes it for granted that the industries that can earn foreign currency are manufacturing industries. But as the worldwide division of labour grows, particularly in social welfare spheres such as medicine, education, rehabilitation training and so forth, there may be the possibility that some countries will develop export-oriented industries in these fields to maintain its economic level. Allocating more resources to welfare industries may even increase the economy's competitiveness.

As the head-on arguments about the balance between growth-competition-investment and welfare-consumption have only begun, there are few opinions on the anti-competitiveness side yet about the total social image of the alternative society. Here we can only comment on the idea of Uchihashi, who refers to workers' collectives as a feasible alternative for Japanese society. Uchihashi thinks that to the extent that the profit motive of traditional type firms continues to be held, the fundamental problems would not be solved: '… if the traditional type of firms were the only one to supply goods and services', and as long as firms are motivated by profit maximization, which the market mechanism compels, such an income transfer structure will be repeatedly created. It then generates depression and unemployment, and a constant danger of under-consumption. If this should be a world where 'people are deprived of places to work in', and if this situation is more apt to happen under increasing competitive pressures, 'they have no other choice but to create places to work by "creating jobs" by themselves' (Uchihashi, 1998, p. 320). Those workplaces managed by workers themselves already exist. He takes notice of such 'symbiotic sectors' as citizens' enterprises, cooperatives, workers' cooperatives, NGOs, and NPOs, and shows that they have already grown to occupy a large sector of the economy. They 'have put on high level of "know-how"'. Supported by 'the accumulated citizens' capital', they have begun to attract the trust of the society. 'They are characterized by "a different principle of conduct" from profit motive or pursuit of economic values' (ibid., p. 323), which is 'unification, solidarity, and cooperation'. The unified development of capital, labour, and management as one body is a workers' collective. Only those who work can contribute to the fund and can participate in the management there. 'Co-owners (contributors) are the co-managers and co-workers' (p. 324). The number of workers exceeded 8% of the total workforce in the US. In Europe the number of workers in workers' collectives alone reached several million, and a trial calculation by ILO shows that the number in the world has reached over one billion (pp. 9-10).

Mondragon Corporation Cooperative, MCC, in Spain provides us with a rough image of a successful workers' collective. This cooperative has financial, industrial, and distributive sub-groups. Its workforce has been growing for the past 15 years from 687 in 1973 to 498,299 in 1998. One of its basic principles is 'Payment Solidarity', which had maintained the income difference by approximately 1 to 3 between the lowest and the highest paid in this body for a long time and has changed to 1 to 6 recently (from the web site). The critical questions are their productivity compared to other 'profit-oriented' firms and their wage levels. The wage levels are determined by paying due attention to the wage levels in the nearby district. As for productivity, the growth of this body itself seems to show good evidence. As long as their productivity keeps pace with other firms the wage levels will not create problems. Although we cannot forecast if they will become the major type of firms, it is at least worth attention as a possibly feasible social image to replace a profit-oriented one.

US

The conspicuous phenomenon accompanying the past two decades' economic development of the US is the constant apprehension about the imbalance between economy and society, particularly the poor-distribution of its wealth. An example of this serious concern about society in the 1980s was that of the US Catholic Church on the income difference and crisis of humanity. A criticism of the increase of income difference resulting from the 'self-help', 'trickle-down' economic policies of the conservative administrations (a large part of which was followed later by the Clinton administrations), was contained in the Message on Economic Justice by the National Conference of Catholic Bishops issued in Nov. 1986 (Isomura et al. 1988). The Message described six moral principles by which to judge social conditions: 1) the criterion for all the economic activities is whether they protect human dignity or not, 2) human dignity can only be realized in human community, 3) everyone has the right to participate in social and economic activities, 4) everyone has obligation to the weak, 5) human rights are fundamental, and 6) a society is responsible for the protection of human dignity and human rights (ibid. p. 9). National priorities were shown as 1) to fulfil the fundamental needs of the poor, 2) to assure employment opportunities, 3) to enlarge opportunities for the poor, and 4) to strengthen family life. The Rev. James E. Hug, S.J., Center of Concern, spoke of the emphasis of this message as 'the difference in income and wealth in the US is morally unacceptable, too' and 'the inequality between the rich and poor countries is ... "shockingly ugly" ' (ibid., pp. 17-8). He asked if 'the economic regime in our country is leaned more toward maximum profit seeking than ... to fulfill human needs', 'if the fruit is equitably distributed', and 'if it is not promoting excess materialism and individualism' (p. 28).

This concern grew in the 1990s and was even addressed with such words as the threat of disintegration of the society. Ex-Secretary of Labour Ministry, Robert Reich, warned of the growing disparity between the rich and poor in his farewell message in 1994.[27] Before he became the Secretary, he had referred to the danger of the deteriorating balance between economy and society: '...we may work in markets, but we live in societies', so it is necessary for a nation's citizens to 'take primary responsibility' for their fellow citizens. But as the traditional regional ties between the 'symbolic analysts' (those who become rich by manipulating numerical or verbal symbols) and the others weaken, there has emerged the question 'whether the habits of citizenship are sufficiently strong to withstand the new global economy' (1991, pp. 193, 202, 207). After having served as the Secretary of the Labour Department, he had to repeat his warning of the disparity between economy and welfare, or economy and society in his farewell speech as follows. Income and wealth difference has grown large: 'The concern about the US in the 21st century ... is about the labour market structure itself. Those in the lowest half to one third in the income distribution have benefited little from prosperity. Average wages after adjusted to inflation ... is still under the level of 1989, which was before the previous recession.' In answering the question of why wages do not rise, he explains that downsizing of firms and continuing mass lay-offs are the reasons why few workers are demanding wage increases even if the labour

---

[27] Reich (1994).

market is tight. He understands that they think it better than losing jobs. With the reduction of wages of workers with prosperity 'the wealthiest 1% owns 39% of all the households' wealth ... 93% of wealth is concentrated on the upper one fifth' (1998).[28]

As for the argument that Reaganomics has succeeded because the wealthy pay more tax today, he points out the regressive character of tax structure. He argues that it is true that the payment from the wealthy has reached the highest in history, but the ratio of it to the overall wealth or to the aggregate incomes is at the lowest level of the post-war period, and it is moving toward a regressive tax system. Thus, he declares that the task of the 21st century US is to stop such a disintegrating trend and proposes: raising education levels and skill levels to assist the schools in poor districts, assistance to lower income groups (enlarging the income tax exemption), and health insurance to cover everyone (now 18% are without any insurance). And he foresees that if such measures are not taken, the disintegrating society will become a fearful one that would need to spend greater expenditure on police, jails, and private security guards. He also foresees the danger of exclusion of the immigrants. He concludes that the real question is whether those who have benefited most from the present prosperity can sacrifice a part of their wealth and enlarge the circle of prosperity to those who have become poor (Nikkei, April 22, 1999).

Perelman (1996) also argued about the danger of the present type of pro-competitiveness US economy and forecasts that it will lead to 'the Haitian road', or 'growth with low wage' economy. He warns that if wages stay low, the pressure for higher productivity and technological progress will fade. Although wages should not grow too high to harm the profit rate, the present wage-profit balance is too uneven. Thus his prescription is to bring about a higher wage economy, which then stimulates technological progress and productivity growth (1996). How to achieve this proper balance becomes the next question. However, as suggested before, the experience of the determined depression and high unemployment rate under the conservative administrations did seem to have weakened the workers' bargaining power even in consistently prosperous years. And what's more, globalization is intensifying downward pressure on union wage rates as companies continue to close unionised factories and move work overseas (*The New York Times* on the web, Oct. 9, 1999).[29]

---

[28] The same reference that fear of unemployment promotes prosperity was shown by Greenspan (1997) and argued by Otsuka (1998) as shown in Chapter 3.

[29] Recruiting new members is still a fundamental problem for the unions. 'Today, unions represent 13.9 percent of the workforce, down sharply from 35 percent in the 1950s' (*The New York Times*, ibid.).

3 QUESTIONS REMAINING

To understand the prospective future of the changing Welfare State today, it was necessary to focus our attention to the question of the balance between economic growth and social welfare. Mishra once wrote, 'Seen as mediating the relationship between production and distribution, or ... between economic and social objectives, social welfare policy in some form or other remains central to modern industrial society ... in this post-crisis period of divergence' (1990, p. 119). Samuelson also wrote that the question of how far we should proceed in redistribution was to be considered because it would start to restrain economic growth of a nation as a whole. He said that, unfortunately, we would have to make a compromise here, we were entering a new era after the 30-40 years development of the Welfare State or mixed economy, and are beginning to calculate seriously if the past income redistribution had been in excess or not.[30] Amartya Sen suggested the possible diversity of the Welfare State today. When asked, 'what are the basic goals of the Welfare States?', he answers that what is important differs from one society to another, and is determined through elections and politics. He says that some countries such as the US does not have a national health insurance system, and some regions, such as Europe, allow high unemployment rates. The area where more is to be spent is determined by political arguments.[31] Although it is necessary to address this differential character of the Welfare State question, it is also important to understand that countries face today the common major choice between the two paths: pro-competitiveness state and pro-Welfare State.

From the arguments discussed in this chapter, we could see positive acceptance or reluctant admission of the pro-competitiveness road on the government leaders' side, and concerns and apprehensions on the part of various writers. The reality is moving along the former. As this question concerns the overall social ideal, it is difficult to reach a clear-cut answer immediately. What is possible now is the comparison of the situations and opinions and infer what option would render maximum satisfaction to society. From what we have seen, the government leaders' views do not seem to have succeeded in this careful comparison of pluses and minuses of the pro-competitiveness path, either. The conclusion among the political leaders has been to pursue the pro-competitiveness path more than ever. Although we have also seen that they are worried about the deteriorating

---

[30] Paul A. Samuelson, Dilemma of the World at the End of the Century, 1996 (Statements at the International Symposium in Osaka, 'Opening the 21st Century – the Roles of the Advanced Countries').

[31] Nikkei, March 21, 1999, in a seminar, Economy and Ethics in Welfare State, convened by National Institute of Social Security and Population Problems and Nihon Keizai Shimbunsha.

social atmosphere and disintegrating society, they do not see that their competitiveness-first strategy as the cause of such problems. This emphasis may well be because considering their positions as politicians, they have to secure 'daily bread' to the people. And especially when they are faced with the globalizing market competition and its pressures, the leaders may well become overwhelmed. It is this danger, of the short-term management of the society failing to achieve the long-term balance, that they are likely to fall into.

Non-governmental observers, not being bound by the short-term 'competitive success' of the economy, are often able to provide broader perspective arguments. In this sense, the most significant of the above views was their deep concern and apprehension about the growing imbalance between economic growth and overall social welfare. The problems revealed there were two: statistically confirmed income or wealth difference between the social groups and spiritually observed anxieties of the society itself. A typical example of the latter was anxieties and apprehensions that would lead to overwork to death (Karoshi). These observations suggest the opposite social image: less competitive and more compassionate society. The Catholic Bishops' Conference, Reich, and Kawahito regarded the present competitive situation as excessive and strongly suggested the necessity to change it. As to the possibility of such an alternative society, George, Miller et al. and Wilding argued for the growing welfare demand and suggested an idea of a 'citizens' Welfare State'. OECD, George and Taylor-Gooby, and Okamoto's arguments supported this by pointing out the productive effects of welfare spending. Although from a different perspective, Uchihashi proposed another alternative way to meet the present problem by creating a new culture of workers' collectives. His argument for improving the income transfer mechanism is also worth being studied further too.

After having seen the necessity to maintain, and if possible to strengthen, the Welfare State in the increasingly insecure and anxious society today as discussed above, we will have to answer the question of its possibility. Before we embark on this task, we will next discuss how urgent it is to maintain or strengthen the Welfare State from the viewpoint of social health. We will look at public opinions and social problems about this issue, which seem to be closely related to this key question of the choice of social balance between growth and welfare, or stability and competition. Thus, we will examine the necessity of the pro-Welfare State route from two viewpoints: the people's explicit preference for the extent of welfare provisions, and their inexplicit expression of the anti- 'pro-competitiveness' society in Chapter 5. By discussing it this way, we will be able to see more clearly the people's preference. Inexplicit expressions, in particular, will add to our understanding of how urgent it is to strengthen the secure feelings for the citizens in the increasingly insecure anti-welfare world.

The image of and path to the alternative Welfare State will be discussed in Chapter 6. Although the argument there will be limited to fundamental characteristics, setting the basic goal will help develop the necessary measures to realize it. We have to answer this question in the difficult conditions of prevailing pro-competitiveness attitudes, and the determination of the business and government leaders today. To change their opinion is actually to change the firms' attitude, but as they are increasingly detached from mother countries, and as governments have less and less power over them, the logical conclusion seems to lie only in restoring a stronger safety net through the people's burden, acceptance of the increasing cost of the welfare provisions by the people themselves. As such, the focus of our consideration in the last chapter will be on the possibility of this route, the citizens' Welfare State.

The conclusion of this chapter: Despite the apprehensions of various discussants concerning the emerging imbalance between economic efficiency and social welfare, the political leaders, although often aware of the social problems, are more inclined to pursue the road of becoming more 'competitive' in the economic globalization. Security is restrained by smaller government, smaller burden on firms and a smaller Welfare State.

5 People's Choice

This chapter questions what is the people's will about the future of the Welfare State.

What are the preferences of the peoples living in the advanced welfare nations today on the social balance between economy and welfare? The theme of this chapter is to examine this question so as to understand what people hope for as a desirable society today. We will start from the general preference for the direction of the Welfare State by looking at the known preferences of peoples in Section 1. It concerns the scale of the Welfare State they prefer today. Although some reservation is made, people's preference today in general seems to be rather for a higher welfare and higher burden society. In evaluating their attitudes, we will also observe some difference among nationalities. We will deal with the inexplicit preferences in Section 2. It deals with people's behaviour, particularly pathological ones, which will confirm that the people's general preference for the stronger Welfare State is further rooted in their unconscious but acute awareness of the necessity of a securer and more reliable social structure.

1 REVEALED PREFERENCES – Higher welfare and higher burden

Before we examine the people's attitude, we have to recognize the importance of the government's effort to call for discussion among the people. If the governments had tried this in the past decade, people could have formed their will on this question more fully and precisely today. George and Miller et al. (1994), discussing the growing welfare demand today, referred to the importance of the people's will as the final cause. Having foreseen an age when the conflict between economic growth and social welfare would become harsh, the Economic Council in Japan at the beginning of the 1980s pointed out the necessity for the formation of national consensus on the overall social image: 'The scale of public spending, including social security, will inevitably increase in the longer run, ... but the extent of the people's burden, which will also inevitably increase, will have to be consented' (p. 241).[1] But this proposition for a national discussion was not realized in its genuine sense. The argument in the following years has been led almost entirely by the government, who argued mostly for restraint

---

[1] *Japan in 2000*, 1982. Long Term Prospect Committee in the Economic Council.

of spending from the budgetary viewpoint and for containing the welfare burden so that it would not hinder economic growth. Of course, they were the elected representatives but as pointed out before, the nature of this question, how to reform the overall society, demands the participation of the whole people in the discussion. There was not sufficient discussion on the part of the people. As mentioned before, this was because of the difficulty of moving away from the traditional ways of thinking up to the 1970s, when economic growth and welfare growth were both realized together.[2]

Given the importance of the question, governments have not been successful in alerting their peoples to the comprehensive nature and scale of the Welfare State issues. As referred to in the previous chapter, this failure is mostly due to their incompetence in understanding the true nature and scale of this question. They were either compelled or wished to believe that when the state faced the malfunction of the market, which was caused by the profit squeeze or harsher global competition, there was no other way but to restore the firms' power or reduce the firms' burden. Even if it had been the correct answer, what was important was to reach this conclusion through popular consent. The governments might have been busy meeting the pressing problems, but they could have posed the core question as to what balance the people wished between growth and redistribution both in the 1980s and 1990s. But with their mind occupied by the 'survival' ethos, they have failed to do so. Although the citizens are ultimately responsible for determining society's future, because the necessary information is mostly in its hands, the governments' failure has been mostly to be blamed for this outcome.

Lacking such a comprehensive, general argument on their side, the following may not be the outcome of conscious comparison between economic growth and social welfare, fully considering the related materials. But we can still get some useful indications about how they feel and think about the present Welfare State and its future. Because of the availability of some materials we will also refer to some countries other than the four – Sweden, the UK, Japan and the US – but our attention here will be mostly focused on these four countries.

Major Issues – High General Support and Different Attitudes in Some Respects

Welfare Provisions

The high general support for the Welfare State has not changed in Sweden

---

[2] Furthermore, an additional reason for Japan would be, ironically, its exceptionally high economic performance in the 1980s through export expansion.

and the UK for the past two decades.[3] In 1984 in Sweden two thirds of the people supported the maintenance or expansion of the public sector and three quarters answered that government intervention was necessary to correct the inequality generated in a market society. In 1983 those who said the social welfare was what they were most proud of in their country were 62% in Sweden and 42% in the UK (Mishra, 1990, p.64). In 1996 the figure for 'very or somewhat proud of social security system' was the same and 65% in Sweden and 48% in the UK in 1997.[4]

Table 5.1 Proud of Welfare State (%)

	1983	1997
Britain	42	48
Sweden	62	65

Source: Mishra 1990 and Jowell et al. *British Social Attitudes,* 1997, 1998.

But in comparison with other options, pride in the social security system ranks rather low in the UK and high in Sweden. Instead, armed forces and history are ranked high in the UK.

Table 5.2 What to be Proud of, 1997 (%)

	Britain	Sweden
Social security system	48	65
Fair and equal treatment	53	43
Economic achievement	43	17
Armed forces	88	33
History	89	69

Source: Jowell et al. *British Social Attitudes,* 1997, 1998.

As to what kind of social welfare policies are the responsibilities of the government, those who chose pensions, employment and medical care as an essential or important responsibility were as high with around 70% to well over 90% in Sweden, the UK and US (Table 5.3). One significant difference between countries was that the high percentage of those who answered 'essential' was 73.5% in the UK compared to 41.9% in the US (Onodera, 1996). In Japan the percentage of 'definitely or probably' was: looking after old people, 83%, everyone can have a job, 49%, and providing medical care, 82% (ibid.). But for unemployment benefit, the figure was very different;

---

[3] Most figures in this chapter are of the Great Britain (excluding Northern Ireland), but as we have used the word "the UK" in the previous chapters, we will use it often here, too.
[4] '... the Scandinavian welfare states continued to enjoy strong support in the early 1990s' (Nordlund, 1997, p. 244).

42% in Norway, 32% in the UK, and 14% in the US.[5]

Table 5.3 Government's responsibility, essential or important, 1985 (%)

	Sweden	UK	US
Looking after old people	96.0	88.2	81.4
Everyone can have a job	93.8	85.4	71.6
Providing medical care	94.6	94.6	77.5

Source: Tom W. Smith, 'The Polls, A Report, The Welfare State in Cross-National Perspective', *Public Opinion Quarterly*, Vol. 51, Fall, 1987.

Table 5.4 Difference in support between income groups, 1990 (%)

Definitely the government's responsibility to provide:

	Britain	Norway
Health care: low income group	85	86
high income group	85	76
Pensions: low income group	84	88
high income group	70	78
Unemployment benefits:		
low income group	43	52
high income group	22	30

Source: Svallfors (ed.) 1995, p.42.

This difference in the support for unemployment benefit is also significant in the high- and low-income groups. This benefit was supported by 43% of the low-income group compared to 22% of the high-income group in Britain. This difference was also observed in Norway, with the higher support at 52% of low-income group compared to 30% of high-income group in 1990 (Table 5.4). These figures were similar in Sweden and the UK in 1997, too (Table 5.5).

In the UK, this difference coincides with the result that 52% thought the unemployed were already well protected, compared to 16% in Norway (Svallfors, ed., 1995, p. 41). In the UK, the support for increased taxes and larger spending on health, education and social benefits has greatly increased during the decade since the early 1980s, from 32% in 1983 to 61% in 1995

---

[5] ISSP 1990 survey, Svallfors (ed.), 1995, p. 35 and Jowell, et al., 1993. According to statistical surveys in Sweden (1992) and Norway (1990), the attitudes toward different expenditures in social welfare in the two countries were similar in medical and health care, support for the elderly people, support for families with children and employment policies. For the question if they would support increased or unaltered public expenditure for the respective items, all of these scored high around 80% to 90%. Support for elderly people scored 96% in Sweden and 99% in Norway (Nordlund, 1997, p. 237).

172

Table 5.5 Income and the attitudes to the unemployed, 1997 (%)

Decent unemployment benefit: Definitely government's responsibility

	Sweden	Britain
High income group	34	18
middle	39	24
low	46	42

Source: Jowell et al., *British Social Attitudes*, 1998, p.68.

(Jowell et al. 1996, p. 187). Spending priorities show that health and education are the two major needs of the people in these years. Support for health care has grown from 63% in 1983 to 78% in 1987 and remained high at 77% in 1995. Support for education has constantly grown from 50% in 1983 to 66% in 1995 (ibid. p. 196).

In the US 67% answered that the social security system in the US faced serious financial problems that must be dealt with by Congress in the next year (the Gallup poll, July 1998). Providing more revenues by increasing social security taxes on people who are working today was much favoured (57%) compared to cutting expenditure by reducing benefits (21%) (March 1998), (Gallup website, Social and Economic Indicators, Social Security).

Japan and the US had divided opinions as to which to prioritise, when in trade-off, inflation or unemployment, but twice as many people in the UK preferred reducing unemployment (Table 5.6).

Table 5.6 Priority, inflation or unemployment (%)

	UK	Japan	US
Inflation	28.3	37.9	39.2
Unemployment	63.5	37.6	44.5

*UK, US: 1985, Japan: 1996.
Sources: UK, US: Smith, 1987; Japan: Onodera, 1996.

Income Difference

The attitudes toward income difference are less similar in these countries than toward welfare provisions (Table 5.7). As we saw in Chapter 3, the post-tax income difference has more or less increased in all of these countries; In the UK, the sense of inequality about income distribution grew constantly from 1983 to 1995. Those who felt there was too much income difference between high and low-income groups was high at 72% in 1983 and grew to 87% in 1995 (Jowell, et al., *British Social Attitudes*, 13th Report, 1996, p. 87). In the US, 'About one-quarter of Americans consider themselves to be have-nots' (Gallup, 1998, Social Audit). Have-nots here are

Table 5.7 Preference of income shares, 1991 (%)

	Equal Shares	No Desert	Income Ceiling
Britain	30	16	39
Japan	39	18	36
US	19	14	17

Equal Shares = agree strongly or somewhat with 'The fairest way of distributing wealth and income would be to give everyone equal shares'.

No Desert = agree strongly or somewhat with 'It is simply luck if some people are more intelligent or skilful than others, so they don't deserve to earn more money'.

Income Ceiling = agree strongly or somewhat with 'The government should place an upper limit on the amount of money any one person can make'.

Source: ISJP (International Social Justice Project) Documentation and Code book, in Svallfors (ed.) 1995, p. 92.

those who have difficulties in making ends meet even for the basic necessities such as food, clothing, housing, etc. Those who answered that they 'worry about household finances all or most of the time' was 26% in 1976, increased in the depression to 35% in 1984, and decreased in the more prosperous time to 21% in 1998.[6]

But such recognition does not necessarily correspond to stronger demand for income equalization. As to the level of desirable income difference, in the US only one out of five people supported equal income distribution and one out of six, an upper limit to income. Although still being a minority, this figure is larger in the UK and Japan. Thirty per cent in the UK and 39% in Japan supported equal distribution, and 39% in the UK and 36% in Japan supported an upper limit (Svallfors (ed.) 1995, p. 92). Japanese and UK societies seem to show quite a different preference from the US here.

As to what is the proper income difference between the highest rank occupation, such as cabinet minister, and the lowest, such as unskilled worker, the answers in the US, the UK and the Netherlands were between four to six times, whereas the answers to the same question between elite and manual worker were between three to four times (Svallfors (ed.) 1995, p. 95). Compared to the vast difference of income in reality, this similarity is somewhat amazing.

---

[6] Japan EPA (1998) concludes that because of the smaller income difference than other nations, Japan still had room for market-oriented reforms (p. 52). But even if this were true, income difference has different significance to the peoples in different countries with different cultures. Tachiki refers to a poll that in Anglo-Saxon countries such as the US or the UK more than 60% preferred a competitive society, in Germany and France 50% preferred an egalitarian society, and in Japan 42% were undecided (*Nikkei*, March 21, 1999). These replies suggest the need to take into account the cultural preference of the extent and content of income difference.

To the question whether it is the government's responsibility to reduce income differences, those who answered definitely yes was 39% in Norway, 42% in Britain in 1990, and 25.4% in Japan in 1996 (ibid., p. 36 and Onodera, 1996). Fourteen per cent of the upper income class and 30% of the middle-income class agreed to it in Britain, but a much higher percentage, 32% of the upper class and 46% of the middle class, agreed in Sweden (Jowell, et al., 1998/99, p. 68). In the US, the cause of poverty was recognized either as lack of effort (43%) or as circumstances beyond people's control (41%). As for the rich people, their success was recognized as being a result of hard work (53%) or circumstances (32%). The US economic system was recognized as basically fair by 74% of 'haves', but by 51% of 'have-nots'. Opportunity was recognized to be plenty (87%) in 1998, 'more than in the past' was 43% and 'about the same' 36% (Gallup, 1998).

In the US, government was expected to have the main responsibility for helping the poor by 32% of the people. But 28% answered that the poor themselves were responsible. Although half the population in the US recognizes that the income difference is due to hard work, those who answered that wealth should be more evenly distributed were relatively higher at between 60% to 70% throughout the years 1984 to 1998. Seventy-nine per cent of those who recognize themselves as 'have-nots' support more equal distribution of money/wealth, while 59% of 'haves' do, too. Whether as mainly responsible or not, those who thought government should help the poor were 65%. The measures to be taken were better education (38%) and more job and skills training (29%). Financial aid was supported only by 12%. Redistributing wealth by heavy taxes on the rich was opposed by the majority, 51% in 1998, about the same figure of half a century ago in 1939, 54%. But those who support it grew from 35% in 1939 to 45%, coming close to those against in 1998. Being traditionally a self-help country, but under the rapidly increasing income difference, the US people appear to have more divided opinions than ever (Gallup, website).

Future Prospect: Higher Welfare, Higher Burden

Generally, the peoples seem to accept higher benefits and a higher burden. In a survey in 1996, the willingness to pay higher taxes for better social services throughout different income quartiles were roughly: 80-70% in the UK, 70-50% in the US, 50-40% in Sweden, 30-20% in Germany, 20-30% in France. We can also generally observe that people in higher taxes countries prefer lower tax and people in lower tax countries think they can afford more (Bonoli, et al., 2000, Figure 4.4). According to the Japan Research General Institute's 'Opinion Poll on Society and Life' (1997), 46% approved 'higher welfare, higher burden', 43% 'moderate welfare, moderate burden', and 9% 'lower welfare, more self-help' (p. 9). Similarly, the opinion poll by the

Social Security Council at the Prime Minister's Office (Dec. 1992–Jan. 1993) showed that 50% were for the maintenance of the present social welfare provision and a higher burden, and 15% for increased provision and higher burden.[7] The Onodera report based on the 1996 International Social Survey Program shows that in Japan 45% was for higher welfare and higher burden, and 26% was for lower welfare and lower burden (Onodera, 1996, p. 54).

The higher income group, in particular, is expected to pay more. In the UK, those who felt that the tax for the high-income group was too low increased significantly from 32% in 1983 to 56% in 1994. Sixty-six per cent of the middle-income group in 1994 thought their tax rate was 'about right', and 76% of the low-income group thought it too high (Jowell, et al., 1996, p. 15). In general, the high-income groups in Europe and the US seem to judge themselves as being able to pay more tax. To the question if the tax level on the high income group is too low, the bottom quartile's answer in 1996 was 'Yes' by 67% in Sweden, 64% in Germany, 46% in the UK, 45% in France, and 44% in the US, and the top quartile's 'Yes' answer was not much different, 58% in Germany, 46% in Sweden, 41% in the UK, 39% in France, and 33% in the US[8] (Bonoli, et al., 2000, Table 4.1).

The ratio of those willing to pay more tax decreases generally as the ratio of social welfare spending to GDP increases. But as in the case of the UK and Italy, although both have the ratio of this spending at around 20%, those who support a higher tax burden in the UK is close to 80% compared to less than 60% in Italy (Svallfors (ed.) 1995, p. 23). As their income levels are similar (GDP per capita, 1996, Keizai Koho Centre, 1998, p. 17), this difference must be explained by some kind of cultural difference. If we generally regard the ratio at which more than 50% accept higher tax burden as the limit to the Welfare State, it would be when social spending reaches around 30% of GDP (cf. ibid., p. 37).[9]

Overall, we can conclude, first, that support among the peoples for the maintenance and strengthening of the Welfare State is generally still high in those countries examined. Secondly, judgement on the acceptable income difference is not much different in Europe and the US. Thirdly, social

---

[7] Japan EPA, *Kokumin Seikatsu Hakusho*, FY1996, p. 221.

[8] But there remains the possibility, as the authors explain, that quite a lot of rich people (because this quartile occupies one fourth of the total population in the research) might not have regarded themselves as rich and may have mistakenly answered Yes. To get a more accurate view, we will have to divide the top quartile into smaller parts. What has to be considered in addition is the 'firms' attitude'. The same person who answered Yes to higher tax in general (both for personal and corporate income) as an individual might say no as an executive of a firm.

[9] Public social protection expenditure as proportion of GDP in 1990 was 33.9% in Sweden, 20.3% in the UK, 14.8% in the US and 11.6% in Japan (UK, 1988) (OECD, 1996, *OECD Economies at a Glance*, pp. 107-8).

spending at 30% of GDP seems to be roughly the common upper limit of welfare spending. Fourthly, there is a difference between countries as to the role of government in addressing income difference, and also a difference as to the support for the respective welfare spending. As such support probably reflects the growing insecurity in the rapidly changing work and welfare conditions, we can foresee that it may well continue to be so in the near future under the globalizing economies.

Related Issues – Polarization, Victimization, Cultural Difference, and Trust in Government

Except for the main issues above, we should also pay attention to such characteristics of the peoples' attitudes as below. First, polarization of 'work incentives' is observed in some parts of the societies such as the UK. On the one hand, working people are working harder. Hours worked per week (employees) increased from 1985 to 1995. Those who work 40 hours or more increased from 26% to 31%, 60 hours or more from 2% to 3%. A part of this change can be explained by business cycles. In prosperous years the employers tend to increase production by having their workers work longer rather than by employing new ones. Thus, the figure for 40 hours or more dropped in the recession years of 1990-93 to around 26-28% (Jowell, et al., 1996, p. 84). Such intensified and longer work hours have caused many cases of Karoshi in Japan. On the other hand, work incentives of some lower income people seem to be declining. It is shown in the steady decline in the willingness of the unemployed to take 'unacceptable' jobs between1983 and 1994. The answer 'very willing' declined from 24% to 9%, 'quite willing' from 31% to 29%, and 'not willing' increased from 41% to 61% (ibid. p. 78). Comparing stable and unstable types of jobs, workers in the former type might fall into this overwork trap so as not to lose their stable jobs in an age of job-insecurity.

Secondly, although the general opinion may be for maintaining or strengthening welfare provisions, the difficult conditions of today may lead the middle and upper income groups to obtain their security in the short run by victimizing the lower income people, such as cutting short their welfare benefits. In the globalizing world, not only the minorities but also the vast majority of the middle-income group would be more vulnerable to more frequent job losses and changes in more competitive conditions. But the reaction of the middle- and upper-income people facing such an insecure environment might first be to secure safety for them. When they are exposed to this vulnerability long enough, it will become clear that this self-help way does not necessarily help them in the longer run and this understanding will eventually lead people in every stratum of society to strengthen the welfare provisions.

Thirdly, different attitudes in the countries above may well reflect cultural differences. Thus, Shiratori points to the influence of cultural characteristics on the Welfare State regimes (Rose and Shiratori, 1986, p. 5). What, how much, and how welfare goods and services are to be supplied related closely to the overall social structure of each country, its culture, history, family structure, etc. An understanding of the totality of the Welfare State does require an awareness of the historical traditions and values prevailing in each society. We can observe two extreme types in the two distinct types of mentalities of Sweden and the US. Allardt points out the close feeling between government and people as a unique factor of the Swedish type Welfare State: 'For centuries people have not felt themselves as being outside the political system. The difference between public and private, so crucial in many debates in the Anglo-American countries, was of minor importance in the Scandinavian countries' (ibid. p. 111). This democratic character is often further attributed to the solidarity fostered in the severe natural conditions that hardly allowed even serfdom to settle down. The concept of solidarity is given the principal position in society: 'The uniqueness of the Scandinavian countries consists not of the size of the non-market sector but rather of the way in which services and benefits are organized, the rules of entitlements, and the absence of a connection between financing benefits and the entitlement to receive benefits' (ibid. p. 108). The relatively small population may also have been an advantage for this solidarity.

This philosophy of solidarity would naturally lead to a Welfare State that aims to assure a normal standard of living for everyone: 'The old liberal belief in the responsibility of the individual has been replaced by collective responsibility to help everyone maintain a normal standard of living' (ibid.). In a market economy, solidarity among the members of society tends to be weakened under its competitive ethos of market mechanism, and the objectives of the Welfare State tend to be limited to the minimum safety nets. How much Swedish and Scandinavian type societies can resist this trend under growing globalization pressures and can give practical expression of the spirit of solidarity or security for the fundamental conditions for life by mutual efforts will show the possibilities for the solidaristic Welfare States today.

In contrast, Glazer understands the characteristic mentality of the US as individuality: 'Americans tend to see social relationships in terms of individual concerns and individual responsibilities. Only those who cannot look after themselves are expected to rely upon the state ... in Scandinavia there is a great sense of social solidarity' (Rose, 1986, pp. 7-9). Where does this difference originate? If we could attribute the latter's characteristic, at least partly, to its severe natural conditions and its smaller population, the former's could also be attributed to its abundant natural resources, less severe climate, and larger population. Another factor to be addressed would be its historical emphasis on the mentality of independence, which was actually the founding motto of this nation both in the Pilgrim years and the Independence War. Although the native Indians and imported African people were excluded from it, its identity has thus been established as 'liberty' and 'freedom'. 'Self-help' has been given in this country an especially strong, positive, and even religious meaning: 'There is a strong American bias in favor of programs for what are conceived to be independent individuals, against the programs for the dependent' (ibid. p. 42).

Such historical, mental and geographical characteristics shape the images of social welfare. In Europe 'a social policy descends from the heavens in which its complete form can be glimpsed'. In the US 'it arises from immediate needs with no necessary hint that a larger picture is to be completed' (ibid. p. 48). Meanwhile, charity is often suggested as a complementary measure for public assistance in many societies, particularly in the US. Having been cut off from the historical feudal traditions, Americans could start their society believing in individual faith and power alone. Without having had to face the critical social conflicts against the feudal age, their naïve faith in individualism could last for more than two centuries. Based on, and restricted by, such a religious character of its foundation, kindness and help to the needy were understood and carried out largely in line with this individuality, and so by their individual wills.[10] Although this tradition was challenged in the 'socially-produced' difficulties in the 1930s, it still is an important factor in the US Welfare State.

Fourthly, as we suggested before, the difficulty of the welfare question in terms of its scale and complexity may hinder the smooth formation of national consensus. In Japan in the last year of the depressed 1990s those who agreed to the mainstream idea of the government, and the financial and industrial world -- that in order to recover from depression the growth of unemployment is inevitable -- was only 34%, and 51% disagreed. Sixty-two per cent answered that firms should put higher priority on securing employment than profit seeking (*Asahi Shimbun*, opinion poll in August 1999). This result shows that the majority of people do not agree with, or at least do not understand, their leaders' ideas. Even if the government is a democratically elected one, if people fail to understand its policies, it may not be much different from a dictatorship. The vagueness of a new social paradigm as a result of the difficulty of the question may thus create distrust

---

[10] The total amount of private donations in the US was 150 billion dollars, which was a little less than one tenth of the federal government's budget, and 400 times as much as the total private donations in Japan. The government helps donations by allowing a high rate of exemption of the personal income tax (Nikkei, Jan. 7, 1999). But the difficulty of personal or private charity is that as it is done voluntarily, it is too unstable in its scale and continuity to save needy people at the proper time.

in government. Distrust in government's policies then may well delay the formation of consensus. As for the US, those who trusted in government most of the time decreased from 76% in 1964 to 25% in 1994 (Giddens, 1998, p. 51), and those who had confidence in the Presidency a 'great deal' or 'quite a lot' was 72% in 1991 and 49% in 1999 (Gallup, Social and Economic Indicators). When detached from the people, the leaders may carry out more unfavourable policies, which will very likely put people off politics even more. This problem can only be solved by obtaining a hopeful and feasible alternative social ideal. Until then the difficulties of the people will continue, even at times taking the appearance of pathological social phenomena as we will see next.

2 HIDDEN PREFERENCES – What increasing pathological social phenomena suggest

The unrevealed preferences for the future of the Welfare States that seem to be hidden in pathological social phenomena are examined in this section. In the following discussion, we will assume that certain social phenomena are taken to be reactions to the prevailing social and economic conditions of the society and could imply certain social preferences of the people.[11] We will consider the possible connection between such social problems and economic structure, particularly the serious pathological social incidents that would occur when the balance between economy and society, or between production and distribution, growth and welfare, and most of all, security and insecurity, is critically at a risk. In this field of research, however, the data are often either of too gross or of too microscopic a nature.[12] But the seriousness and acuteness of the problems today demand that we tackle this problem. As we do not have an established method to solve this question, all we can do is to try to approach the problem as closely as possible through the available aggregate and microscopic data. But of course from what we have been arguing so far, the focus will be on the effects of this changing economic and social structure – brought about by the anti-welfarism and, pro-competitiveness since the 1980s – on the people and their living

---

[11] As discussed in Chapter 2, the core of human relationship is in the cooperative relationship in production and distribution. In this sense most of the social phenomena, even emotional reactions, are interpreted as the reflections of this underlying cooperative relationship, or productive and distributive social structure. As such, certain pathological social phenomena are understood to reflect the social members' unrevealed satisfaction or dissatisfaction with this structure, especially when they are concerned with the security and insecurity feelings of the peoples.

[12] For example, discussing the trend of school violence, Moore and Tonry say, 'Unfortunately, the academic capability to illuminate the nature of the problem and the range of possible solutions is limited. Available data … are far too gross … to offer either powerful explanations of the past or precise predictions about the future' (Moore and Tonry, 1998, p. 2).

conditions.[13]

Whether the cooperative relationship is satisfactory or not can probably be observed by the people's reactions toward others. When this relationship is maintained satisfactorily, the social members react to each other in a friendly manner. But when it turns into an obstructive one and hinders the members from pursuing happiness, it becomes hostile. When this hostility comes through a too complicated structure of the society, the disadvantaged members might fail to see ways to improve it, become desperate and act anti-socially. They might harm either themselves or others. As the happiness from belonging to society is so strong, the dissatisfaction and despair from exclusion could be as strong, too. We can here recall Adam Smith's exaltation of happiness as being appreciated by others: 'whatever may be the cause of sympathy ... nothing pleases us more than to observe in other men a fellow-feeling with all the emotions of our own breast' (Smith, 1976B, p.13). This high evaluation of human relationships can be glimpsed today in a questionnaire of a research study that included 'people' and 'society' as the major welfare indicators for the quality of life: 'Other people ... most people are in great need of attachment to other people or solidaristic relations'. Also important is 'Society', the participation in decisions and activities influencing his or her social life, safety, etc.[14] Taken together, humans or their aggregate body, 'society', can be the major source of happiness or unhappiness for individuals. Poverty or insecurity is not just a matter of income or goods. Loss of income or security is also the loss of human relationships, which causes unbearable agony to humans and may even generate disintegration of society.

As discussed in Chapter 2, the critical factor that determines whether the cooperative relationship is satisfactory or not is equity and human fellowship in society and its first indication is in the extent of security that one obtains as one's individual share in the social goods, either as income or social benefit. They are particularly critical in a market economy. When these two virtues – equity and human fellowship – or their applied form, security, are realized, people can have the sense of being treated rightly (both when they are strong and when they are weak), and humans can continue their cooperative relationship and their society. When not, what they feel first is fear and anxiety. It may be the fear of losing one's job. It may be the fear of one's children being unable to live better lives than one's own. Or it may be the fear of decreasing old age

---

[13] We have such works as of Miringoff and Miringoff (1999) or Oliver James (1995 and 1998). The former tries to deal with the indices of 'social health' in the US, and the latter adopts a clinical approach to the psychological effect of the changing UK society.

[14] Research conducted by the Research Group for Comparative Sociology at the University of Helsinki in the 1970s about the peoples in Denmark, Finland, Norway, and Sweden. A third is 'Nature', to what extent people have the opportunity to enjoy nature (Allardt in Rose, et al., 1986, p. 119).

pensions. Combined and taken together, there is a growing fear of insecurity that seems to prevail in many of the Welfare States today, as shown below. When such feelings continue without being properly addressed, the members come to regard their relationship as hostile. What caused the civil revolution was the dissatisfaction with too much income difference and too much inequality between the aristocrats, citizens and serfs. Merciless exploitation of the employees by the employers in the 18th and 19th centuries caused the workers' resistance and brought about the establishment of social reforms. Destructive damages accompanying market mechanism and severe business cycles led to government's responsibility for full employment and social welfare. These are the outcomes of dissatisfaction through the ages. But until these remedial reforms are found and implemented, this dissatisfaction may find a different way of expressing itself, which seems to be the pathological social phenomena of today.

The phenomena we will see next seem to suggest the necessity today to increase security in this uncertain, unclear age. When the leaders or society in general cannot notice its seriousness or show the proper answers, it generates the despair of people and their detachment from and even hatred of society and its members. Anxiety, dissatisfaction, despair and hatred, generated through such a process, seem to be growing and causing the pathological social phenomena observed in both adults and children in many societies today. They seem to suggest that there is an urgent necessity to reinforce security in today's ever-more competitive and insecure society and the only way we can realize it would be to strengthen the Welfare State.

Excess Competition and Pathological Social Phenomena

In the argument below we will see look at general characteristics of social pathology and examine the respective conditions of the four countries. Here, by pathological social phenomena are meant the fatal incidents that occur when humans are losing or have lost the human bond to others or to themselves.[15] When the fear of people being victimized by violent crimes, many children being killed by bullying, or hundreds of adults killing themselves in Karoshi prevails, it shows that the fundamental human relationship has deteriorated and changed from a cooperative to a hostile one among fellow human beings, between pupils or students, or between employers and employees, to the point where they cannot recognize each other as fellow humans any more. Serious incidents of these kinds are often dealt with as personal cases, but the problem today is that this incident of

---

[15] As far as humans can observe themselves as purposive entities, we can talk about the bond between a person and himself/herself. Suicide can only happen when the subject can recognize oneself as an object, which does not happen in animals.

'in-humanization', which used to be observed mostly among the 'exceptional few', seems to be happening in the common and 'ordinary' social members. When these exceptional pathological incidents occur among the ordinary majority of people, it does suggest a huge and serious malfunction of the society itself, a flawed human relationship and the necessity of fundamental treatment for the society as a whole, not only its individuals members.

A competitive urge and lack of security, hence the distrust of their cooperative relationship, seem to be the underlying cause for various pathological social phenomena. As referred to in Chapter 2, the competitive urge is a natural by-product in a market mechanism. As it is principally an 'invisible' mechanism, participants can only feel at ease when they earn a lot of money by 'winning' in the labour or commodity market. This insecurity-driven competitive urge is the intrinsic characteristic of a market economy. This insecurity is reduced by a social remedy, the Welfare State. And the problem today is that this remedy seems to be becoming insufficient. When the market mechanism is not balanced by countervailing measures, it undermines the two critical virtues for a human society -- equity and human fellowship. This insecurity affects the children, too. Driven by insecurity, the anxious parents in the insecure jobs and living conditions push their children harder to do well at school. This push is not aimed at the genuine growth of their own children but at their survival over the others. The pressurized children come to regard other children and humans as mere competitors and at worst, as enemies. Instead of friendship hatred is born and prevails. The relationship between parents and children becomes perverted and unnatural. The close relationships, which used to grow in the association between adults and children, are undermined. After they grow up under the overwhelmingly competitive urge, what the humans face now is the real battlefield. Merciless competition threatens them there. All this was what the people used to try to avoid when they started to follow the Welfare State path. The following incidents today seem to show that the two decades of political and economic processes have been a retreat toward this more insecure and inhumane society. Such deterioration seems to have permeated the whole of society. We can observe it in the behaviour of both children and adults.

The discussion by Pfeiffer of juvenile crime provides a helpful starter for this argument. Based on a review of the studies of the US and 10 European countries (Austria, Denmark, England and Wales, France, Germany, Italy, the Netherlands, Poland, Sweden and Switzerland), Pfeiffer concludes that juvenile crime has increased heavily since the mid-1980s in most of these countries, and a substantial cause seems to be the growing 'winner-loser' cultural background, where many disadvantaged youth feel themselves fated to be losers (Pfeiffer, 1998): '... police-recorded youth violence, especially robbery and serious forms of bodily harm committed by people under eighteen, has increased strongly since the mid-1980s in almost all of the countries surveyed. Particularly high growth rates have been recorded in Italy, Sweden, Denmark, Germany, and the Netherlands. By contrast ... total recorded youth crime has risen less strongly... Second, in all countries surveyed, crimes of violence committed by young adults (eighteen to twenty) or by adults in general have increased far less rapidly since the mid-1980s' (ibid., p. 256). The reason for youth crime is not the same as before: 'Many analysts no longer accept that the youth crime developing under these social circumstances results from a transient crisis of adolescence ... Rather, it would seem that this is a manifestation of a situation of lasting social exclusion' (ibid., p. 258). One substantial factor in increased youth violence seems to be 'an increase in social inequality that is particularly pronounced in the juvenile world' (ibid., p. 257). The discrepancy between increasing inequality and growing consumerism is suggested to be the reason for these crimes: 'Materialistic societies make consumption a goal for all of their members.' '... the lifestyle of the rich, tantalizingly displayed in the media, increasingly serves as the key model for young people, particularly among people whose social situations make realization of such lifestyles difficult ... one possible consequence is that the people concerned will resort to crime as a means of attaining their culturally determined goals and conforming to more general social conditions' (ibid., pp. 301-2). Data on the 'widening material and social gulfs' within society seems to suggest that this is what is happening today.

In addition to the growing consumerism and inequality, he further suggests that the lack of or weakening of the counter influences, which are the traditional supportive societies and political solidaristic groups, may be aggravating the situation: '... political movements in the past acted as an integrating factor. The family, school, a steady job, and socially integrative leisure-time groups are referred to as the once-existent supportive societies. Political parties and trade unions drew up programs with strong utopian elements. Young lower-class people were highly organized in these groups and placed their hopes in them. Nowadays, with the collapse of "real socialism," utopian ideals have lost credibility. Trade unions and left-wing political parties are thus in danger of losing their integrative power as a vehicle for the hopes and aspirations of the poor' (ibid., p. 303). In the absence of this 'solidaristic' social image, and thus of role models for the youth, television and videos can easily become a 'problematical source of orientation for many juveniles' (ibid., p. 305).

The following figures show a part of this growing social pathology in the four countries. All show a worsening crime trend between the mid-1980s and 1990s. Serious crime (Table 5.8) against the person represents the peak of dissatisfaction; underlying these crimes are harmful intentions toward other humans. Alcohol and drugs (Table 5.9) are in this sense secondary, directed

184

Table 5.8 Serious crimes
(murders, violent crimes and armed robberies, per 100,000 inhabitants)

	1987-88 average	1995	1996
Sweden	55	117	124
UK	72	96	144
Japan	3	17	17
US	225	647	598

Source: IMD, 1990, 1998, and 1999.

Table 5.9 Alcohol and drugs
(employees' productivity, not reduced by alcohol, drug abuses and other addictive substances)

	1987	1995
Sweden	67.9	76.7
UK	67.9	65.0
Japan	90.7	79.6
US	39.0	50.4

Source: IMD, 1990, 1998.

toward injuring oneself. As observed below, the US easily leads the rest in both scores. As for alcohol and drug problems, they have gone down in Sweden and the US, remained the same in the UK and worsened in Japan. Sweden's figure for serious crime has increased more than twice in these years but its pace dropped in 1995-96. The UK's figure has just doubled in these years, and showed a sharp increase in 1995-96. Japan showed the best performance in this respect in absolute terms, but its pace of increase between the middle of 1980s and the 1990s was the highest. The condition of the serious crimes in the US society is astonishing both in absolute level and relative growth pace.

Below, the pathological social phenomena among the citizens in Sweden, the UK, Japan, and the US are introduced and discussed, in all of which countries these problems have become more or less prominent in recent years. The situation of the latter three countries seems to deserve serious attention as the political leaders themselves have admitted (Chapter 4).

SWEDEN

Crime The rate of crime overall has increased little in the past four decades. The numbers in prison per 100,000 inhabitants aged 15-67 years was 143 in 1960, 157 in 1970, 147 in 1980, 172 in 1990, and 164 in 1994 (Nordic Council, 1997, p. 333). As for homicide, 'The level ... has been fairly

constant in Sweden since the mid 1970s, fluctuating between 230 to 140 ...
annually.' Burglaries have remained at a similar level since the mid-1970s as
well. The number of car thefts doubled from 1980 to 1989 but decreased
from roughly 70,000 in 1991 to 61,000 in 1993 (Wirkstrom and Dolmen,
website).

Children and youth The problems concerning children and youth do not
appear to be as prominent as in the other three countries. But if any
symptoms of pathological social phenomena were to be observed in this
country, it would be in this sphere. The report of the Children's Ombudsman
in Sweden may be understood to describe somewhat unfavourable
conditions for them. According to the report, 'Swedish children are among
the healthiest in the world', and generally the statistics of the conditions of
Swedish children and youth show 'a fairly bright picture'. But there can be
observed some ominous symptoms, too: 'Juvenile crime does not ... appear
to have increased during the second half of the 20th century, but there has
apparently been a growth of violent juvenile crime'. Although still below the
level of the 1970s, youth drug abuse has increased since the mid-1980s.
Bullying is a serious problem for many children and young persons. About
100,000 pupils are bullied every year. Although the number of children
affected has been roughly the same since the 1980s, elements of physical
violence are reported to have increased.

A significant warning seems to be shown particularly in children's
mental health. A 1996 survey in Stockholm showed that some 12% of pupils
in the 23 schools investigated were considered to have psychosocial
problems. Mental illness among children and youth is becoming increasingly
visible. The number of first-time visits to mental hospitals within the County
of Stockholm rose by nearly 64% since 1991 (Ombudsman, website).

In Sweden, too, the positive correlation between mentality and
unemployment has been observed (Bjorklund and Eriksson, 1998). If
Sweden experiences a high rate of unemployment in the near future, this may
add to the pathological social phenomena in Sweden, too.

Although we can observe these symptoms, it is still not clear if they are
connected with any increasing competitive urge in this society, as can be
clearly observed in the following countries. It would also be too hasty to
connect directly all of these problems with the economic difficulties of the
early 1990s and the resulting huge unemployment and economic hardship
alone. But as the Ombudsman's report points out, economic difficulties most
probably played some role through reduced welfare provisions, such as
worsened school conditions or reduced incomes of the parents of the
children. However, judging from its still higher level of social protection, it
would be argued that the most threatening factor for the adults and the young
today, the over-competitive pressures or insecurity feeling, does not seem to
have grown as much as in the other three countries. Although the above

conditions indicate somewhat worrisome symptoms, the relatively high social welfare protection seems to support their lives both physically and mentally. Although they are all facing the problem of rapidly changing market competition conditions, the strength of the safety net in this country still seems to differentiate the depth and extent of the peoples' anxieties from the less protected.

THE UNITED KINGDOM

It seems that in the UK today, excessive competitive urge and anxiety are slowly growing, or have started to prevail in society, possibly at a serious level. We have seen that the policies in the 1980s and 1990s under the Conservative and Labour governments have put a strong emphasis on competitiveness. It has been emphasized as a motto for everyday life and international trade. But, unfortunately for the people, this shift of balance from state protection to private competition seems to have failed to bring about a well-balanced society between the economic sphere and the overall welfare of society. As shown in Chapter 3, the accomplishment in the UK for these decades has been more conspicuous in the economy than in social welfare. As a result of this balance shift between the competitive way of life and a lifelong security, a feeling of insecurity has been fermenting among individuals.

Crime The growth of crime is supposed to be one serious result of this social imbalance in the UK. The 'extent and therefore the normality of crime' has generated 'the sense of social crisis and pessimism' (George and Wilding, 1999, p. 186). Total offences recorded by the police have risen in the past decade in England and Wales from less than 4000 in the last half of the 1980s to more than 5000 in the mid-1990s. Of these, violent offences against the person have kept increasing. Drug offences have risen drastically from a little more than 10,000 in 1976 to well over 90,000 in 1995 (ibid. pp. 170-172). When we look at the longer trend, the situation has clearly worsened. Notifiable offences per 100,000 persons have constantly increased from 1958 to 1987 and increased dramatically from 1988 to 1991. Although it was decreasing from 1991 to 1997, it does not show a halt to this long-term increase. More serious is the increasing trend of violent crime and homicide. Violent crime per 100,000 remained around 100 during the 1960s, increased to between 200 and 300 in the 1970s, and further accelerated from 1987 to 1997. The number of offences initially recorded as homicide per one million population has taken a similar course. It was around between 6 and 8 in the 1960s but has constantly increased since the end of 1960s and is around 12 to 14 in the first half of the 1990s. Twice as many people are killed today than in the 1960s. One characteristic among criminals is the shift of the peak age from 14 in 1958 to 18 in 1997; the peak age of the number of males found guilty or cautioned for indictable offences per 100,000 persons was 14 at about 3000 in 1958, but 18 at over 9000 in 1997. About 85% to 90% of offenders found guilty or cautioned are males (Rick Taylor, website).

Depression Recently, psychological studies dealing with psychiatric illnesses related with economic stress are observed: 'With a world-wide recession, unemployment remains a significant risk factor for psychiatric illness' (Tennant, 1994, pp. 207-8). As for the sensitivity of suicidal behaviour to social factor, Kirmayer and Jarvis suggest that social and political factors may be more important than economic factors (Kirmayer and Jarvis, 1998, p. 186). Based on this psychiatric clinical perspective, James (clinical psychiatrist) compares Britain in the 1950s and present (James, 1998). Drawing on much medical evidence, he argues that the chemical substance serotonin is at the basis of modern people's depression. Serotonin is a material that works between two synopses to convey electrical signals in the brain. It works to restrict the animal instinct, causing depression or anger when it is in short supply. In this thesis, depression and anger are the twins, born from the same chemical phenomenon. And what is relevant to our argument is that animals, and probably humans, too, tend to lose a certain amount of serotonin when they are ranked low in their society.

In James' thesis these negative reactions to ranking are what is actually happening in human society today. James draws on various medical materials and observes that this anti-social mental sickness, typical of which is depression, has increased in the UK since the 1950s. Thus, to compare oneself with others and feel low self-esteem are said to be the main cause of depression. Present capitalism, along with its past development, is suggested as one of the major causes of creating this sense of lower ranking. Increasing comparison and declining attachment, such as to families, neighbourhood, etc, are actually prevailing in the industrialized world today. Societies are becoming more and more ranking-obsessed. Although in his conclusion he is cautious in connecting mental problems and social condition, his argument seems to explain the increasing pathological social phenomena above.

An earlier observation of strengthening of competitiveness and market force, both in the economic sphere and leaders' words, suggests this connection by circumstantial evidence. The analytical framework of social virtues presented in Chapter 2, that human society can only continue when it realizes both equity and human fellowship, also suggests this connection. It has been argued there that the sense of being fairly treated is the basis of our support for our society and this feeling is obtained when the two social virtues are fulfilled. This has been the major reason for our creation of the Welfare State, which would help realize these virtues. The more a society becomes market-oriented, the more it increases the competitive feeling in every walk of life, thus making most of the people feel more sensitive to their rank. As income differences increase, more people come to feel ranked and left behind. Insecure feelings and anxiety are inevitable.

Thus, he suggests that if 'advanced capitalism has mercilessly exploited our instinct to rank ourselves against each other', our hope to resist it is also 'our instinct for cooperation' (p. 343). The growing competitive urge does seem to be the key to understanding these phenomena. The remedy of our instinct 'for cooperation' would be effective to ameliorate this competitive urge when practised, and an important part of it should be to re-establish the stronger Welfare State.

Children and youth; youth violence Youth homicide rate in England and Wales is lower than in Sweden and higher than in Japan for 1992-95 (Miringoff and Miringoff, 1999, p. 115). The same figures are much lower than those of the US. But when we look at some microscopic aspects, the two murder cases in Japan and the UK are surprisingly similar and suggestive of the depth of pathological deterioration of some youth in these societies. The murder case committed by five male and female teenagers, in Leeds, the victim being a girl of the same age (*The Guardian*, May 29, 1999), was in every aspect of the details a sheer repetition of a murder case that occurred in Japan several years ago. The killers were all dropouts from school and had no other fun other than to bully the victims to death. The cases of the two students in the UK who killed themselves from exam fear show another resemblance in these two countries, too (*The Times*, July 15, 1999). These cases suggest that the lives of children in the UK have come under more pressure, which can be interpreted as a result of the changing of the social environment toward a more competitive society. As children come to understand that their living conditions are becoming more insecure, they would try to use education more as their survival tool. And if the adult lives that they finally reach after this hard work at school does not quite seem worthwhile, their general dissatisfaction grows. The article by a student in Birmingham explains the condition of the young people around him. They use drugs because 'teenagers want to forget they've got to revise or hand in an essay. Many of those in work want to relieve the boredom of their daily lives.' They 'use drugs because there is little else to do' (*The Guardian*, May 29, 1999). This exactly coincides with what some Japanese girls said when interviewed on why they practised prostitution.

Youth suicide Although increasing, youth suicide remains rather low in the UK. Its rate between ages 15 to 24 has increased by 80% between 1980 and 1992. There were 280 suicides among men of this age, which is quite high compared to 5 from Aids, 173 from cancer, 10 from heart disease and 84 from drug abuse in 1996 (BBC on the web, Feb. 25, 1999). When compared with the US, Sweden, and Japan, the rate for the UK (England and Wales) is the lowest, the US being twice as much, Sweden and Japan in between (Miringoff and Miringoff, 1999, p. 90).

Bullying Bullying among children has long been in existence, but the fatal character of recent days may reflect the increasing stress in childhood: '... ten per cent of primary children and four per cent of those in secondary schools are bullied once a week – 350,000 8-10 year olds and 100,000 secondary school pupils countrywide. It is estimated that 1.3 million children a year are involved in bullying' (BBC on the website, *Bullying, A Survival Guide*; BBC Education, Aug. 12, 1999). 'Many bullies are almost as prone to depression, and even more likely to have strong suicidal urges than those they bully', a Finnish investigation published in the *British Medical Journal* suggests. 'Bullying experts say that this is because bullies often have low self-esteem, or unhappy home lives' (BBC website, Aug. 6, 1999). About ten school children commit suicide because of being bullied in the UK every year (ITV, *Walking on the Moon*, Aug. 29, 1999). When school becomes a place that is more competitive-oriented than ever, it is a breeding ground for a low self-esteem among more children. A competitive urge at school can be generated for children both by witnessing the hardship and insecurity of their parents and by being directly urged to 'succeed' in their results.[16]

Behind these cases can be observed weakened, or even broken relationship among adults and also among the youth. The social image of the individualized, fractured, and atomised human relationship may well be described as war between all. Losing the common purpose or common social image, and instead everything they learn and everything they do become their weapons to survive against others, the school days and adulthood seem to be less and less attractive. This kind of pathological way of life seems to be spreading from lower to upper middle classes in the 'flexible' but more insecure societies.

The main feature of this background change of human relationship is probably the 'winner-loser' culture that has been created and introduced since the 1980s (James, 1995). He investigated the relationship between the increase in youth crime and violence and a growing social and economic cleavage in British society. In a broad re-analysis of criminal survey data, he concluded that the more a society develops a 'winner-loser' culture, the more juvenile violence increases. He argues that this culture is the true outcome of deliberate governmental policies: '... while variations in the business cycle and changes in the reporting of violent crime may have caused a small proportion of the increase since 1987, they are insignificant compared with the medium-term factor, government economic and social policies during the 1980s. They caused the increase in low-income families

---

[16] In this sense, the Labour government's emphasis on education today may bring with it a danger of an increase in this competitive urge at school. David Almond, a winner of the Library Association Carnegie Medal, the Booker prize, laments the creativity being stifled at school today, and even predicts that in 50 years' time 'the concentration on assessment, accreditation, targets, scores, grades, tests, profiles will be seen as a kind of madness' (*The Times*, July 15, 1999). He himself had been teaching English to children with special needs.

that created the rise in juvenile violence after 1987. They also created a winner-loser culture which may well have been influential in encouraging young men to interpret and express the new inequality in a violent manner' (p. 114).

This winner-loser culture may well be labelled as a new stigmatisation of the poor, which exalts only economic success. He understands that this culture took hold in the mid-1980s. Under this culture, where 'previously people of low income were regarded with respect and no blame attached to their low status, the new culture judged them inadequate morally, intellectually and emotionally. The word "loser" replaced words like "disadvantaged" as a common way of denoting them. The winner-loser culture may have caused a change in the way males in the poorest sections of British society interpreted the new inequalities: when feeling frustrated and angry, it may have made them more likely to respond with physical violence' (p. 2). 'It can be argued that if you put someone in a situation where they are very likely to fail and then sneer at them for doing so, you must not be surprised if they react with hostility' (p. 131). Although it is difficult to find the clear-cut evidence for this interpretation, much circumstantial evidence seems to suggest a substantial connection between them, social and mental conditions.[17]

Anxiety in the middle class In this more competitive and more riskful society, UK people in general are living in a rapidly changing social environment. There the risk of exclusion from jobs, especially from more secure ones, gives rise to feelings of insecurity and makes the desire to join the 'comfortable majority' even more urgent. Dominic Hobson argues that UK society is now living under such key words as 'miserable, envy, inequality, insecure feeling' of the middle class in 'more competitive markets'. He suggests that if the middle class can no longer rely on the company or the trade union or the Welfare State to underwrite its standard of living – and its happiness – it must learn to save and to live off its savings (Hobson, 1999, pp. 690-1 and *The Sunday Times*, July 18, 1999). This last comment of self-help coincides with what I argued above that when people are battered by the invisible market force, thereby finding it difficult to feel safe or secure, they can't help focusing on their self-interest. It even compels

---

[17] As a clinical psychiatrist, he mentions that whether or not 'these policies (since the 1980s) were the "right" ones (economically or socially) is ... another matter which will no doubt tax political economists for many a year to come'. We have to evaluate the success of a society by not only economic but also human success. The ultimate criterion for judging the balance between them seems to lie in our commonsense satisfaction. We cannot measure correctly the aggregate satisfaction of the social members, but as Bentham argued, when it (satisfaction or dissatisfaction) grows and reaches a critical point in a society, the need to change the society would become apparent to everyone (see Tsukada, 1998, p. 66).

them to subconsciously deny their natural sense of human fellowship. They become self-centred and save up for themselves, which promotes further the sense of 'self-help', thus making a vicious circle.

The Paradox of Prosperity (the Salvation Army, 1999) studies the trend of social issues in the UK in the future, and forecasts a more stressful society by 2010. It foretells an increase of living standards by around 35% but it also foresees a society where the wealth gap becomes more pronounced and the professional classes are put under increasing pressures, longer working hours and inadequate pensions (pp. 6-7). The report's explanation for the co-existence of macro-economic prosperity and individual misery is growing inequality and 'meaningless' work (pp. 13-21). And the key factor behind them seems to be insecurity. Growing inequality causes this feeling of relative insecurity to grow in the lower paid groups, and middle class workers will also have the feeling of insecurity as possible job-losers ('30% of workers express some degree of concern that their job may not be secure over the next twelve months' (p. 19)). The feeling of insecurity is aggravated by their fear of low pension benefits. They feel that they have to earn more for their old age by themselves. These insecurity feelings make them work the longest hours in Europe today: '59% of the UK citizens are now burdened excessive time pressure'. 'Worryingly, 37% of people feel their working hours are still increasing while 55% believe that they have been subjected to more pressure at work in the past three years' (pp. 17-18). As a result, '82% of the UK population (15 and over) claims to suffer from stresses' and 'Almost a quarter of the population claim to have suffered a stress-related illness in the past year'. There was an increase of absence from work, largely attributed to the stress under which they work (p. 21). They feel that they have been missing precious hours with their families, particularly with children (p. 25), but these pressures keep them in the 'rat-race' life style more than ever. The pressure or the 'competitive urge' becomes much harsher under the growing competition in the globalizing world of today.[18]

And the safety net of the Welfare State seems to have failed so far to meet this problem. The stagnant pension level, increasing education fees and barely improving health provisions etc increase the insecure feelings. Thus the negative effect of the competitive urge overwhelms one's life, making it a more stressful one. It is a natural human reaction, and it often deepens into depression. The human motive for hard work may be stimulated by feelings of fear, but when it grows excessively, it starts to cause serious social

---

[18] *Monitoring Poverty and Social Exclusion 1999*, the New Policy Institute, reported that poverty increased during the first year of the Labour government, particularly in the north. It said that the number of people receiving less than 40% of the average national wage rose by a million to 8 million during the two years to April 1998 and health inequalities have continued to worsen (BBC, website, Dec. 8, 1999).

pathologies, and disintegration of society itself.

Remedies; Government's stance Such a trend then, by the nature of this problem, can only be remedied by strengthening the Welfare State or welfare provisions. As Oliver James proposes, 'a more Scandinavian attitude to society, ... or a notion of co-operative capitalism' will be necessary (*The Independent*, Sep. 15, 1999). The pathological social phenomena above seem to suggest the necessity to shift its weight more toward security, welfare, and stability of people's lives. Can the government succeed in it? The difficulty lies in its basic stance. We saw it already in the principal ideas of Tony Blair. It seeks for 'both economic growth and cohesion'. These are desirable targets. But the problem is that they have to pursue them within their stance to 'win' in the global competition. The force of the market to reinforce competition among the firms and so in the workers and citizens has been very strong. Although the present government tries to achieve the two goals together, the discrepancy between politics and economy in and outside the country makes it difficult. The present stance of the government contains significant danger in this sense. Without finding a breakthrough in this contradictory path, the UK society is apt to follow the scenario of the Salvation Army report.

JAPAN

As for Japan, too, quite a few incidents are noted as signs and symptoms of its pathological phenomena over the last two decades. A large number of cases of bullying to death by middle high school students, high school students and even by elementary school pupils, violence and murders against tramps or homeless people by youngsters, impulsive murder of a teacher by a middle high school student, hundreds of cases of overwork to death, and most of all, the Aum case of 1995 that turned many young people into fanatical murderers (Aum Supreme Truth Cult, 12 killed, and 5000 injured in the subway attack by toxic gas. Quite a few people had been allegedly murdered inside the group). What is common in all these incidents is that they have come to happen among 'ordinary' school children and 'ordinary' adults. This is the same as in the school violence in the US as we will see next.[19] The motives for these crimes and incidents seem to be some blind anxiety and hate, not against particular persons but toward people in general or society itself. It may suggest a weakened human bond in this society in general. The causes for these incidents that we can infer are competitive pressure on the one hand and insecurity on the other. Little noticed because of their intangible nature, they keep accumulating. And when people find

---

[19] It surprised people that among the top ten senior members of the Aum cult, four had graduated from natural science graduate schools, and two were medical doctors.

themselves facing them alone, they feel despair and are induced to rebel against the anonymous society itself.[20]

Crimes Homicide incident rate per 100,000 in 1996 for Japan was 1.0 compared to 7.4 in the US and 2.6 in the UK (Ministry of Justice, website). The general crime rate has stayed much lower in 1970-94 (Ueda et al. 1998, p. 107) than in the UK and US but we can observe an increasing trend since the mid-1970s. The number of penal code crimes per 100,000 was 1.6 in 1960, increased to 1.9 in 1970, decreased to as low as 1.4 in 1975, but since then has increased to 2.0 in 1993 (Japan Statistical Bureau, 1970, 1973/74, 1977, 1981, 1996). The mid-1970s, which was the watershed to the lower economic growth period, also became the turning point of crime increase, too. As we saw in Chapter 3, this was the period when Japan sought to 'survive' by winning export competition and at the same time restraining welfare provisions.

Death by overwork The most conspicuous pathological social phenomenon in Japan is the numerous cases of overwork to death (see also the related argument by Kawahito in Chapter 4). This is no doubt the result of fear of losing jobs in an insecure society. Also related is the suicide by the despair from having lost jobs. According to Kawahito (1998), the researches at Tokyo, Osaka, and Aichi found a close relationship between unemployment and suicide rates (p. 96). He points out not only the economic but also the spiritual damage to the people: 'Why suicide rate increases with unemployment rate ... seems to be related with the spiritual imbalance caused by job losses and the prevalence of anxieties of losing jobs among the people. And as the high unemployment rate continues in depression, the submission of the workers to the firms grows and fatigue from work both in mind and body increases. As the employment situation is expected to worsen more, suicide among Japanese people may increase furthermore' (pp. 96-7). As in the case of the UK, under the pressure and fear of losing jobs a larger part of private lives become subject to the sacrifice for the 'survival in the competition' today. The number of those newly employed by firms who answered they would think more of working late than dating once decreased from 80% in 1981 to 60% in 1991, but in the prolonged depression in the 1990s increased sharply to more than 70% in 1996. It decreased a little in 1997 when the economy recovered a little. 'This fluctuation shows that the submission of young workers to firms increases as the economic and employment situation becomes worse' (Kawahito, 1998, p. 182). In the UK, too, the correlation between male unemployment rate and parasuicide is pointed out by Platt and Kreitman (research at Edinburgh, 1968-82, Platt and Kreitman, 1985, p. 123). As for the recent overall suicide rate in Japan, it is

---

[20] In the Aum case, one culprit stated that their anti-social crimes were a resistance to the Mammonism prevailing in Japan, although regretting what they had finally done.

also moving in a related manner with the unemployment rate (*Asahi*, June 29, 1999). Among the 33,000 who committed suicide in 1998, those whose causes are categorized as 'economy', 'livelihood', or 'work', were about 8,000.

Competition among firms One director of a mental hospital in Tokyo describes the unduly 'restructuring pressure', where the firm manoeuvres to have the workers tender resignations: '... the "bullying" at firms these days are terrible. For example, an office worker is ordered to move to sales front. [They are divided into work groups.] They evaluate the turnover by groups. The group the person is attached to is ranked low because he/she is not used to the work. He/she is bullied by other members in the group, and feels like quitting the job. 'Restructuring depression' is an artificial illness.' The chief secretary of Tokyo Management Union says 'after the bubble burst, as sales turnover decreases, firms started to change its cost structure more suitable for the American standard in the intensifying competition, and tried to make profit quickly. The first thing they did was to downsize the workforce. Those who earn high salaries became the first targets.' Against such a policy of firms, a unique critique is raised that it should be a kind of 'violation of contract', because they used them cheaply while young and then they wished to discharge them because they became expensive, betraying the workers' traditional expectation. Discharge for downsizing is strictly restricted by law in Japan, and discharge by reason of age is also prohibited or restricted in Europe and the US. So the firms look for more efficient ways to downsize. Bullying to retirement is an answer, and of course it costs less (ibid.). And that these things are happening even when firms are not on the verge of bankruptcy give rise to the sense of dissatisfaction and anger among those dismissed.[21]

Juvenile crime Juvenile crime had decreased in the longer run since 1960 but threatens to surge again since the mid-1980s. Juvenile homicide (arrested) decreased from 423 in 1960 to 198 in 1970 and 45 in 1980 but is hovering around 70 to 80 in the early 1990s. Juvenile robbery also decreased from 2646 in 1960 to 1089 in 1970 and 533 in 1985 but increased in the early-1990s to 713 in 1993 (Japan Statistics Bureau). Drug abuse by younger people has also increased dramatically recently.

Suicide and School violence Middle high and high schools in Japan (ages 12 to 18) have been regarded as having serious trouble for the past two decades. Frequent incidents of suicide because of being bullied and school violence have been the major causes. Similarly to juvenile crime, school violence has almost constantly increased from 2148 in 1985 to 8169 in 1996

---

[21] In the restructuring boom, a 51-year-old employee was bullied at workplace – your salary is as much as of four dispatched temporary workers and retired. A 50-year-old was obliged to quit, but being unable to find a new job, he felt like committing suicide, and but with advice from his wife consulted a doctor (*Asahi*, Oct. 10, 1999).

in middle high schools and from 642 in 1985 to 2406 in 1996 in high schools. The increase was particularly conspicuous in middle high schools in 1993-96 (Ministry of Education, *White Paper 1998*). School bullying is reported to have decreased between 1986 and 1993. But the continued suicide because of bullying obliged the Ministry of Education to research the incidents more precisely and the number reported more than doubled in 1994-96. About 50 middle high school students have committed suicide every year in 1974-92. Truancy has also jumped from 7,704 in 1975 to 49,212 in 1993 (PHP, 1995, p. 314).

It is a widely held view in Japan that behind these incidents is the competitive pressures on the students about the test results and entering famous universities. Although the children are told to be friends with each other, they cannot help knowing that what they are really expected to do is to win the race to the elite universities. Quite a few of them come to realize that they are lagging behind in this race as early as in the third or fourth grade of elementary school (6-12 years of age). When they face the high school entrance exam at 15 they all know whether they are in the 'safer life' course or not. The inferiority feeling covers most of the students by the time they enter high schools.[22]

Breakdown of classroom discipline The recent incidents of uncontrollable classes in elementary and middle high schools are being given much attention in Japanese society. In these incidents, children become uncontrollable as a class for even the experienced teachers, some of who are even giving up their careers. This problem is new in the educational culture in Japan. The common phenomena in these incidents seem to be the lack of the control of their own impulses and sentiments by the children.[23]

The loss of prospect of success for the future seems to lie at the bottom of many of these incidents. Kawakami (1999), through his experience of teaching children over thirty years, points out that especially for the past decade, both in society and at home Mammonism and egoism have grown considerably and so has elitism for higher degrees, too (pp. 85, 211):[24]

---

[22] Concerning the recent incident in which a mother killed a rival mother's two-year-old child, exam stress has been referred to as 'a significant factor in a series of suicides and stabbings and a breakdown in classroom discipline' (*The Guardian*, Nov. 27, 1999). Similar problems may be occurring in the UK when the society speaks too much of GCSE scores and lower score pupils lose confidence.

[23] The interim report of the Study Group of Classroom Management (Chairman, Shigeru Yoshida, President of the National Education Research Institute) poses a different view. It assigns 70% of the causes to the inadequate abilities of the class teachers, and 30% to causes that class teachers are unable to cope with (*Asahi*, Sep. 9, 1999).

[24] As education as well as other aspects of life becomes overwhelmed by the competitive ethos, children seem to have lost their liveliness. A photographic record of them shows how Japanese children's mode of life and facial appearance have changed over the high economic growth period in the 1950s to 1970s (Higashi, 1992).

196

'About eight out of ten children are destined to be "losers" by the age of 15. When they knew they would not be able to enter elite high school, their hopes to become social elite are shut up. Once the children of working class used to be able to find jobs that were not bad after graduating schools' but not any more (*Newsweek Japan*, Nov. 18, 1998, p. 34). The growing threat of a jobless society and also the chilly prospect of an inadequate social safety net seem to have become the sources of these anxieties.

Loss of compassion Having lived in this environment, children in Japan seem to have lost much of their sensitivity to human fellowship. According to the international comparative research on compassion (Shisei, Nakazato, et al.), youth in Japan are ranked the lowest in the seven countries, the US, China, Korea, Poland, etc. (Respondents: 6000 middle and high school students. They were asked if they would help those who fell down in front of them, give seats to the elderly in vehicles, engage in voluntary works, etc.) Approval of drugs, prostitution and materialism was conspicuously high among Japanese children. It is observed that the degradation of this kind of consciousness became prominent after the 1980s. Shibazaki commented on the causes of this result as 'homes, which were supposed to be the place to learn basic morals and comforts, have become a mere aggregate of personal rooms, and schools that lost the reproductive function of social norms have become mere hopeless bondage for those young people who could not catch up in the career competition.' 'The problem is that the atmosphere surrounding the lives of Japanese people are being filled up with the competitive principle among individuals, and it is getting rid of every aspect of society where they come across public interest and mutual living' (Shinzo, Shibazaki, Nikkei, Nov. 23, 1998).

Distrust of adult generations Being plagued by this continuous pressure in the Japanese educational system, children increase their distrust of and dissatisfaction with the adult who does not see the problem or try to help them out of this hardship: 'Why do not teachers and parents do anything to the entrance exam wars although they know it is wrong?' is a latent voice among them. The same was heard in the high school revolts in the 1970s but it was in a more explicit form of accusation. Having failed to solve this problem in the following years the distrust among children seems to be directed inward until they erupt in a catastrophic manner such as bullying or school violence.

Regaining the balance of society As shown above, most of the problems seem closely related to the competitive urge and insecure feelings that have come to dominate the society. Frequent occurrences of similar pathological social incidents can only be understood as being caused by such an underlying cause in the social fabric. What is necessary is to change this excessive competitive urge in the society. If the problem is in the imbalance of economic growth and security for all, or excessive competitive urge in the

197

society and lack of countervailing measures, we have to change the balance for the better. Civil society is basically nothing but an organization of humans for mutual security. As Rousseau said, a society must always pay equal amount of attention 'to the security of the least of its members' as to the rest of them. 'So little is it the case that any one person ought to perish for all, that all have pledged their lives and properties for the defence of each, in order that the weakness of individuals may always be protected by the strength of the public, and each member by the whole State.' 'The security of individuals is so intimately connected with the public confederation that, apart from the regard that must be paid to human weakness, that convention would in point of right be dissolved, if in the State a single citizen who might have been relieved were allowed to perish, or if one were wrongfully confined in prison, or if in one case an obviously unjust sentence were given. For the fundamental convention being broke, it is impossible to conceive of any right or interest that could retain the people in the social union'. '... being subjected to the duties of the state of civil society, without enjoying even the common privileges of the state of nature, and without being able to use their strength in their own defence, they would be in the worst condition in which freemen could possibly find themselves, and the word "country" would mean for them something merely odious and ridiculous' (Rousseau, 1973, pp.131-2).[25] The pathological social phenomena we have seen, and will see when we discuss the US case, too, can be understood to be a type of this revolt against the disintegrating social consent. Although the present condition of many countries seems to threaten this fundamental understanding, and although the disadvantaged people might feel powerless when they witness the powerful firms and governments not following this principle, what they should recollect is this original understanding of what a society is.

Too much security? Yasuo Takeuchi argued the opposite. He accused the 'overgrown' Welfare State in Japan and argued that the excess of the Welfare State had created the crimes. He argued like Friedman that the 'bear the burden if you can, receive the benefit if you need' type welfare society has created the hotbed of crime. 'It is wrong that a society which does away with excessively protective socialism becomes a bloody, "the survival of the fittest" society, which is full of crimes. Devastation and crimes are the

---

[25] Thus, we should recognize the necessity for the government to save the needy from the viewpoint of responsibility, not from paternalism, for a large part of it is being caused by the social system itself. The homeless people would say 'I am in this miserable condition now, and it's my fault. I don't blame others'. But this abandonment of hope is wrong because it fails to recognize that a society is based on the consensus for every member's happiness and is at least partially responsible for his/her difficult condition. It is generally so because any particular social structure has the defect of favouring some particular type of people appropriate to it, and it is the same in a market economy in which only those who are fit for profit-making in this particular social structure can flourish.

outcomes of a society where people have nothing to be afraid of under sufficient affluence and excessive protection. This is easily understood by looking at Japan today' (1998, p. 57). But cross-national comparisons clearly show the opposite evidence: 'The industrial societies that have done the most to blunt the inequalities produced by the market system have low rates of crimes' (James, 1995, p. 66). When we take into account those various incidents discussed above, they seem to suggest their close connection with insecurity and anxiety rather than the overflowing security from abundant welfare provisions.

Government's posture Thus, the pathological anti-social phenomena that have been observed frequently since the 1980s in Japan among children and adults alike all seem to be closely related to the growing stress and competitive urge in society as a whole. What is therefore suggested from this finding is the need to reduce the competitive urge and increase security by strengthening the safety net. The government needs to recognize this imbalance, which it fails to do at present. This inadequacy is reflected in the government's recognition of and response to the UN recommendation on the serious conditions of Japanese children. The Convention on Children's Rights was adopted by the UN in 1989 and has been ratified by every country except two, the US and Somalia. Japan ratified it in 1994. Countries are required to report on their relevant policies within two years. The Japanese government made a report in 1996 and wrote 'there are no problems among Japanese children.' An NGO, DCI (Defence For Children International, established in 1979) Japan handed in their own report, too. The Committee on Children's Rights in the UN concluded from these reports that they were concerned that 'Japanese children are exposed to stresses in the educational system which press upon them excess competition and are suffering from growth defect'. The Committee recommended Japan to reform its policies for children in May 1998.

Japanese people today regard the public insurance system insufficient to meet their anxieties. The research by the Centre for Life Insurance and Culture shows that 99.2% are anxious about its adequacy.[26] Recent relief policy to those victims of serious natural disasters is another example that has increased the people's anxieties. The Relief Law for the Victims of Natural Disasters was enacted in April 1998, three years after the Hanshin earthquake, and a small amount of money was paid to the victims.[27] This small amount and the delay of enactment reflected the unwillingness of the government, which had originally asserted that insurance of private property should be the individuals' responsibility. Although this assertion might

---

[26] Respondents, 5000 males and females between 35 and 74 of age in the Capitol area (*Asahi*, June 28, 1999).

[27] It was quite small for those who had to bear the burden of paying for two loans, not only for the newly bought house but also for the destroyed one.

appear fair, in such a case it is rather neglecting the important building block of a society, human fellowship. When middle-income people are deprived of their homes with huge still outstanding loans left, it is almost a death sentence for them. When a society ignores such a hardship, the people would feel that this is not a 'fair opportunity' society. Although a new law was enacted, the anxiety of people at the prospect of a serious natural disaster is not completely eased.

Although the people are the ultimate sovereign in determining social direction, government is in practical terms the most capable and responsible for it. But when the question is too big, the government often loses its ability to follow the right path. In such a case, the people have to undertake this responsibility. Although modern society is supposed to function for 'the greatest happiness of the greatest majority', it can maintain this principle only when the majority of people can support it. And the problem is that we are not sure of what kind of society is desirable and possible today with the firms and governments being obsessed by excessive neo-liberalism and globalizing competition, which is overwhelming the people. From what we have seen above, Japanese people are unable to cope with this question for the future of their society, either,

US

As with the nations described above, the US also shows some serious symptoms of the disintegration of human relationships. As seen before, inequality in income, declining average income and the larger number of uninsured people are the dark side of the US economy today, compared to its prosperous side of low unemployment. Thus, the US seems to have shown two characteristic facets in the past two decades: a growing economy and deteriorating social bond. As Miringoff shows, the positive side of the growing economy is reflected, for example, in increased life expectancy or lower infant mortality. The dark side is reflected in increases in violent crimes, teenage suicide, uninsured health care coverage, inequality, child poverty, or child abuse (Miringoff and Miringoff, 1999, p. 45). Although the country is gaining wealth as a whole, it is also gaining anxiety and anger in the same process. This seems to be the bird's-eye view of this society. Although it is ranked high in terms of global competitiveness, when looked at from the viewpoint of 'the social health of the nation', whether it is following the right path or not is doubtful (as Miringoff and Miringoff show by the 18 figures, ibid. p. 45). The seriousness of the worsening performance in the social sphere even seems to seriously offset the bright economic accomplishment of the US society today.

Thus Glazer's view still seems true: 'The uniqueness of the United States consists not only in the lateness and the incompleteness of its social policy system, but also in the scale of its social problems. Are the two related? It would appear so.' '... the facts that suggest a more severe problem in the United States are ... measures such as the amount of crime, of youth unemployment among minorities, of broken families, of illegitimate children, and the condition of the neighborhood in the great cities ...' (Glazer in Rose, et al., 1986, p. 47). All these phenomena coincide with the problems raised by the President himself a decade later and what we are often witnessing today.

Violent crime Violent crime – murder, non-negligent manslaughter, forcible rape, robbery, and aggravated assault – increased from the 1970s to 1990s. Crime rate per 100,000 population was 363.5 in 1970 but increased to 634.1 in 1996. Although the number decreased between 1991 and 1996, the level in the mid-1990s was still very much higher than in the 1970s (Miringoff and Miringoff, 1999, p. 111) and it is quite possible that 'the recent declines could well be reversed' (Blumstein and Rosenfeld, 1998, p. 1216). The rise in convicted prisoners (Dec. 31, state and federal institutions) is astonishingly high. It was still as low as 93 per 100,000 resident population in 1972, but increased to 133 in 1979 and skyrocketed from 130 in 1980 to 427 in 1996 (Miringoff and Miringoff, 1999, p. 204).

In youth homicide in 22 selected industrial nations, the US ranks top by far, N. Ireland second, and the rest follow far behind (ibid. p. 115). The following is the list of gun shootings in the US at work-related or hate-related incidents in 1999. The high frequency of this kind of incident seems to suggest the existence of weakening human relationships in the adult society as well as in childhood as we shall see later.[28]

Table 5.10 Recent workplace shootings

Apr. 15	Utah	Library	3 dead, incl. gunman
June 11	Mich.	Clinic	3 dead, 4 wounded
July 12	Geo.		7 dead, incl. gunman
July 29	Geo.	Workplace	13 dead, incl. gunman
Aug. 10	Cal.	Jewish CC	5 wounded
Sep. 15	Texas	Church	8 dead, incl. gunman
Nov. 3	Hawai	Workplace	7 dead
Nov. 3	Wash.	Workplace	2 dead, 2 wounded

Source: BBC on the web, Sep. 16, Nov. 3. 1999.

Anti-social terrorism We can observe some serious anti-social incidents

---

[28] Those who believed there was more crime in the US are still over half the population. Those who expected 1998 to be a year of rising crime rate were 53% in Jan. 1998, and falling crime rate, 42% (Gallup, website, social and economic indicators: crime issues).

in the US, as in the case of Japan. One of these incidents that can compare with that of the Aum sarin incident in Japan was that of Unabomber in the same year, who was arrested in 1995. Similar to the criminals in the Aum case, the bomber also believed he was acting for society. He believed that 'The Industrial Revolution and its consequences have been a disaster for the human race. They have ... destabilized society, have made life unfulfilling'. People are destined to become 'mere cogs in the social machine', and 'it had best break down sooner rather than later' (The Unabomber Manifesto, *The Washington Post*, Sep. 19, 1995). His act of indiscriminate killings has no excuse, and neither does that of the Aum culprits. But what we should pay attention to is the similarity of their background anxieties in their condemnation of the present societies in these countries. Even though we are all convinced the Unabomber was wrong in the measures he took in facing the problem, the true question is that it would be hard for most of the people to completely ignore his grief and despair about the ways our societies function today. And as Miringoff and Miringoff say, the overall social condition that gives rise to such anxieties is not given enough attention yet, not as much as that given to economic indicators (Miringoff and Miringoff, pp. 11-12).

Children and youth; youth suicide Youth suicide rate, deaths per 100,000, aged 15-24, was the highest among the four countries in 1992-95 (Miringoff and Miringoff, p. 90). In the past three decades it has gradually increased from 8.8 in 1970 to 12.0 in 1996. The rate was 13.9 for white males and 10.5 for black males in 1970. In the 1980s while that of white males increased to over 20, which of black males stayed relatively low. Although it is still lower than that of white males in 1996, it has showed a sharp increase from the middle of 1980s to the middle of 1990s, closing the gap of the 1980s rapidly (ibid. p. 197).

School violence Among the many similar examples of youth violence in the industrialized world, frequent school violence in the US is the most prominent. Journals in several countries have often focused on this issue in recent years, as in Germany, *Der Spiegel*, Nr. 15. 1998, with the title of 'Die Kleinen Monster, warum immer mehr Kinder kriminell werden', or in *Newsweek*, April 8, 1998, Japanese version, 'That Day School became a battlefield'. The school shootings in the US are the worst examples of this kind. As the latter article suggests, the reason why these juvenile crimes have been so shocking is not only by their massacre type violence but also by the fact that they have happened in the 'ordinary' schools, which had long been taken as 'sacred'. 'In the beginning, America's public schools were supposed to be the cure for violence and social order.' A Massachusetts Senate committee declared in 1846 that, while a poorly educated child might turn to delinquency, one 'placed under the care of judicious men, taught to labor, be furnished with a good moral and intellectual education ... would, in nine cases out of ten, perhaps, become a good citizen'.[29]

The targets here are not goods but the humans, friends and teachers. To harm other humans seems to be the purpose there. In this sense they are the worst example of 'hate' crimes, which are not hate toward any particular person or restricted minority groups but indiscriminate people or 'society' itself. What makes us worried and puzzled most is this character of these incidents: 'By 1989, awareness of the problem had developed to the point that the president and the nation's governors … acknowledged it in a set of national education goals to be reached by the year 2000. Goal 6 calls for schools to be free of drugs and violence and able to offer a safe, disciplined learning environment'. But the problem was that 'educators and other public officials remained divided or confused about how to pursue such a goal' (Anderson, 1998, p. 319).[30]

Facing this tragic situation, *Crime and Justice, A Review of Research*, compiled a volume on 'Youth Violence' in 1998, which was mostly on the US issue. Moore and Tonry wrote, 'Something extraordinary seemed to be happening to American teenagers in 1995 when this volume was conceived' (p. vii). 'For a decade now, the United States has been besieged by an epidemic of youth violence. At a time when the overall crime rate has been stable or falling, violence committed by and against youth rose sharply during the late 1980s and early 1990s. Both frightened and disheartened, society wants to understand what is happening to its young people' (p. 1). The changing character of school violence should be noted: 'There is a broad agreement among educators that the nature of school violence has changed for the worse in recent years, an aspect of the issue not always revealed in the compilation of incident statistics.' According to the National School Boards Association survey, 'many [teachers] apparently felt the increase was more qualitative than quantitative' (Anderson, 1998, p. 329).[31]

G. M. Stennis et al. found 105 school-associated violent deaths in the US during two consecutive school years between 1992 and 1994. Seventy-six were students and 12 were staff. Homicide was the predominant cause of death (81%). The deaths occurred at 101 different schools in 25 states. They understand that 'Many common approaches to reducing school-associated violence – such as security cameras, metal detectors, and random locker searches – would have little effect beyond the immediate environment of the school building', and recommended developing a comprehensive approach to prevent violence among young people.[32] According to Frank Zimring,

---

[29] Menacker, Julius, 'Public Schools and Urban Youth Disorder', *School Safety*, Spring, 1995, p. 4, cited in Anderson, 1998, p. 318.

[30] Six national assessments of school violence in 1978-96 are in Anderson 1998, pp. 322-3.

[31] This qualitative change, often for the worse and for younger children, is also common in the cases in Japan.

[32] Press release by American Medical Association Science News, June 12, 1996, website.

University of California, Berkeley, the Jonesboro deaths brought the number of fatal school shootings to 201 since his group began counting in 1992 (*The Japan Times Weekly*, April 18, 1998).

But some figures show a different picture: 'Youth firearm violence is way down from its 1993-94 peak'. They show that youth homicide arrests in general fell by 20% – from 3,192 to 2,172 – between 1994 and 1996. According to the *Journal of American Medical Association*, August 4, 1999, school violence in the US declined from 1991 to 1997 for the students in grades 9 through 12 surveyed. Among the major findings were that carrying a weapon such as a gun, knife or club anytime in the past 30 days decreased from 26.1% in 1991 to 18.3% in 1997 – a relative decrease of 30%, and participating in a physical fight anytime during the past 12 months decreased from 42.5% in 1991 to 36.6% in 1996 (CNN on the web, Aug. 5, 1999).

But the medical report's authors warned against interpreting the figures too optimistically. They added, 'this study did not find significant decrease in the percentage of students feeling too unsafe to go to school' (ibid.). '... experts differ sharply on the basic question of whether the Jonesboro incident was an isolated, if deeply tragic, aberration – a contradiction to the welcome decline in national homicide rates – or part of a worrisome new pattern or trend.' As for the question what was the biggest problem at school concerning physical security, those who answered 'violence' were 22% in 1994 and down to 14% in 1999 (*The New York Times*/CBS News poll of teenagers, *The New York Times* on the web, Oct. 20, 1999, conducted Oct. 10-14, 1999). Those who knew someone who had been shot in the past five years were 40% in 1994 and 34% in 1999. The reasons why violence happens at school were: 'pride/being made fun of' was cited the most, 22%, and 'people don't get along/argue' was 10%. Those who answered that what happened in Littleton, Colorado, could happen at their own schools were 52%. Parents who feared for their children's' safety at school were increasing from 24% in 1997, 37% in 1998, 55% in 1999, April, and 47% in August (Gallup). Those adults who answered that the kind of incident at Littleton could happen in their communities were 37% (very likely) and 37% (somewhat likely). As to the cause and prevention, 32% answered that parental involvement/responsibility was the most important in preventing it. To the question 'there has been an increase in violence in the nation's public schools over the last decade. How important do you consider each of the following as a cause for this violence ...?', more than 70% answered increased use of drugs, growth of youth gangs, easy availability of weapons, and a breakdown in the American family, such as an increase in one-parent and dysfunctional families [33] (Gallup, social and economic indicators:

---

[33] As for the trust in social institutions, Gallup poll shows that the most trusted institution in the US is now military (68%), then church (58%) in June 1999. The figure for church was

children and violence). The views are somewhat different among children and parents, but the fact that half the children think that such a tragedy could happen at their schools seems to show the continuing seriousness of the problem.

Table 5.11 below lists recent school shootings in the US. The incidents in 1998 and 1999, one of which was the worst 'senseless killing' that occurred on April 22, 1999, in Littleton, Colorado, seem to suggest that the situation has not improved in recent years. It is reported that 29 were killed in eight school shootings since 1997. Today these incidents even seem to be fused into the 'culture' of the society, with people being unable to understand their 'cause'. The word 'senseless' killing shows this feeling of powerlessness. But this very 'senselessness' and cruelty seems to show the key. It appears senseless by the ordinary criterion of personal violence. But when we think of it as hate toward the society itself, as we have been reasoning from the social imbalance view, we may be able to understand it more clearly. From this perspective the adult terrorist such as Unabomber and these young shooters are both terrorists against society itself. They feel agony but do not know its cause. Thus they just destroy what appears to them its source: society itself and people around them. They then turn into mere

Table 5.11 Recent school shootings in the US, 1997-99

1997 Feb	Ark.	Bethel	age 16	2 dead 2 wounded
1997 Dec	Ken.	West Paducah	age 14	3 dead 4 wounded
1997 Oct	Miss.	Pearl	age 16	3 dead 7 wounded
1998 Mar	Ark.	Jonesboro	age 11, 13	5 dead 11 wounded
1998 May	Ore.	Springfield	age 15	4 dead 20 wounded
1998 Apr	Penn.	Edinboro	age 14	1 dead 2 wounded
1999 Apr	Colo.	Littleton	age 17, 18	13 dead 23 wounded
1999 Nov	Geo.	Conyers	age 15	6 wounded

Sources: CNN. com, June 10, 1998, *USA Today*, Apr. 23, 1999, *The New York Times* on the Web, May 21, Sep. 5, 1999.

68% and military 58% in 1975 (Social and economic indicators: confidence in institutions).

terrorists. The victims of society now turn into assailants, without addressing the underlying cause.

Background factors As Hagedorn points out, we have to tackle these problems in the 'cultural and structural factors'. He refers to the discrepancy between the apparent affluence of the society and individual difficulty in achieving it, especially among poor boys: 'In recent decades, most Americans have reduced associations with neighbors and replaced them with TV and the mass media …' The ever-present contrast between media images of the rich and famous and limited real-life chances has been one factor that has encouraged many poor young men to 'make their money' by 'any means necessary'.[34] Although he mainly refers to the gang culture today, the problem of 'this one-sided emphasis on profits' is probably not a culture limited to the gang groups alone but also one permeating the whole of society. The intensified 'winner-loser' culture of our society, being particularly celebrated and promoted since the 1980s, as we saw both in the UK case (Oliver James) and in the Japanese case (school bullying and Karoshi), seems to run strongly through the US incidents also.

We can observe some reactions to this imbalance in such attitudes as that toward job security and school grades in the US. Although in the growing, low unemployment economy total dissatisfaction with the things going on in the US decreased from around 80% in 1979-80 to roughly between 40 and 50% in 1999, the feeling of job insecurity has remained high. Those who felt it very likely that they might lose jobs or be laid off in the next twelve months remained about the same throughout this quarter of a century: 14% in 1975, 11% in 1979, 18% in 1982, 14% in 1991, and 12% in 1998. Those who thought it not at all likely was 59% in 1975, 53% in 1989, 62% in 1990, 51% in 1996, and 60% in 1998. It means that a constant 40% of the employed have worried about losing their jobs in this period and 10% to 20% seriously so. This shows a somewhat different picture of US prosperity and the increasing satisfaction in general (Gallup).[35] This feeling of insecurity in the parents results in pressure upon their children to get safer jobs. Those who felt 'a lot of pressure' from their parents to get good grades increased from 22% in 1994 to 37% in 1999. Including 'some pressure', the figure becomes

---

[34] Hagedorn (1998), pp. 368-9.

[35] Economic cycle affects their attitude significantly. The years when the dissatisfaction figure rose over 70% were 1992, 1993, and 1996 in this period. Except for 1996, these years coincide with the years when the economy was down. Economic conditions were rated 'excellent' (20%) and 'good' (47%) in Sep. 1999, while the same figure was 1% and 11% in Apr. 1992 (Gallup, social and economic indicators, work and workplace). Among children, those who felt growing up was harder than for their parents was 53% in 1989, then there was a jump after the economic downturn in the early 1990s to 70% in 1994 but then it decreased in the recovery to 48% in 1998, and 43% in 1999 (*The New York Times*/CBS News poll of teenagers (*The New York Times* on the web, Oct. 20, 1999), conducted Oct. 10-14, 1999).

206

quite high at 78%. Also 78% answered getting good grades was very important in 1999.[36] Until we address the significance of insecurity and the competitive urge in society, these pathological incidents would continue to happen, first accumulating in the most disadvantaged and erupting in and spreading through the weaker part of our social fabric next. The proper way to address this problem is thus to enhance the secure feeling of the peoples, both children and adults. The priorities people give to strengthening public domain seem to suggest their hopes in this sense. In general, the educational system, social security finance, crime, health care system ranked high at around 70% as the top priorities for the nation, and Medicare finance and poverty followed them at 62% and 57% respectively (Princeton Survey Research / Pew Research Center 1/99, from Public Agenda online, 1999).

Every society must retain two major virtues, equity and human fellowship, and institutions to embody them. This is true for US society, too. When a society adopts market mechanism as its wealth-creating system, it is inevitably exposed to the destructive tides of this mechanism to erode these pillars. We have invented the Welfare State mechanism to offset this effect. But since the 1980s this offsetting force has been restrained, and social resources have been directed more toward market mechanism. What is happening in the US today seems to indicate that this change was rather an advance to the unbalanced society when evaluated by the overall social health. Despite its comforting effect of a low unemployment rate, reduced security in the society, which helps growth in the economy and firms, seems to have been eroding the vital health of a nation as a whole.[37]

Some Concluding Remarks for this Chapter

The pathological social phenomena seem the most conspicuous in the US, then in Japan and the UK, and the least in Sweden. Violent crime, school shootings, workplace shootings, and youth suicide in the US, school bullying and overwork to death in Japan, and mental depression in the UK are the symptoms we could observe as the possible outcomes of insecurity and anxiety in the ever more increasing competitive urge in those countries. Every security in life – secure jobs, attachment to families and neighbours, friendship at school, cooperation at firms – seem to be being eroded behind the thick curtain of a 'more competitive' and 'fit-for-survival' social ethos. Insecure feelings and anxieties are construed to be the common causes of

---

[36] *The New York times*/CBS, ibid.

[37] Alfie Kohn points out the negative influence of the 'number one-ism' particularly in educational life in the US (*No Contest*, revised ed., 1992). Elliott Currie warned of the effects of 'the unleashing of the market', 'its full social and personal consequences will not be felt until many years down the road: as the children of the Reagan legacy grow into adolescence and young adulthood bearing the wounds of public neglect' (Taylor (ed.) 1990, p. 314).

these pathological social incidents. The kind of anti-social crime directed toward the society in general could also be interpreted as resulting from the instinctive anger toward a society that should but cannot ensure security and ease to every member of the society. This instinctive sense of unfairness and imbalance is based on more tangible and material causes – the fear of insecurity in job opportunities and the fear for a less solidaristic, and more self-help oriented, social welfare system.[38]

The seriousness of these incidents today suggests the urgent need for remedies. And if our diagnosis that they have been caused by the insecurity, which followed the weakening of the Welfare State, is right, the remedy is to re-establish it. Once there might have been a case where the growth of the Welfare State hindered higher growth and thus eroded its financial basis. But we should understand that the past two decades' movement toward neo-liberalism and globalization has not enhanced but eroded the social balance. We can argue this by the present pathological social incidents. These pathological phenomena are similar and the causes – economic and welfare policies – also appear much alike in the four countries, especially in the more competitive-oriented three. The only explanation for this common problem seems to be the imbalance between the two delicate factors in the market economy-based society, competitive urge and insecurity. The performance of the US and the UK might look desirable in economic terms. But we should judge a society by its overall condition. The condition of the 'social health', or the overall happiness of the people of the societies -- the extent of security which the people could enjoy, and the extent of equity and human fellowship which the people would hope for as much as, and sometimes more than, economic efficiency – seems to suggest an excessive shift toward competitiveness or insufficient social security in these years. Considering the pro-business postures of the governments of these countries, the sufferings of the peoples as examined above do not seem likely to be reduced much in the near future.

If our understanding of the situation is right, what is necessary today is to regain somehow the fundamental balance of our society between growth and security. If we could understand that the Welfare State should have, or regain, the role to complement the defects of market mechanism for a proper social balance, our task today is clearly to maintain or strengthen it. Shifting more social resources to this direction would be necessary and so will be reinforcing the workers' bargaining power by strengthening their position. Revising the bargaining method so that the major three players, the government, the employers and the employees, could be responsible for the

---

[38] 'The present situation is one characterised by an increase in labour market insecurity'. Under such a condition 'Those who cannot riot will continue to suffer quietly' (MacGregor, 1999, p. 96).

208

economy would be helpful, too. But most of all strengthening the safety net would be the most urgent. The seriousness of the present pathological social phenomena strongly suggests it. It must be strong enough so that no one falls through it and so they can feel secure in society.

But how can we realize it? To realize this goal, we will need more protective labour laws and a higher-level welfare spending. As seen in Chapters 3 and 4, the pro-business and pro-competitiveness trend is strong both in the business world and governments. Governments' power and even their will to control firms seem severely restricted by the economic globalization. Thus the governments' attitudes seem rather reserved. Facing the emergency and seriousness of our social problems on the one hand, which seem to have reached a critical condition today, and restrictive conditions on the other, what measures remain and are possible for reinforcing the Welfare State? Our argument will seek to answer this last question in the next chapter.

The conclusion of this chapter: The great majority of people show a preference for higher security, that is a higher burden and higher welfare society. The urgent necessity for a higher security society is also suggested by the harmful pathological social phenomena in both adults and children today.

6 Toward a Citizens' Welfare State

This chapter questions what we can and should do to maintain or strengthen the Welfare State in the unfavourable economic and political conditions surrounding it today.

1   RESTORING THE SOCIAL BALANCE – Long-term prospect

The task of this chapter is to propose a measure to reinforce the Welfare State in the difficult conditions of today. In the chapters above, I have argued that a society needs three virtues and the Welfare State has been necessary to support equity and human fellowship in a market mechanism society (Chapter 2), that the Welfare State mechanism has been weakened and market mechanism strengthened in the past two decades (Chapters 3 and 4), and that this trend or shift of balance has created serious social problems and has undermined the above-mentioned fundamental social balance between economy and society to a critical point (Chapter 5). We are entering a society full of insecure feelings. The growing competitive urge and competitive ethos, accompanied by growing insecurity such as retrenched social welfare provisions, insecure employment, restricted wages, larger income difference, are, after all, generating serious negative effects on the overall welfare of the people and creating insecurity both physically and mentally.[1] Anxieties about social welfare, employment, and income are growing. 'People are demanding more from government. That is understandable; the current economic and social environment is in many respects perceived as harsher and more unforgiving to the less successful or less healthy than it has been since current systems of social protection were introduced' (OECD, *A Caring World*, 1999, p. 4).

We have seen that the enlarging global market and intensifying global

---

[1] 'In contrast to the general reluctance to reduce benefit levels, there has been a much greater willingness to tighten programme eligibility. Greater attention is being placed on ensuring that potential recipients satisfy the core criteria of disability, sickness and unemployment. There are risks if these measures are taken to extremes as overly rigorous and inflexible rules can lead to people in need being excluded from assistance – contrary to the objective of many countries to reduce the incidence of social exclusion' (OECD, 1999, p. 124).

competition are increasing the mobility of firms and instability of employment. Accordingly, the policies 'allowed' for the governments have become lower corporate taxes, lower wages or a more 'flexible' labour market to attract capital. Thus we have seen that governments in the four countries have started to reduce the firms' tax burden in recent years to meet global competition. This means a possible decrease of government's revenue, hence less scope for welfare spending. The question here about how to reinforce the Welfare State is, then: how can we reinforce a Welfare State in an unfavourable budget situation of 'corporate tax cutting competition' among countries?

First, we will consider the long-term prospect of this question. It concerns the possibility for a government to resist the globalizing market power. How or can we change the weaker government position in the near future? Imagine that the people succeeded in electing a new government that would favour more welfare provisions. If the government, say, of the UK, the US or Japan thus radically changed its stance and tried to reverse the policy trend and raise corporate tax rate, aiming at enlarging the welfare provision resources, would it succeed? It would not, because the present powerlessness of governments derives from the firms' mobility over borders. It means pro-Welfare State policies in one area in the world cannot succeed. Firms and capital will only change their locations. For this reason, for any 'new' government to successfully meet this problem, it is necessary for each of them to unite by establishing an international governing body.[2] Regional unification is in progress such as in the EU or the NAFTA, etc. Cooperation in the financial sphere is also in progress. But such a movement still largely remains regional and slow. In the meantime the problem remains.

Another possibility for a society to resist globalizing business power is to look at employees' power. Being essential factors of both production and consumption, their voice possibly has a major influence on the social movement. Of course, this voice is powerless if fragmented, thus it must be united. As the firms' overriding power today derives from globalization, if the workers can unite worldwide, they would be able to exert greater influence, possibly an equal bargaining power. But this movement seems to be made difficult at present, first by the decline of the labour movement in many industrialized countries, and secondly by the ongoing polarization of the workers into two industries, the newer higher paid high-tech and lower paid service industries. A large part of the middle class workers who were in manufacturing industries and in the middle management class have been

---

[2] As for the possible bodies for 'global governance', such as regional or worldwide international cooperation, both of public and private sectors, see Nicola Yeates, 'Social Politics and Policy in an Era of Globalization', *Social Policy and Administration*, Vol. 33, No.4, Dec. 1999.

driven to the service industries today. This is the fragmentation of workers into smaller workplaces, which make unification more difficult.

But even under this negative prospect, dominance of the globalizing firms will end sooner or later with the disappearance of two kinds of resources: natural resources and cheaper labour. Natural resources are already being questioned as to the absolute amount available and also on the relative pace at which they can be consumed, which will be increasingly determined by environmental considerations. As for labour, as a lower wage workforce in the world becomes more employed, a worldwide levelling up of wage levels will occur. At present, during this globalization or intensely competitive era, profit can and must be directed and re-invested immediately into highly profitable developing countries. Competitive pressure in the world market demands this for any international firms. As a result, very high growth rates will be achieved in these countries. These developing countries will then grow quickly, and the demand for labour will exceed supply. Under this movement, the wages in these countries and regions will increase fast and catch up with those of developed countries. This rapid catch-up of wage levels has been the case in developing Asian countries, which now necessitates foreign firms to move to relatively lower wage countries in the region, and will continue in other developing countries, too.[3]

Disappearance of low-wage frontiers means the end of the dominance of management over labour. At this stage workers will regain fairer and more equal bargaining power. Global pro-labour institutions and agreements that will continue to grow in the meantime, necessitated by the hardships brought about by the globalization movement, will help achieve this. This new power relationship will create a new stage, something that we might call 'the international corporatism' among the governments, globalized management and globalized labour unions. It will help secure and create a desirable social balance between efficiency and equity, and human fellowship, hence a new welfare system or a new Welfare State worldwide. This new corporatism among the employers, employees, and government is nothing but the restoration of democratic management of a society through consensus on the basis of a completely globalized market for the purpose of realizing a well-balanced society.

A newly balanced society, balanced between production and consumption, will be allowed to emerge or to be created. This well-balanced society or a new Welfare State will follow the traditional goals of the Welfare State again: to realize the best balance between market mechanism and society as a whole. The insecurity that people had to accept in the

---

[3] As an economy grows, GDP per capita tends to converge. Lower wages will catch up with those of the first runners (Japan Economic Council, Globalization Working Group, Appendix Figure). Also Barr, 1998, p. 412, note 5.

globalization era will be overcome. Policies for secure employment and a strong enough safety net for livelihood will be implemented. The burden on the firms' side will be raised again, to match the people's fairer and more democratic choice between production and consumption. As the firms will be released from their obsessive pursuit for higher profit of the 'competitiveness-first' era, this course will be welcomed not only by the pro-Welfare State citizens but also by the firms themselves. Being able to share the responsibility for the overall social welfare with the workers and governments, the firms would actually feel more proud, and also relieved this time for not being driven by the short and narrow-sighted pressures of a global survival race.

Although such a new Welfare State realized on international corporatism would be the inevitable future, how long will it be before it is actually realized? As its critical factor is the catching up of the wages in the newly invested countries, it will take a few more decades. A new question then arises. What to do in the meantime? Can we realize a better social balance? Even if we can expect its recovery in a long run, we also need to realize it in the near future, too. We have already seen its ample and urgent necessity in Chapter 5. How can we do it?

2   RESTORING THE SOCIAL BALANCE – Short-term prospect

The only solution we can put into practice in today's unfavourable situation seems to be to strengthen the present Welfare State by higher burden on citizens themselves. Strengthening the present Welfare State through the citizen's own burden, by accepting higher taxes or social contribution and spending it for a safer and securer Welfare State, seems to be the only possible way to survive the anti-welfare and excessively competitiveness-oriented era today. If our reasoning in the previous chapters is right – if every society needs a proper balance between efficiency, equity and human fellowship, if market mechanism has an intrinsic tendency to make efficiency override the other two virtues, if the Welfare State has been made to countervail this defect, if anti-welfare statism after the 1980s, both by neo-conservatism and intensifying globalization, has caused serious imbalance between them, if this imbalance has generated critical pathological social phenomena in our societies, and if the fundamental countervailing power, labour power, will take many more years to revive, gather force and meet this problem fully – the only measure we can put into practice now will be this, defending our society by our own burden, hence, the Citizens' Welfare State.

It will mean higher taxes or social contribution from the citizens. Most of the politicians today are reluctant to proceed with this choice. They are afraid of proposing it, partly believing in the further necessity for a 'higher competitiveness' by their country and partly because of the middle class's hatred of higher taxes. But the people's explicit support for a stronger Welfare State and their strong aversion to the present imbalance of society, which is expressed in pathological social phenomena, seem to suggest that this would be the course that people would agree to. 'There is a constituency of potential support for an alternative among the increasingly insecure middle classes, who are concerned about the future for their children and about their own futures in old age or when redundancy strikes, as well as among those most obviously damaged by poverty and inequality. They could be attracted to a revised form of social insurance which linked increased contributions to social expenditure ... A combination of self-interest, altruism and fear could once again lead to support for social solidarity' (MacGregor, 1999, p. 96). Although the problem of unfairness concerning the lighter burden of firms remains, this road to a more secure life will be supported as an emergency measure by the majority of the people. The present obstacles to people accepting this plan are probably the insecurity of today's life itself, which urges them to save for themselves, and the 'self-help' ideology since the 1980s. But we have seen that this path has generated serious social imbalance. If the government and the people can understand the structure of the question and convince themselves of the seriousness of the problem and the desirability of the alternative path, the government's proposal for this path will be strongly welcomed by the people.

What kind of burden – taxes or social security contributions – would be preferable depends on the condition of the society. Depending on the cultural difference among the countries, the amount and composition of taxation and social contribution necessary to realize the proper balance in each country varies.[4] It might be to raise personal income tax or consumption tax, or it could be increasing social security contribution rates. The composition should be carefully studied and proposed, but the most important is to ensure people the security necessary today. When this kind of plan is properly proposed, it is likely to be accepted by the people. Sweden's case, together with the other Scandinavian countries, still seems to show this possible acceptance of a higher burden by the people when it assures a higher level of security. We saw the deep-rooted virtue of security in its policies and the overall social life there, and this may be the very virtue we need to realize fully in this age of insecurity today. Realizing security and strengthening the safety net will be the main goal and measure of the Citizens' Welfare State

---

[4] Recently 'The defining characteristic of personal income tax reforms has been to lower the top rates of marginal taxation and to broaden the personal income tax base. However, simultaneously, pressures to finance social spending have led to *increases* in social security contribution rates' (OECD, 1999, p. 39).

today.[5] What leads us along this path is the understanding of the seriousness of the present problems, the origin of them, and the possible alternative today, which we have debated above.

The conclusion of this chapter: In the long run a stronger Welfare State supported by both management and labour will be re-established when economic globalization has spread out and no cheaper labour is left in the world market. But to realize a stable and secure society in the meantime, a strengthening of the Welfare State through the citizens accepting a higher burden is necessary. The pathological social phenomena in the previous chapter emphasize its urgency.

---

[5] Such measures will also support economic growth through stronger consumption, higher productivity (easier workforce rearrangement), larger workforce, and less expenditure for law and order, etc. It will even contribute to a less commercialized way of life by blunting its emphasis on economic efficiency.

Conclusion

The arguments of this book consist of three major parts: first, the argument on fundamental social structure featuring efficiency, equity and human fellowship in Chapter 2, which also provides the analytical viewpoint for the following chapters, secondly, the analyses of the changing spheres of the Welfare State and related arguments in Chapters 3 and 4, and thirdly, the argument on the people's preferences in Chapter 5. The argument in Chapter 6 about the Citizens' Welfare State is the logical and inevitable conclusion derived from the previous ones.

We can summarize these arguments as follows:

Chapter 1: With the 1970s as the watershed, post-war industrialized societies changed into a lower growth rate economy, which then made the growth of the Welfare State difficult. In a conflict between limited economic resources, the Welfare State has had a setback. Why and how much the Welfare State should change concerns the fundamental relationship between economic growth and social welfare, and past studies have shown the necessity to clarify this further.

Chapter 2: As the question of the Welfare State is related to the whole structure of our modern society, we need to have an analytical framework for the overall social structure itself. Good balance between efficient production and proper distribution has always been the fundamental question for a society. A useful viewpoint for this question is to analyse it through the balance between three fundamental virtues of society: efficiency of production on the one hand and equity and human fellowship of distribution on the other. Civil society has adopted market mechanism but this has the intrinsic bias toward more efficiency in production and less equity and human fellowship of distribution. The Welfare State has been devised to meet this fundamental defect of market mechanism.

Chapter 3: The Welfare State kept growing until the 1970s (Sweden, the UK, Japan, the US). But the turbulence in the 1970s gave birth to anti-welfarism or neo-liberalism. Its economic and social policies then pushed society toward market mechanism too far and thus toward too much insecurity. Emerging economic globalization further aggravated this imbalance.

Chapter 4: The postures of the government leaders predict that this imbalance will continue in the coming years. But arguments for the necessity and possibility to change this trend are apparent, too.

Chapter 5: People's will, both expressed explicitly in opinion polls and demonstrated in pathological social phenomena, shows that we should make progress toward an alternative society today, for maintaining and strengthening the Welfare State to regain the social balance that we have lost in the past two decades.

Chapter 6: The long-term prospect is to re-establish the Welfare State by the growth of the governments' and workers' powers and the dissolution of a low wage workforce. And as these take time, we need a short-term remedy, namely to create a more secure Welfare State through the citizens' burden, namely the citizens' Welfare State.

I would like to conclude my arguments here with some other observations for the readers. First, this book is an attempt to relate economy with society, particularly market mechanism to the overall social structure. It has been motivated by the perception that a fundamental change is happening today in the post-war industrialized societies, in which once intertwined economic and social factors in the Welfare State are being torn apart. In a socio-economic analysis of the present and future of the Welfare State today, forming or regaining a total social image – where it is leading, and where it can lead – will be the essential for us in order to live through these tumultuous years of the pro-efficiency and insecure globalization era. This understanding and a hope to reconnect them form the basis of this study. So this book covers such interdisciplinary fields as philosophical arguments and causal relations between economic factors and social pathology, and both merit and demerit will derive from this analytical method itself.

The conclusion of this book: In industrialized countries the anti-welfarism of neo-liberalism and economic globalization has tilted the social balance too much toward market mechanism and economic efficiency in the past two decades. This imbalance has put society in a serious condition today. In the long-term prospect we can expect a new Welfare State on international corporatism to emerge. And in the short-term prospect, in order to cope with the problem in the strong globalization trend of today we need to rebuild the proper balance by building the citizens' Welfare State.

Appendix:
Statistical Tables for Sweden UK, Japan, US

STATISTICAL TABLE FOR SWEDEN - 1

Sweden	GDP growth rate *1	Per capita income growth *2	Unemployment rate *3	Inflation rate *4	Interest rate,C.B. *5	Current account % of GDP *6	Financial balance % of GDP *7
1960	3.3						
61	5.3						
62	3.9						
63	6.0						
64	6.8						
65	3.8		1.2				4.3
66	2.2		1.6				
67	3.4		2.1				
68	3.6		2.2	1.9			
69	5.0		1.9	2.7			
70	6.6		1.5	7.0			4.4
71	0.9		2.5	7.4			5.2
72	2.3		2.7	6.0			4.4
73	4.0		2.5	6.7	5.9	2.8	4.1
74	3.2		2.0	9.9	7.0	−1.0	1.9
75	2.6		1.6	9.8	6.0	−0.5	2.7
76	1.1		1.6	10.3	8.0	−2.1	4.5
77	−1.6	−1.9	1.8	11.5	8.0	−2.6	1.7
78	1.8	1.5	2.2	10.0	6.5	−0.3	−0.5
79	3.8	3.6	2.1	7.2	9.0	−2.2	−2.9
80	1.7	1.5	2.0	13.7	10.0	−3.5	−4.9
81		−0.2	2.5	12.1	11.0	−2.4	−5.4
82	1.0	1.0	3.1	8.6	10.0	−3.3	−3.1
83	1.8	1.7	3.5	8.9	8.5	−0.8	−0.5
84	4.0	3.9	3.1	8.0	9.5	0.8	−0.8
85	1.9	1.8	2.8	7.4	10.5	−1.0	−0.8
86	2.3	2.1	2.7	4.2	7.5		1.0
87	3.1	2.8	1.9	4.2	7.5		6.0
88	2.3	1.8	1.6	5.8	8.5	−0.3	4.5
89	2.4	1.7	1.3	6.4	10.5	−1.6	5.9
90	1.4	0.5	1.5	10.5	11.5	−2.8	4.3
91	−1.1	−1.7	2.7	9.3	8.0	−1.9	−1.0
92	−1.4	−2.0	5.8	2.3	10.0	−3.6	−7.5
93	−2.2	−2.8	9.5	4.6	5.0	−2.2	−11.3
94	3.3	1.8	9.8	2.2	7.0	0.4	−8.3
95	3.9		9.2	2.5	7.0	2.1	−4.3
96	1.3		10.0	0.5	3.5	2.3	−0.2
97	1.8		9.9	0.5	2.5	3.2	2.4
98			8.3				4.7
99			7.2				

STATISTICAL TABLE FOR SWEDEN - 2

Sweden	Exc.rate 1SDR= Kroner *8	Social security contrbtn *9 (% of GDP)	Tax and SSC *9	Total tax revenue % of GDP *10	Corporate income tax, % of GDP *11	Employers SSC as % of GDP *12	Total of *11 and *12
1960				27.2			
61							
62							
63							
64							
65				35.0	2.1	3.1	5.2
66							
67							
68							
69	5.2						
70	5.2	11.5	55.0	39.8	1.8	4.7	6.5
71	5.3						
72	5.1						
73	5.5						
74	5.0						
75	5.1	12.8	57.6	43.4	1.9	8.0	9.9
76	4.8						
77	5.7						
78	5.6						
79	5.5						
80	5.6	19.5	65.0	48.8	1.2	13.5	14.7
81	6.5	20.4	66.6				
82	8.0	19.8	66.5				
83	8.4	19.8	68.8				
84	8.8	19.3	68.9				
85	8.4	19.1	70.2	50.0	1.7	11.9	13.6
86	8.3	19.3	73.2				
87	8.3	18.8	76.5	55.4			
88	8.3	19.2	75.1	54.8			
89	8.2	20.8	76.5	55.5			
90	8.1	21.8	78.5	55.6	1.7	14.5	16.2
91	7.9	21.7	75.2	52.7			
92	9.7	20.5	70.5	49.9	1.5	14.5	16.0
93	11.4	19.1	70.4	49.9	2.2	12.8	15.0
94	10.9	19.7	70.3	50.3	2.7	12.5	15.2
95	9.9	19.9	67.5		3.1	12.4	15.5
96	9.9	22.2	73.2				
97	10.6						
98							
99							

Sweden	Real H. earnings, mfg.,yearly growth *13	Unit labour cost, mfg *14	Industrial disputes *15	Operating surplus mfg,gross *16	Operating surplus, mfg,trspt, commn, *16	Gross C. formation % of GDP *17
1960						24.7
61						24.2
62						24.1
63						24.2
64						26.3
65			4			26.9
66			352			25.7
67			0			24.8
68			1			24.0
69			112			24.3
70			156			25.2
71			839			22.4
72			11			21.7
73			12			20.7
74			58			23.9
75			366			23.3
76			25			22.2
77	−4.3	11.1	87			20.1
78	−1.1	8.4	37			17.2
79	0.5		29			19.6
80	−4.3	9.5	4479	21.7	29.0	21.3
81	−1.4	10.5	209	19.3	27.5	18.2
82	0.1	3.5	2	24.8	31.2	17.6
83	−1.7	3.2	37	29.0	33.8	17.2
84	1.4	3.6	41	30.5	33.4	17.8
85	0.2	8.6	504	28.9	32.0	19.2
86	3.0	6.3	683	31.3	33.3	17.9
87	2.2	4.6	15	31.4	32.9	18.9
88	2.1	5.0	797	30.5	32.9	19.9
89	3.3	7.2	410	30.2	33.0	21.9
90	−1.0	8.7	770	27.1	31.1	21.3
91	−3.5	8.0	22	23.6	29.8	17.9
92	2.3	−0.6	28	24.0	31.7	16.5
93	−1.3	−7.6	190	32.7	36.2	13.3
94			52	35.9	38.1	14.1
95			627			15.4
96			61			14.6
97						14.1
98						
99						

UK	GDP growth rate *1	Per capita income growth *2	Unemploy ment rate *3	Inflation rate *4	Interest rate,C.B. *5	Current account % of GDP *6	Financial balance % of GDP *7
1960	5.0						
61	3.0						
62	0.8						
63	4.5						
64	5.3						
65	2.2		2.3				-0.4
66	2.0		2.3				
67	2.7		3.4				
68	4.1		3.1	4.7			
69	2.1		2.9	5.5			
70	2.3		3.0	6.4			2.9
71	2.0		3.6	9.4			1.3
72	3.5		4.0	7.1	9.0		-1.3
73	7.4		3.0	9.2	13.0	-1.3	-2.7
74	-1.7		2.9	15.9	11.5	-3.8	-3.8
75	-0.7		4.3	24.2	11.3	-1.4	-4.5
76	2.8		5.6	16.5	14.5	-0.7	-4.9
77	2.4	2.3	6.0	15.8	7.0	-0.1	-3.2
78	3.5	3.7	5.9	8.3	12.5	0.6	-4.4
79	2.8	2.7	5.0	13.4	17.0	-0.2	-3.2
80	-2.2	-2.3	6.2	18.0	14.0	1.4	-3.4
81	-1.3	-1.3	9.7	11.9	14.5	2.8	-2.6
82	1.5	1.6	11.1	8.6	10.0	1.6	0.4
83	3.6	3.5	11.1	4.6	9.0	1.1	-0.2
84	2.5	2.2	11.1	5.0	9.5	0.4	-0.6
85	3.5	3.2	11.5	6.1	11.5	0.7	0.5
86	4.4	4.1	11.5	3.4	11.0	-0.2	0.4
87	4.8	4.5	10.6	4.1	8.5	-1.2	1.2
88	5.0	4.7	8.7	4.9	13.0	-3.5	3.3
89	2.2	1.8	7.3	7.8	15.0	-4.3	3.4
90	0.4	0.2	7.1	9.5	14.0	-3.3	0.8
91	-2.0	-2.6	8.8	5.9	10.5	-1.4	-0.7
92	-0.5	-0.9	10.1	3.7	7.0	-1.7	-4.5
93	2.1	1.9	10.5	1.6	5.5	-1.6	-5.8
94	4.3	3.5	9.6	2.5	6.3	-0.2	-4.2
95	2.7		8.7	3.4	6.5	0.5	-2.8
96	2.2		8.2	2.4	6.0	-0.3	-1.5
97	3.4		7.0	3.1	7.3	0.5	0.9
98			6.3		6.3		3.2
99			6.1		5.0		

STATISTICAL TABLE FOR UK - 2

UK	Exc.rate 1SDR= Sterling *8	Social security contrbtn *9 (% of GDP)	Tax and SSC *9	Total tax revenue % of GDP *10	Corporate income tax, % of GDP *11	Employers SSC as % of GDP *12	Total of *11 and *12
1960				28.5			
61							
62							
63							
64							
65				30.4	2.2	2.3	4.5
66							
67							
68	0.4						
69	0.4						
70	0.4	7.9	49.2	36.9	3.3	2.6	5.9
71	0.4						
72	0.5						
73	0.5						
74	0.5						
75	0.6	9.8	47.1	35.5	2.4	3.7	6.1
76	0.7						
77	0.6						
78	0.6						
79	0.6						
80	0.5	9.7	49.1	35.3	2.9	3.4	6.3
81	0.6	10.4	52.7				
82	0.7	10.8	53.4				
83	0.7	11.1	52.4				
84	0.8	11.1	52.3				
85	0.8	11.0	52.0	37.9	4.7	3.4	8.1
86	0.8	11.2	52.2				
87	0.8	11.2	51.8	37.2			
88	0.7	11.1	51.8	37.1			
89	0.8	10.4	50.7	36.2			
90	0.7	10.2	50.6	36.4	3.9	3.6	7.5
91	0.8	10.6	50.5	35.8			
92	0.9	10.3	48.0	35.4	2.6	3.7	6.3
93	0.9	10.3	46.1	33.6	2.4	3.5	5.9
94	0.9	10.3	46.9	34.1	2.7	3.5	6.2
95	1.0	10.4	49.0		3.3	3.4	6.7
96	0.8	10.2	49.2				
97	0.8						
98							
99							

223

UK	Real H. earnings, mfg.,year-ly growth *13	Unit labour cost, mfg *14	Industrial disputes *15	Operating surplus mfg,gross *16	Operating surplus, mfg,trspt, commn, *16	Gross C. formation % of GDP *17
1960				29.5	31.7	18.6
61						18.3
62						17.0
63						17.3
64						20.4
65			2925			19.8
66			2398			19.2
67			2787			19.7
68			4690		30.8	20.4
69			6846			19.9
70			10980			19.5
71			13551			19.1
72			23909			18.5
73			7197			21.9
74			14750	19.9	25.7	22.1
75			6012			18.6
76			2384			20.3
77	-4.8	12.1	10142			19.8
78	5.7	15.1	9405			19.5
79	1.9	17.8	29474			19.7
80	-0.1	22.0	11964	19.1	31.3	16.8
81	1.0	10.5	4266	17.9	33.3	15.1
82	2.4	4.4	5313	21.2	36.4	15.6
83	4.2	-0.5	3754	23.5	39.2	16.4
84	3.6	2.4	27135	23.5	40.4	17.3
85	2.9	5.5	6402	25.6	40.4	17.2
86	4.1	4.5	1920	26.7	37.1	17.1
87	3.7	5.1	3546	25.9	37.7	18.0
88	3.4	1.2	3702	28.2	38.2	20.3
89	0.9	5.7	4128	29.6	38.6	21.0
90	-0.1	2.1	1903	27.4	36.2	19.2
91	2.2	6.4	761	23.8	33.5	16.1
92	2.7	5.1	528	25.0	34.3	15.3
93	2.9	2.5	649	27.4	36.7	15.0
94			278	30.1	39.7	15.5
95			415			16.1
96			1303			15.8
97						15.7
98						
99						

STATISTICAL TABLE FOR JAPAN - 1

Japan	GDP growth rate *1	Per capita income growth *2	Unemployment rate *3	Inflation rate *4	Interest rate,C.B. *5	Current account % of GDP *6	Financial balance % of GDP *7
1960	13.3						1.7
61	14.5						
62	7.0						
63	10.5						
64	13.1						
65	5.1		1.2				0.5
66	10.5		1.3				
67	10.4		1.3				
68	12.6		1.2	5.4			
69	12.1		1.1	5.2			
70	9.4		1.1	7.7			1.7
71	4.2		1.2	6.4			1.1
72	8.4		1.4	4.9			-0.1
73	7.9		1.3	11.7	9.0		0.5
74	-1.2		1.4	23.1	9.0	-1.0	0.4
75	2.6		1.9	11,8	6.5	-0.1	-2.8
76	4.8		2.0	9.4	6.5	0.7	-3.7
77	5.3	3.7	2.0	8.2	4.3	1.6	-3.8
78	5.1	3.9	2.2	4.2	3.5	1.7	-5.5
79	5.2	4.7	2.1	3.7	6.3	-0.9	-4.7
80	3.6	2.8	2.0	7.8	7.3	-1.0	-4.4
81	3.6	2.8	2.2	4.9	5.5	0.4	-3.9
82	3.2	2.5	2.4	2.7	5.5	0.6	-2.0
83	2.7	2.0	2.6	1.9	5.0	1.8	-1.8
84	4.3	3.6	2.7	2.2	5.0	2.8	-0.1
85	5.0	4.3	2.6	2.0	5.0	3.8	1.0
86	2.6	2.0	2.8	0.6	3.0	4.3	0.7
87	4.1	3.6	2.8	0.1	2.5	3.9	2.0
88	6.2	5.8	2.5	0.7	2.5	2.7	2.7
89	4.7	4.3	2.3	2.3	4.3	2.2	3.6
90	4.8	4.5	2.1	3.1	6.0	1.5	3.7
91	3.8	3.9	2.1	3.3	4.5	2.0	3.4
92	1.0	0.8	2.2	1.7	3.3	3.0	2.1
93	0.3	-0.5	2.5	1.3	1.8	3.1	-0.9
94	0.6	0.3	2.9	0.7	1.8	2.8	-2.3
95	1.5		3.1	-0.1	0.5	2.2	-3.1
96	3.9		3.4	0.1	0.5	1.4	-3.5
97	0.9		3.4	1.7	0.5	2.3	-2.3
98			4.1				-4.9
99			4.7				

Japan	Exc.rate 1SDR= Yen *8	Social security contrbtn *9 (% of GDP)	Tax and SSC *9	Total tax revenue % of GDP *10	Corporate income tax, % of GDP *11	Employers SSC as % of GDP *12	Total of *11 and *12
1960				18.2			
61							
62							
63							
64							
65				18.3		1.7	5.8
66							
67							
68	357.7						
69	357.8						
70	357.7	5.4	24.3	19.7		2.3	7.5
71	341.8						
72	327.9						
73	337.8						
74	368.5						
75	357.2	7.5	25.7	20.9	20.6	3.2	7.5
76	240.2						
77	291.5						
78	253.5						
79	315.8						
80	258.9	9.2	31.3	25.4		3.8	9.3
81	256.0	9.8	32.5				
82	259.2	10.0	33.1				
83	243.1	10.0	33.4				
84	246.1	10.1	34.0				
85	220.2	10.4	34.4	27.6		4.2	10.0
86	194.6	10.6	35.5				
87	175.2	10.6	37.0	29.7			
88	169.4	10.6	37.9	30.3			
89	188.5	10.8	38.4	30.7			
90	191.2	11.4	39.2	31.3		4.7	11.5
91	179.1	11.6	38.7	30.8			
92	171.5	11.9	36.8	29.2		4.9	9.9
93	153.6	12.1	36.5	29.1	14.9	5.1	9.4
94	145.6	12.5	35.7			5.0	9.1
95	152.9	13.2	36.6			5.2	9.5
96	166.8	13.2	36.2				
97	175.3	13.7	37.4				
98		14.3	37.4				
99		14.3	36.6				

Japan	Real H. earnings, mfg.,year-ly growth *13	Unit labour cost, mfg *14	Industrial disputes *15	Operating surplus mfg,gross *16	Operating surplus, mfg,trspt, commn, *16	Gross C. formation % of GDP *17
1960				55.1	50.1	32.4
61						37.8
62						34.4
63						34.8
64						34.9
65			5669			32.0
66			2742			32.6
67			1830			35.5
68			2841		51.3	36.8
69			3634			37.6
70			3915			39.0
71			6029			35.8
72			5147			35.5
73			4604			38.1
74			9663	47.1	42.8	37.3
75			8016	,		32.8
76			3254			31.8
77	0.6	5.6	1519			30.8
78	1.9	1.0	1358			30.9
79	3.6	-1.4	930			32.5
80	-0.6	2.5	1001	43.7	42.0	32.2
81	0.6	2.7	554	42.5	42.7	31.1
82	1.8	-0.4	538	42.6	40.9	29.9
83	1.1	0.2	507	42.1	40.2	38.1
84	1.5	-2.1	354	43.1	41.8	28.0
85	1.1	-2.3	264	43.3	42.4	28.1
86	0.8	6.9	253	42.3	42.1	27.2
87	1.6	-5.5	256	42.8	43.2	28.5
88	3.8	-3.8	174	43.9	44.1	30.4
89	3.4	-0.8	220	44.3	44.1	31.3
90	2.2	0.3	145	43.8	43.4	32.3
91	0.2	0.5	96	43.8	42.9	32.2
92	-0.7	5.6	231	40.8	40.8	30.8
93	-1.1	2.5	116	37.8	38.6	29.7
94			85			28.7
95			77			28.6
96						29.9
97						28.5
98						
99						

US	GDP growth rate *1	Per capita income growth *2	Unemploy-ment rate *3	Inflation rate *4	Interest rate,C.B. *5	Current account % of GDP *6	Financial balance % of GDP *7
1960	2.2						0.7
61	2.6						
62	5.2						
63	4.1						
64	5.3						
65	5.8		4.4				0.2
66	5.9		3.6				
67	2.9		3.7				
68	5.1		3.5	4.1			
69	2.7		3.4	5.4			
70			4.8	5.9			-1.0
71	3.1		5.8	4.3			-1.8
72	4.8		5.5	3.3			-0.3
73	5.2		4.8	6.2	7.5	0.5	0.6
74	-0.6		5.5	11.0	7.8	0.1	-0.3
75	-0.8		8.3	9,1	6.0	1.1	-4.1
76	4.9		7.6	5.7	5.3	0.2	-2.2
77	4.5	3.4	6.9	6.5	6.0	-1.7	-1.0
78	4.8	4.0	6.0	7.6	9.5	-0.7	0.0
79	2.5	0.9	5.8	11.3	12.0		0.5
80	-0.5	-1.3	7.2	13.5	13.0	0.1	-1.3
81	1.8	1.2	7.6	10.3	12.0	0.2	-1.0
82	-2.2	-3.1	9.7	6.1	8.5	-0.4	-1.7
83	3.9	2.7	9.6	3.2	8.5	-1.3	-2.4
84	6.2	5.7	7.5	4.3	8.0	-2.5	-1.0
85	3.2	2.2	7.2	3.5	7.5	-3.0	-1.1
86	2.9	1.8	7.0	1.9	5.5	-3.4	-1.4
87	3.1	2.2	6.2	3.7	6.0	-3.5	-0.5
88	3.9	3.0	5.5	4.1	6.5	-2.5	0.0
89	2.5	1.8	5.3	4.8	7.0	-1.9	0.5
90	0.8	0.2	5.5	5.4	6.5	-1.6	-0.5
91	-1.0	-1.5	6.8	4.2	3.5	-0.2	-1.0
92	2.7	1.4	7.3	3.0	3.0	-1.0	-2.2
93	2.2	2.3	6.9	3.0	3.0	-1.4	-1.4
94	3.5	3.1	6.1	2.6	4.8	-1.9	-0.2
95	2.0		5.6	2.8	5.3	-1.8	0.3
96	2.8		5.4	2.9	5.0	-1.9	1.1
97	3.8		4.9	2.3	5.0	-2.1	2.3
98			4.5				3.3
99			4.2				

STATISTICAL TABLE FOR US - 2

US	Exc.rate 1SDR= Dollar *8	Social security contrbtn *9 (% of GDP)	Tax and SSC *9	Total tax revenue % of GDP *10	Corporate income tax, % of GDP *11	Employers SSC as % of GDP *12	Total of *11 and *12
1960				26.5			
61							
62							
63							
64							
65				25.8	4.0	1.8	5.8
66							
67							
68	1.0						
69	1.0						
70	1.0	6.4	34.4	29.2	3.6	2.3	5.9
71	1.1						
72	1.1						
73	1.2						
74	1.2						
75	1.2	8.0	34.4	29.0	3.0	2.9	5.9
76	1.2						
77	1.2						
78	1.3						
79	1.3						
80	1.3	8.7	35.7	29.3	2.9	3.2	6.1
81	1.2	9.3	36.9				
82	1.1	9.6	36.1				
83	1.0	9.3	35.1				
84	1.0	9.3	34.5				
85	1.1	9.5	35.0	28.7	2.0	3.6	5.6
86	1.2	9.7	35.2				
87	1.4	9.7	35.9	29.9			
88	1.3	10.0	35.3	29.5			
89	1.3	9.9	36.0	29.7			
90	1.4	10.0	35.9	29.4	2.1	3.6	5.7
91	1.4	10.2	35.8	29.5			
92	1.4	10.2	35.1	29.6	2.0	3.6	5.6
93	1.4	10.2	35.4	29.7	2.2	3.6	5.8
94	1.5	10.2	35.8		2.5	3.7	6.2
95	1.5	10.2	35.9		2.6	3.6	6.2
96	1.4	10.1	36.5				
97	1.3						
98							
99							

US	Real H. earnings, mfg.,year-ly growth *13	Unit labour cost, mfg *14	Industrial disputes *15	Operating surplus mfg,gross *16	Operating surplus, mfg,trspt, commn, *16	Gross C. formation % of GDP *17
1960				25.2	30.9	18.4
61						17.7
62						18.5
63						18.8
64						18.8
65			23300			20.0
66			25400			20.2
67			42100			19.0
68			49000			18.4
69			42869			18.8
70			66414			17.3
71			47589			18.3
72			27066			19.4
73			27948			20.2
74			47991	22.0		19.3
75			31237			16.8
76			47859			18.4
77	2.1	5.3	35822			20.0
78	1.0	8.1	36922			21.2
79	-2.5	9.1	34754			21.3
80	-4.3	12.7	20844	22.2	32.1	19.3
81	-0.5	6.0	16908	23.6	33.0	20.2
82	0.2	5.2	9061	22.8	32.6	17.8
83	0.6	0.5	17461	24.9	34.6	17.8
84	-0.2	1.9	8499	26.8	36.7	20.4
85	0.3	1.8	7079	26.2	36.3	19.4
86	0.2	1.5	11861	27.1	35.6	18.8
87	-1.8	-4.0	4469	29.2	37.1	18.3
88	-1.2	1.6	4381	30.7	37.6	17.5
89	-1.8	3.4	16530	31.4	37.7	17.5
90	-2.0	3.5	5926	30.5	37.2	16.3
91	-0.9	3.0	4584	29.7	36.6	14.8
92	-0.6	2.0	3989	29.1	36.1	15.2
93	-0.4	0.1	3981	29.9	36.7	16.2
94			5022			17.5
95			5771			17.1
96			4889			17.2
97						17.9
98						
99						

Sources for Statistical Tables

*1 Real GDP, OECD, *Historical Statistics*, 1992, 1996. IMF, *International Financial Statistics Yearbook*, 1990, pp. 162-3, 48; 1996, p. 50.

*2 Real GDP per capita, *Hist. Stat.*, 1992, 1996.

*3 OECD, *OECD Economies at a Glance*, 1996, 31. *Main Economic Indicators*, September 2000.

*4 Consumer price indices. *Hist. Stat.*, 1992, 1996.

*5 Central Bank Discount Rate, end of period, % per annum. IMF, *International Financial Statistics Yearbook*, 1990, pp. 106-7; 1998, pp. 104-5. Money and bill rates, London clearing banks base rate (end of the year). Until 1982 minimum lending rate of Bank of England. CSO *Annual Abstract of Statistics*, 1985, pp. 96, 98. *Monthly Digest of Statistics*, Nov. 1998, Sept. 1999.

*6 IMF, *International Financial Statistics Yearbook*, 1990, pp. 154-5; 1998, pp. 152-3.

*7 General government financial balances. OECD, *Economic Outlook*, Dec. 1988, p. 178; June 1999, p. 256. GNP/GDP.

*8 IMF, *International Financial Statistics Yearbook*, 1998, pp. 14-15.

*9 OECD, *Revenue Statistics*.

*10 OECD, *Hist. Stat.*, 1992, 1996.

*11 OECD, *Revenue Statistics*.

*12 OECD, *Revenue Statistics*.

*13 OECD, *Hist. Stat.*, 1992, 1996.

*14 ibid.

*15 Days not worked, 1000. ILO, *Yearbook of Labour Statistics*, 1975, 1982, 1989-90, 1997.

*16 OECD, *Hist. Stat.*, 1992, 1996.

*17 IMF, *International Financial Statistics Yearbook*, 1998, pp. 162-3.

Bibliography

Adema, Willem (1999), *Labour Market and Social Policy*, Occasional Papers No. 39, Net Social Expenditure, OECD: Paris.

Akama, Yusuke (1989), 'Fukushi Kokka no Zaisei Futan – OECD Shokoku no Hikaku Bunseki', *Kikan Shakai Hosho Kenkyu*, Vol. 25, No. 3, Todai Shuppankai: Tokyo. (Japanese, 'Fiscal Burden of the Welfare State', *Quarterly Journal of Social Security Research.*)

Allardt, Erik (1986), 'The Civic Concept of the Welfare State in Scandinavia', in Rose, Richard and Rei, Shiratori (eds), *The Welfare State East and West*, Oxford University Press: Oxford.

Anderson, David C. (1998), 'Curriculum, Culture, and Community: The Challenge of School Violence', in Moore, Mark H., and Tonry, Michael (eds), *Youth violence*, Issued as: *Crime and justice: a review of research*, Vol. 24, University of Chicago Press: Chicago.

Atkinson A. B. et al. (1995), *Income Distribution in OECD Countries*, Social Policy Studies No. 18, OECD: Paris.

Bacon, Robert William, and Eltis, Walter (1976), *Britain's Economic Problem: Too Few Producers*, Macmillan: Basingstoke.

Baldassarri, Mario, Paganetto, Luigi, and Phelps, Edmond S., (eds) (1996), *Equity, Efficiency and Growth: The Future of the Welfare State*, Macmillan: Basingstoke.

Barr, Nicholas (1998), *The Economics of the Welfare State*, third edn, Oxford University Press: Oxford.

Bentham, Jeremy (1948), *A Fragment on Government: an Introduction to the Principles of Morals and Legislation*, Blackwell: London.

Bjorklund, A. and Eriksson, T. (1998), 'Unemployment and mental health', *Scandinavian Journal of Social Welfare*, Vol. 7, No. 3, July, Munksgaard International: Copenhagen.

Blair, Tony (1996), *New Britain – My Vision of a Young Country*, Fourth Estate: London.

Block, Fred (1987), 'Rethinking the Political Economy of the Welfare State', in Fred Block et al., *The Mean Season; the attack on the Welfare State*, Pantheon Books: New York.

Blumstein, Alfred and Rosenfeld, Richard (1998), 'Exploring Recent Trends in U.S. Homicide Rates', in *Journal of Criminal Law and Criminology*, Vol. 88, No. 5, Fall, 1998, Northwestern University, School of Law: Baltimore.

Bonoli, Giuliano, George, Vic, and Taylor-Gooby, Peter (2000), *European Welfare Futures – Toward a Theory of Retrenchment*, Polity Press: Cambridge.

Brown, Lester R. (1998), *State of the World 1998*, The World Watch Institute, W. W.

Norton & Company: New York.

Budge, Ian, Crewe, Ivor, McKay, David, and Newton, Ken (1998), *The New British Politics*, Longman: Harlow.

Chatterjee, Pranab (1999), *Repackaging the Welfare State*, NASW Press: Washington, D.C.

Christiansen, Hans (1996), 'Denmark The Costs of the Welfare State', *The OECD Observer*, No. 199, April/May, OECD: Paris.

Clinton, William Jefferson (1996), *Between Hope and History – Meeting America's Challenges For the 21st Century*, Random House: Harrisonburg.

Ericsson, Robert (1986), 'Fukushikokka wa Keizaikiki wo Norikoeru', *Nihon Keizai Kenkyu Centre Kaiho*, June 15, Nihon Keizai Kenkyu Centre: Tokyo. (Japanese, 'The Welfare State will muddle through the Economic Crisis', *Newsletter of Japan Research Centre of Economy*).

Esping-Andersen, Gosta (1990), *The Three Worlds of Welfare Capitalism*, Polity Press: Cambridge.

--------------(1996), 'After the Golden Age: Welfare State Dilemmas in a Global Economy', in Esping-Andersen, Gosta, (ed.), *Welfare States in Transition – National Adaptations in Global Economies*, Sage: London.

--------------(ed.) (1996), *Welfare States in Transition – National Adaptations in Global Economies*, Sage: London.

European Communities (1999), *Social protection – expenditure and receipts: European Union, Iceland and Norway,* Office for Official Publications of the European Communities: Luxembourg.

Euzeby, Chantal (1998), 'Social security for the twenty-first century', *International Social Security Review*, Vol. 51, 1/98, General Secretariat of the I.S.S.A.: Geneva.

Feldstein, M. (1974), 'Social Security, Induced Retirement and Aggregate Capital Accumulation', *Journal of Political Economy*, Vol. 82, No. 5, University of Chicago Press: Chicago.

Fittoussi, Jean-Paul (1996), 'Welfare State: Leaner or Starved? Competitiveness and Social Cohesion', in Baldassarri, Mario, Paganetto, Luigi, and Phelps, Edmond S., (eds), *Equity, Efficiency and Growth: The Future of the Welfare State*, Macmillan: Basingstoke .

Friedman, Milton, and Friedman, Rose, (1979), *Free to Choose: A Personal Statement,* Harcourt Brace Jovanovich: New York.

Galbraith, Kenneth E. (1988), *Capitalism, Communism, and Co-existence*, NHK: Tokyo.

--------------(1993), *The Culture of Contentment*, Penguin: Harmondsworth.

George, Peter (1985), 'Towards a Two-dimensional Analysis of Welfare Ideologies', *Social Policy & Administration*, Vol. 19, No. 1, Spring, Blackwell: Oxford.

George, Vic, and Wilding, Paul (1984), *The impact of social policy*, Routledge: London.

--------------(1985), *Ideology and Social Welfare*, Routledge: London.

--------------(1993), *Welfare and Ideology*, Harvester Wheatsheaf: New York.

233

--------------(1999), *British society and social welfare – Towards a sustainable society*, Macmillan: Basingstoke.

George, Vic (1998), 'The Recent and Future Development of European Welfare States', *Nihon Fukushi Daigaku Kenkyu Kiyo*, Vol. 98-1, Feb., Nihon Fukushi Daigaku: Mihama. (*Journal of the Research Institute of Japan University of Welfare.*)

--------------, and Howards, Irving (1991), *Poverty Amidst Affluence – Britain and the United States*, Edward Elgar: Aldershot.

--------------, and Miller, Stewart (eds) (1994), *Social Policy Towards 2000 – Squaring the Welfare Circle*, Routledge: London.

--------------, and Taylor-Gooby, Peter (eds) (1996), *European Welfare Policy – Squaring the Welfare Circle*, St. Martin's Press: New York.

Giddens, Anthony (1991), *Modernity and Self-Identity – Self and Society in the Late Modern Age*, Polity Press: London.

--------------(1994), *Beyond Left and Right – The Future of Radical Politics*, Polity Press: London.

--------------(1998), *The Third Way – The Renewal of Social Democracy*, Blackwell: London.

Gilbert, Neil (1983), *Capitalism and the Welfare State – Dilemmas of Social Benevolence*, Yale University Press: New Haven.

Ginsburg, Norman (1982), *Divisions of Welfare – A Critical Introduction to Comparative Social Policy*, Sage: London.

Glazer, Nathan (1986), 'Welfare and "Welfare" in America', in Rose and Shiratori (eds), 1986, Oxford University Press: New York.

Glennerster, H. (1998), 'Which Welfare States are most likely to survive?', *International Journal of Social Welfare*, Vol. 8, No. 1, Jan., Blackwell: Oxford.

Glyn, Andrew and Sutcliffe, Bob (1972), *British capitalism, workers and the profits squeeze,* Penguin: Harmondsworth.

Golub, S. (1995), 'Not So Absolutely Fabulous', *The Economist*, November 4, Economist Newspaper: London.

Gould, Arthur (1993), *Capitalist welfare systems, a comparison of Japan, Britain, and Sweden*, Longman: London.

Hagedorn, John M. (1998), 'Gang Violence in the Post-industrial Era', Moore and Tonry (eds), *Youth violence*, Issued as: *Crime and justice: a review of research*, Vol. 24, University of Chicago Press: Chicago.

Hayek, F. von (1976), *The Mirage of Social Justice,* as *Law, Legislation and Liberty*, Vol. 2, 1976, Routledge: London .

Heclo, Hugh (1990), 'Toward a New Welfare State?' in Heidenheimer, Arnold J. et al., *Comparative public policy: the politics of social choice in America, Europe, and Japan*, St. Martin's Press: New York.

Heclo, Hugh and Madsen, Henrik (1987), *Policy and Politics in Sweden – Principled Pragmatism*, Temple University Press: Philadelphia.

Higashi, Nobuhiro, (ed.) (1992), *Shouwa no Kodomotachi*, Gakushu Kenkyusha:

Tokyo. (Japanese, *Children in Showa era.*)

Hills, John (1997), with Karen Gardiner and the LSE Welfare State Programme, *The future of welfare – A guide to the debate*, revised edition, Joseph Rowntree Foundation: York.

Hobson, Dominic (1999), *The National Wealth – Who Gets What in Britain*, HarperCollins: London.

Hug, James E., (1988), 'Kaihou to Handan wo Shikibetsu Shinagara' (Japanese, 'Distinguishing liberation and judgement'), in Isomura et al. (1988), *Imakoso Keizai Seigiwo*, Mikuni Shobo: Tokyo. (Japanese, *Economic Justice Now.*)

Hughes, Kirsty (ed.) (1993), *The Future of UK Competitiveness and the Role of Industrial Policy*, Policy Study Institute: London.

Hyde, Mark, Dixon, John, and Joyner, Melanie (1999), 'Work for those that can, security for those that cannot: The United Kingdom's new social security reform agenda', *International Social Security Review*, Vol. 52, 4/99, General Secretariat of the I.S.S.A.: Geneva.

ILO, *World Employment*, 1995, 1999, ILO: Geneva.

ILO, *Yearbook of Labour Statistics*, 1975, 1980, 1985, 1990, 1997, ILO: Geneva.

IMD, *The World Competitiveness Yearbook*, 1990, 1998, 1999, IMD: Lausanne.

Isomura, Naonori et al. (1988), *Imakoso Keizai Seigiwo*, Mikunishobo: Tokyo. (Japanese, *Economic Justice Now.*)

Ito, Mitsuharu (1999), 'Nihon Keizai Ushinawareta Junen', *This is Yomiuri*, March 1999, Yomiuri Shimbunsha: Tokyo. (Japanese, *Japanese Economy, the Lost Ten Years.*)

James, Oliver (1995), *Juvenile violence in a winner-loser culture, socio-economic and familial origins of the rise in violence against the person*, Free Association.

--------------(1998), *Britain on the Couch – Why We're Unhappier Compared With 1950 despite Being Richer, A Treatment for the Low-Serotonin Society*, Arrow: London.

Japan Keizai Seisaku Gakkai (Economic Policy Association) (ed.) (1980), *Annual Report 1980*, Keiso Shobo: Tokyo.

Japan Keizai Kikakucho (EPA, Economic Planning Agency) (ed.) (1998), *Nihon no Shotoku Kakusa – Kokusai Hikaku no Shiten kara*, Okurasho Insatsukyoku: Tokyo. (Japanese, *Economic Research Institute of Economic Planning Agency of Japan (ed.), Income Difference in Japan – International Comparative Study.*)

Japan EPA Sogo Keikakukyoku (Planning Bureau) (ed.) (1982), *Zusetsu 2000nen no Nihon*, Nihon Keizai Shimbunsha: Tokyo. (Japanese, General Planning Bureau of Economic Planning Agency of Japan (ed.), *Japan in 2000.*)

--------------(1997), *Data de Yomu Nihon no Keizai Kozo – Choki Suii, Shorai Tenbo, Kokusai Hikaku*, Toyo Keizai Shinposha: Tokyo. (Japanese, *Economic Structure of Japan in Data – Long-term trend, Future Prospect, International Comparison.*)

Japan EPA Chosakyoku (Research Bureau) (1998), *Keizai Yoran*, Okurasho Insatsukyoku: Tokyo. (Research Bureau of Economic Planning Agency of Japan, *Statistical Digest of Economy* 1998.)

Japan Somucho Tokeikyoku (Management and Coordination Agency Statistics Bureau), *Statistical Yearbook of Japan*, Bureau of Statistics of the Office of the Prime Minister: Tokyo.

Jichitai Mondai Kenkyjo (Research Institute of Local Government) (1998), *Shakaihosho No Keizaikoka Shisan*, Jichitai Kenkyusha: Tokyo. (Japanese, *A Trial Calculation of the Economic Effects of Social Welfare.*)

Jiten Kanko Iinkai (ed.) (1989), *Shakaihosho, Shakaifukushi Jiten*, Rodo Junposha: Tokyo. (Japanese, *Encyclopaedia of Social Security*, Encyclopaedia committee (ed.).)

Jowell, Roger et al. (1993), *International Social Attitudes, the 10th British Social Attitudes report*, Gower: Aldershot.

--------------, *British Social Attitudes*, 1997, 1998, Gower: Aldershot.

Kameyama, Sanae (1998), *Teion Kankei*, Wave Shuppan: Tokyo. (Japanese, *Low Temperature Relationship.*)

Kato, Hiroshi (1996), 'Chiisana Seifu to Kozokaikaku', *Kikan Shakai Hosho Kenkyu*, Vol. 33, Winter, Todai Shuppankai: Tokyo. (Japanese, 'Small Government and Restructuring', *Quarterly Social Security Research.*)

Kawahito, Hiroshi (1998), *Karoshi*, Iwanami Shoten: Tokyo.

Kawakami, Ryoichi (1999), *Gakko Hokai*, Soshisha: Tokyo. (Japanese, *The Collapse of School.*)

Keizai Koho Centre (1998), *Japan 1998 An International Comparison*, Japan Institute for Social and Economic Affairs: Tokyo.

Keynes, J. M. (1926), *The End of Laissez-Faire*, Hogarth: London.

King, D. and Waldron, J. (1988), 'Citizenship, Social Citizenship and the Defence of Welfare Provision', *British J. of Political Science*, vol. 18, C. U. P.: London.

Kirmayer, L., and Jarvis, E. (1998), 'Cultural Psychiatry: from museums of exotica to the global agora', *Current Opinion in Psychiatry*, Vol. 11, No. 2, March, Current Science: London.

Klein, Rudolf and O'Higgins, Michael (1988), 'Defusing the Crisis of the Welfare State: A New Interpretation', in T. Marmor and J. Mashaw (eds), *Social Security: Beyond the Rhetoric of Crisis*, Princeton University Press: Princeton.

Kohn, Alfie (1992), *No Contest*, revised edn, Houghton Mifflin: Boston.

Lazar, Harvey and Stoyko, Peter (1998), 'The future of the Welfare State', *International Social Security Review*, Vol. 51, 3/98, General Secretariat of the I.S.S.A.: Geneva.

Lindblom, Charles Edward (1977), *Politics and markets, the world's political economic systems*, Basic Books: New York.

MacGregor, Susanne (1999), 'Welfare, Neo-Liberalism and New Paternalism: Three Ways for Social Policy in Late Capitalist Societies', *Capital & Class* 67 Spring, Conference of Socialist Economists: London.

Mapel, David (1989), *Social Justice Reconsidered*, Illinois University Press: Urbana and Chicago.

Marklund, S. (1996), 'Must the Welfare State diminish to survive? – Post-industrial society and deregulation theory', *Scandinavian Social Welfare*, Vol. 5, No. 3, July, Munksgaard International: Copenhagen.

Marshall, Alfred (1961), *Principles of Economics*, Ninth edition, Vol. I, Macmillan: London.

Marshall, T. H. (1963), *Sociology at the crossroads, and other essays*, Heinemann: London.

Martin, W. E., (ed) (1981), *The economics of the profit crisis, papers and proceedings of the Seminar on Profits held in London on 1 April 1980*, H.M.S.O.: London.

Maruo, Naomi (1986), 'Fukushikokka ni okeru Shijo to Keikaku', *Keizaigaku Ronsan* – Chuo Daigaku –, Vol. 27, No. 1-2, March, Chuo University: Tokyo. (Japanese, 'Market and Planning in the Welfare State', *Economic Journal* – Chuo University.)

--------------(1994), 'Fukushikokka no Restructuring', *Chuo Daigaku Keizai Kenkyujo Nenpo*, Vol. 25-I, Chuo Daigaku: Tokyo. (Japanese, 'Restructuring of the Welfare State', *Chuo University Economic Research Institute Annual Report*.)

---------------(1999), 'Sweden no Koteki Shikin Tonyu to Keiki Kaifuku', *Shukan Shakai Hosho*, No. 2016, Dec. 7, Shakaihoken Hoki Kenkyukai: Tokyo. (Japanese, 'The Investment of Public Money and Economic Recovery in Sweden', *The Weekly Social Security*.)

Masumura, Machiko (1998), 'Sweden no Keizai Kozo Henka to sono Kadai', *Keizaigaku Ronsan*, Vol. 38, No. 5-6, March, Chuo Daigaku: Tokyo. (Japanese, *The Transformation of Economic Structure in Sweden and Its Tasks, Economic Journal* – Chuo University.)

Mcleod, Jay (1995), *Ain't No Makin' It*, Westview: Boulder.

Mima, Takahito (1994), 'Thatcher Seiken kano Fukushi Kokka', *Hokkai Gakuen Daigaku Keizai Ronshu*, Vol. 42, No. 2, Sept, Hokkai Gakuen Daigaku Keizai Gakkai: Sapporo. (Japanese, 'The Welfare State in the Thatcher Administration', *Hokkai Gakuen Daigaku Journal of Economics*.)

Miringoff, Marc, and Miringoff, Marque-Luisa (1999), *The Social Health of the Nation – How America is Really Doing*, Oxford University Press: New York.

Mishra, Ramesh (1984), *The Welfare State in Crisis*, Wheatsheaf: Brighton.

--------------(1986), 'Social Analysis and the Welfare State: Retrospect and Prospect', in Elsen Oyen (ed.), *Comparing Welfare States and their Futures*, Gower: Aldershot.

--------------(1990), *the Welfare State in Capitalist Society: policies of retrenchment and maintenance in Europe, North America and Australia*, Harvester Wheatsheaf: New York.

Misztal, Barbara A. (1996), *Trust in Modern Societies*, Polity Press: London.

Mitchell, Deborah (1992), 'Welfare States and welfare outcomes in the 1980s', *International Social Security Review*, Vol. 45, 1-2/1992, General Secretariat of the I.S.S.A.: Geneva.

Mitsuhashi, Tadahiro (1989), *Thatcherism*, Chuoukouronsha: Japan. (Japanese.)

Moore, Mark H., and Tonry, Michael (eds) (1998), *Youth violence*, Issued as: *Crime and justice: a review of research*, Vol. 24, University of Chicago Press: Chicago.

Myles, John (1996), 'When Markets Fail: Social Welfare in Canada and the United States', in Esping-Andersen, Gosta (ed.) (1996).

Nagaoka, Nobutaka (1992), 'Sweden Shakai Minshushugi no Doyo to Kakushin', *Osaka Keidai Ronshu*, Vol. 43, No. 2, July, Osaka Keizai Daigaku: Osaka. (Japanese, 'The Disturbance and Reformation of Swedish Social Democracy', *Journal of Osaka University of Economics.*)

Nakamae, Tadashi (1998), *Mittsu no Mirai – Suitai ka Saisei ka, Nihon no Scenario* Nihon Keizai Shinbunsha, Tokyo. (*Japanese, Three Futures for Japan – Perish or Rebirth – Views from 2020.*)

Nickell, Stephen, and Layard, Richard (1998), *Labour market institutions and economic performance*, London School of Economics & Political Science, Centre for Economic Performance: London.

Nakamura, Yuichi, and Ichibangage, Yasuko (eds) (1998), *Sekai no Shakai Fukushi, Sweden, Finland*, Junposha: Tokyo. (Japanese, *Social Welfare in the World; Sweden, Finland.*)

---------------(1999), *Sekai no Shakai Fukushi the UK*, Junposha: Tokyo. (Japanese, *Social Welfare in the World, the UK.*)

Navarro, Vincente (1998), 'Neoliberalism, "Globalization", Unemployment, Inequalities, and the Welfare State', *International Journal of Health Services*, Vol. 28. No.4, Baywood: Farmingdale.

---------------(1999), 'The Political Economy of the Welfare State in Developed Capitalist Countries', *International Journal of Health Services*, Vol. 29, No.1, Baywood: Farmingdale.

Nihon Research Sogo Kenkyujo (ed) (1997), *Shakai to Seikatsuni Tsuiteno Kokumin Ishiki – Kokumin no Kadai Ninshiki to Kitai –*, Nihon Research Sogo Kenkyujo: Tokyo. (Japanese, Japan Research General Institute (ed.), *Opinions of the People on Society and Life – Recognition of the Tasks and Expectations of the People*, 1997.)

Nikkei; Nihon Keizai Shimbun: Tokyo. (Japan Newspaper of Economy.)

Ninomiya, Atsumi (1997), '21seiki no Shakai Hosho to Shingata Fukushi Kokka heno Tenbo', *Sogo Shakai Fukushi Kenkyu*, No.11, June, Sogo Shakai Fukushi Kenkyujo: Osaka. (Japanese, 'Social Security in 21st Century and A Perspective toward A New Welfare State', *General Research of Social Welfare.*)

Niskanen, William. A. (1996), 'Welfare and the Culture of Poverty', *Cato Journal*, Vol. 16, No. 1, Cato Institute: Washington D.C.

Nordic Council (1996), *Yearbook of Nordic Statistics 1996, Nordic Council: Stockholm.*

Nordlund, A. (1997), 'Attitudes towards the Welfare State in the Scandinavian countries', *Scandinavian Journal of Social Welfare*, Vol. 6, No.4, Oct, Munksgaard International: Copenhagen.

OECD (1981), *The Welfare State in Crisis,* OECD: Paris.

--------------(1983), *Positive Adjustment Policies Managing Structural Change*, OECD: Paris.

--------------(1991, 1992), *Economic Outlook 50*, Dec. 1991, 52, Dec. 1992, OECD: Paris.

--------------(1992), *Historical Statistics 1960–1990*, 1992, OECD: Paris.

--------------(1994), *New Orientations for Social Policy*, OECD: Paris.

--------------(1996a), *Economic Studies*, No. 27, 1996/II, OECD: Paris.

--------------(1996b), *Historical Statistics 1960–1994*, OECD: Paris.

--------------(1996c), *OECD Economies at a Glance – Structural Indicators*, 1996, OECD: Paris.

--------------(1999), *A Caring World – The New Social Policy Agenda*, 1999, OECD: Paris.

Okamoto, Yuzo (1990), *Denmark ni Manabu Yutakana Rogo*, Asahi Shimbunsha: Tokyo. (Japanese, *Lessons from Rich Old Days in Denmark*.)

--------------(1996), *Fukushi wa Toushidearu*, Nihonhyoronsha: Tokyo. (Japanese, *Welfare is Investment*.)

Okazawa, Fumio (1991), *Sweden no Chousen*, Iwanami Shoten: Tokyo. (Japanese, *The Challenge of Sweden*.)

Olsen, Gregg M. (1996), 'Re-Modelling Sweden: The Rise and Demise of the Compromise in a Global Economy', *Social Problems*, Vol. 43, No. 1, Feb., Society for the Study of Social Problems: Syracuse.

Olsson Hort, Sven E. (1997), 'Sweden: Towards a 21st Century Post-Modern People's Home?' in Koslowski, Peter, and Follesdal, Andreas (eds), *Restructuring the Welfare State – Theory and Reform of Social Policy*, Springer-Verlag: New York.

Onodera, Noriko (1996), 'Seifu eno Kitai to Kakawari – ISSP Kokusai Kyodo Chosa "Seifu no Yakuwari" Nihon Chosa kara', *Hoso Kenkyu to Chosa*, Nov., Nihon Hoso Shuppan Kyokai: Tokyo. (Japanese, 'Expectation from Government and Participation – from the ISSP international research "the role of government" in Japan', *Broadcast Research and Public Opinion*.)

Otsuka, Hideyuki (1998), '"Fuan Kaikyu" to "Koyo Fuan Paradigm"', *Roudou Souken Quarterly*, No. 30, Spring, Roudou Undou Sougou Kenkyujo: Tokyo. (Japanese, '"Anxious class" and "Anxious employment paradigm"', *Quarterly of General Research of Labour*.)

Perelman, Michael (1996), *The Pathology of the U.S. Economy*, St. Martin's: New York.

Pfaller, Alfred, Gough, Ian and Therborn, Göran (1991), *Can the Welfare State compete? a comparative study of five advanced capitalist countries*, Macmillan: London.

Pfeiffer, Christian (1998), 'Juvenile Crime and Violence in Europe', in *Crime and Justice: A Review of Research*, Vol. 23, University of Chicago Press: Chicago.

PHP Kenkyujo (ed.) (1995), *Suuji de Miru Sengo 50nen Nihon no Ayumi*, PHP Kenkyujo: Tokyo. (Japanese, *Japanese Progress in the Post-war 50 years in*

239

Figures, PHP Research Institute.)

Pierson, Christopher (1998), *Beyond the Welfare State – the New Political Economy of Welfare*, second edn. (And first edn, 1991.) Polity Press: London.

Platt, S., and Kreitman, N. (1985), 'Parasuicide and unemployment among men in Edinburgh, 1968-82', *Psychological Medicine*, No 15, C.U.P.: London.

Plotnick, Robert D., Smolensky, Eugene, Evenhouse, Eirik, and Reilly, Siobhan (1998), 'Inequality and poverty in the United States: The twentieth-century record', *Focus*, Vol. 19, No. 3, Summer-Fall, Institute for Research on Poverty, University of Wisconsin: Madison.

Price Waterhouse World Firm Services BV, Inc. (1997), *Individual Taxes – A Worldwide Summary*, 1997 edition, Price Waterhouse: London.

---------------(1997), *Corporate Taxes – A Worldwide Summary*, 1997 edition, Price Waterhouse: London.

Rawls, John (1971), *A Theory of Justice*, The Belknap Press of Harvard University Press: Cambridge.

Reich, Robert (1991), 'What Is a Nation?' *Political Science Quarterly*, Vol. 106, The Academy of Political Science: New York.

---------------(1994), 'The Fracturing of the Middle Class', *New York Times*, August 31, The New York Times Company: New York.

Rhodes, Martin (1996), 'Globalization and West European Welfare States: A Critical Review of Recent Debates', *Journal of European Social Policy*, 1996, Vol. 6, No. 4, Longman: Essex.

Rinji Gyosei Chosakai (Rincho) (1983), *Saishu Houkoku*, Rinji Gyosei Chosakai: Tokyo. (Japanese, *Final Report*, Temporary Administrative Investigation Committee.)

Robson, W. A. (1976), *Welfare State and Welfare Society*, Allen and Unwin: London.

Rose, Richard and Shiratori, Rei (eds) (1986), *The Welfare State East and West*, Oxford University Press: New York.

Rose, Richard (1986), 'The Dynamics of the Welfare Mix in Britain', in Rose et al., *The Welfare State East and West*, Oxford University Press: New York.

Rousseau, Jean Jacque (1973), 'A Discourse on Political Economy', in *The Social Contract and Discourses*, translated by G. D. H. Cole, revised and augmented by Brumfitt, J. H. and Hall, John C., Dent: London.

Sakurai, Hitoshi (1997), 'A Lot of Hard Trials of Sweden, a Highly Developed Welfare State: The Necessity to Normalize the State and Integrate the Family', *Shokei Gakusou*, Vol. 44, No. 2, Dec., Kinki Daigaku Shokei Gakkai: Higashi Osaka. (*Journal of Business and Economics*.)

Salvation Army, The (1999), *The Paradox of Prosperity*, The Henley Centre: London.

Shibata, Yoshihiko (1996), *Sekai no Shakai Hosho*, Shin Nihon Shuppansha: Tokyo. (Japanese, *Social Security in the World*.)

---------------(1998), *Nihon no Shakai Hosho*, Shin Nihon Shuppansha: Tokyo. (Japanese, *Social Security in Japan*.)

Shirota, Jun (1997), 'Sweden no EU Kamei to Fukushi Kokka no Saihensei', *Ritsumeikan Kokusai Kenkyu*, Vol. 10, No. 1, May, Ritsumeikan Daigaku Kokusai Keizai Gakkai: Kyoto. (Japanese, 'The Affiliation of Sweden into EU and the Restructuring of the Welfare State', *Ritsumeikan International Study*.)

Smeeding, T. M. (1997), 'American Inequality in a Cross National Perspective: Why Are We So Different', Working Paper No.157, Luxembourg Income Study, Harvester Wheatsheaf: New York.

--------------- and Gottschalk, Peter (1998), 'Cross-national income inequality: How great is it and what can we learn from it?' *Focus*, Vol. 19, No. 3, Summer-Fall, Institute for Research on Poverty, University of Wisconsin: Madison.

Smith, Adam (1976A), *An inquiry into the nature and causes of the wealth of nations*, Clarendon Press: New York.

----------------(1976B), *The Theory of Moral Sentiments*, edited by D. D. Raphael and A. L. Macfie, Oxford University Press: Oxford.

Smith, David (1992), *The British Economy Survey*, Vol. 22, No. 2, Autumn, Oxford University Press: Oxford.

Smith, Tom W. (1987), 'The Polls A Report, The Welfare State in Cross-National Perspective', *Public Opinion Quarterly*, 51, Fall, Princeton University Press: Princeton.

Soros, George (1997), 'The Capitalist Threat', *The Atlantic Monthly*, Feb., The Atlantic Monthly: Boston.

Stephens, John D. (1996), 'The Scandinavian Welfare States: Achievements, Crisis, and Prospects', in Esping-Andersen, Gosta (ed), *Welfare States in Transition – National Adaptations in Global Economies*, Sage: London.

Svallfors, Stefan, ed. (1995), *In the Eye of the Beholder – Opinons on welfare and justice in comparative perspective*, The Bank of Sweden Tercentenary Foundation: Umea.

--------------- and Taylor-Gooby, Peter (eds) (1999), *The End of the Welfare State? – Responses to state retrenchment*, Routledge: London.

Takeuchi, Yasuo (1998), 'Kyoso no Muchi de Kitaenaose', *This is Yomiuri*, July, Yomiuri Shimbunsha: Tokyo. (Japanese, *Re-forge with the Whip of Competition*.)

Takashima, Susumu (1995), *Shakai Fukushi no Rekishi*, Minerva Shobo: Kyoto. (Japanese, *The History of Social Welfare*.)

Taylor, Ian (ed.) (1990), *The Social Effects of Free Market Policies*, Harvester Wheatsheaf: New York.

Taylor-Gooby, Peter (1996), *The Response of Government*, in George & Taylor-Gooby (eds), *European Welfare Policy – Squaring the Welfare Circle*, St. Martin's Press: New York.

Tawney, R. H. (1923), *The Acquisitive Society*, G. Bell and son: London.

Tennant, Chris (1994), 'Life-even stress and psychiatric illness', *Current Opinion in Psychiatry*, Vol.7, No.2, July, Gower Academic J.: Philadelphia.

Tezuka, Kazuaki (1996), 'Koutaisuru EU Fukushi Kokka', *Sekai*, Aug., Iwanami Shoten: Tokyo. (Japanese, 'EU Welfare States in Setback'.)

241

Thatcher, Margaret (1993), *The Downing Street Years*, HarperCollins: London.

Tilton, Timothy (1991), *The political theory of Swedish social democracy, through the Welfare State to socialism*, Clarendon: New York.

Titmuss, R. (1968), *Commitment to Welfare*, Allen and Unwin: London.

Tsukada, Hiroto (1983), 'Kasenka to America Keizai', *Hitotsubashi Kenkyu*, Vol. 8-2, Hitotsubashi Daigaku Daigakuin Gakuseikai: Tokyo. (Japanese, 'Oligopoly and American Economy – on the effect of oligopoly on prolonging depression'.)

---------------(1997), *Economic System and Distributive Justice – On its Analytical Framework*, Yamaguchi University Economics Association: Yamaguchi.

---------------(1998), *Shakai System to Shiteno Shijo Keizai – Shijo Keizai System no Saikochiku no Tameni*, Seibundo: Tokyo. (Japanese, *Market Economy as a Social System – For the reconstruction of market economy system*.)

Uchihashi, Katsuto (1995), *Kyosei no Daichi*, Iwanami Shoten: Tokyo. (Japanese, *The Earth of Symbiosis*.)

---------------(1998), *Doujidai eno Hatsugen, 1, Nihon Kaikakuron no Kyojitsu*, Iwanami Shoten: Tokyo. (Japanese, *Opinions to the Contemporary, 1, Truth and False of Reformatory Arguments on Japan*.)

Ueda, Atsuo et al. (1998), *Japan 1998 An International Comparison*, Keizai Koho Centre: Tokyo.

UN the United Nations Development Programme (1999), *Human Development Report 1999*, Oxford University Press: New York.

UK Office of National Statistics, *Annual Abstract of Statistics*, 1983, 1993, 1997, 1999, H.M.S.O.: London.

Uzuhashi, Takafumi (1995), 'Fukushikokka no Ruikei ron to Nihon no Ichi', Hosei Daigaku *Ohhara Shakai Mondai Kenkyujo Zasshi*, No. 445, 12/1995, Hoseidaigaku Shuppankyoku: Tokyo. (Japanese, 'Typology of the Welfare States and the Location of Japan', *Journal of Ohhara Social Problems Research Institute*.)

Walker, Robert (1998), 'The Americanization of British welfare: A case study of policy transfer', *Focus*, Vol. 19, No. 3, Summer-Fall, Institute for Research on Poverty, University of Wisconsin: Madison.

Watanabe, Hiroaki (1996), 'W. Korpi no Fukushi Kokkaron to Sweden Fukushikokka no Keisei Katei (1)', *Nagoya Daigaku Housei Ronshu*, July, Nagoya Daigaku Hogakubu: Nagoya. (Japanese,' W. Korpi's theory of the Welfare State and Formation of Swedish Welfare State 1', *Journal of Law and Politics of Nagoya University*.)

Weber, Max (1930), *The protestant ethic and the spirit of capitalism*, translated by Talcott Parsons; with a foreword by R. H. Tawney, Allen: London.

Winter, J. M., and Joslin, D. M. (1972), *R. H. Tawney's Commonplace Book*, University Press: Cambridge.

Worswick, G. D. N. (1991), *Unemployment: A Problem of Policy – An Analysis of British Experience and Prospects*, Cambridge University Press: Cambridge.

Yeates, Nicola (1999), 'Social Politics and Policy in an Era of Globalization: Critical

Reflections', *Social Policy & Administration*, Vol. 33, No. 4, Dec., Blackwell: Oxford.

Yokoyama, Juichi (1986), '"Fukushi Kokka" no Kiki to Shakai Hosho Seisaku no Tenkan', *Ritsumeikan Keizaigaku*, Vol. 35, No. 3, Aug., Ritsumeikan Daigaku Keizai Gakkai: Kyoto. (Japanese, 'The Crisis of "the Welfare State" and the Transformation of Social Welfare Policy', *Ritsumeikan Economics*.)

Zaidan Houjin Yano Koutaro Kinenkai (ed.) (1997), *Sekai Kokusei Zue* 8th edition, 1997/98, Kokuseisha: Tokyo. (Japanese, *Statistics of the Nations 1997/98*.)

Websites

21 Seiki Nihon no Koso Kondankai (Prime Minister's Commission on Japan's Goals in the 21st Century): http://www.kantei.go.jp/jp/21century/index.html

American Medical Association Science News, June 12, 1996: http:// jama.ama-assn. org/

Asahi Newspaper: http://www.asahi.com/

BBC: http://www.news.bbc.co.uk/

CNN: http://www.cnn.com/QUICKNEWS/

Gallup: http://www.gallup.com/poll/index.asp

Globalization Working Group Report: http://www.epa.go jp/99/e/ 19990629e–global-e.html

Gwartney, James, et al. (1998) The Size and Functions of Government and Economic Growth, JEC Study, April: http://www.house.gov/jec/ growth/function/ function.htm

ISA Facts & Figures 1998, ISA: http://www.sa.se/default.cfm?page=/automotive/ team/ team.htm

KPMG: http://www.tax.kpmg.net/

Keidanren: http://www.keidanren.or.jp/ tax affairs: http://www.keidanren.or.jp/ english/policy/pol068s.html

Keizai Kikakucho (EPA, Economic Planning Agency): http://www.epa.go.jp/e-e/ menu.html

Keizai Senryaku Kaigi, Japan (the Economic Strategy Council): http://www.kantei. go.jp/ foreign/senryaku/990317report.html

Kokumin Seikatsu Kyoku, Kokumin Seikatsu Hakusho 1996 (White Paper on the Livelihood of the People): http://www.epa.go.jp/j-j/doc/s8honbun-j-j.html

Monbusho (Ministry of Education, Japan) White Paper 1998: http://www.monbu. go.jp/hakusho/1999jpn/j2-ch03.html#2.03

Mondragon CC: http://mondragon.mcc.es/ingles/menu_ing.html

New York Times: http://www.nytimes.com/

OECD: http://www.oecd.org/

OECD in Figures, 1997, 1999: http://www.oecd.org/publications/figures/e_38-39_ taxation.pdf

Ombudsman, A report from the Children's Ombudsman in Sweden to the Committee on the Rights of the Child regarding the second periodic report of Sweden, June 1998: http://www.bo.se/barnombudsmannen/eng/bo_report_ 1998. html

SAF (Swedish Employers' Confederation): http://www.saf.se

Sangyo Kyosoryoku Kaigi, Japan (the Industrial Competitiveness Council): http://www.kantei.go.jp/jp/sangyo/index.html

Taylor, Rich, Forty Years of Crime and Criminal Justice Statistics, 1958 to 1997, Research Development Statistics: http://www.homeoffice.gov.uk/red/pdfs/40 years.pdf

US Social Security Administration: http://www.ssa.gov/statistics/ssptw97.html

Vedder, Richard K., Gallaway, Lowell E. (1999) Unemployment and Jobs in International Perspective, Joint Economic Committee Study, April 1999: http://www.house.gov/jec/employ/intern.pdf

Wirkstrom, Per-Olof H. and Dolmen, Lars, World Factbook of Criminal Justice Systems, Sweden: http://www.ojp.usdoj.gov/bjs/pub/ascii/wfbcjswe.txt

Index

247

liberalism 53, 123, 146n, 200, 208, 216, 217
Lindbrom, Charles E. 153
LO 151
Longevity 143
Low Pay Commission 122
low self-esteem 188, 190

Major 116, 170
Malthus 54
market mechanism x, xi, 2, 34n, 37n 39, 41, 58, 60, 76, 108, 109, 121, 128, 143-8, 161n, 162, 178, 182-3, 207-17
and the Welfare State 8, 23
better-fit-for 31
Adam Smith on 33
Marshall on 36
favoured virtue of 40
market society 3, 7, 8, 35, 40, 45, 109, 112, 120, 171
fitted for 57
market-makers 118
Marshall, Alfred 33-4, 36
Marshall, T. H. 48
Maruo, Naomi 67, 68n, 70, 151
materialistic societies 184
means tests 114
measure question 8
medical insurance 7
meritocracy 26
middle class society 115
Military Assistance Act 55
Miller, Stewart 22, 75, 80, 154-5, 157, 167, 169
minimum wage 50, 54, 57, 121, 155
Miringoff 181n, 189, 200-2
Mishra 13, 17, 38, 92, 153, 166, 171
Mitchell, Deborah 18, 19
Miyazawa 126
mobility of firms 7, 211
Mondragon 163
monopoly 35, 54
Moore, Mark H. 181, 203
Myrdal 112

nation states 23, 48
National Health Service 53, 73, 79
national minimum wage 77
nationalization clause 76

natural advantages 27, 30
Navarro, Vincente 91, 230
neo-classics 5
neo-conservative 5, 15
neo-conservative economics 5
neo-liberalism 146n, 200, 208, 216
neo-liberal policies 75
Net operating surplus 73, 95
Net profit rate 73
net social protection 71
New Deal 56
Niskanen, William A. 146, 230
non-wage labour costs 117
nuclear weapons 11

Obuchi 125-7, 129, 130, 138, 141
O'Higgins, Michael 16, 17
Ohira 126
Okamoto, Yuzo 162, 167
old age pension 4, 7, 50, 52, 54-7, 71, 155, 158n, 182
Older Americans Act 56, 57
Oughton 73, 95, 96
output-capital ratio 96
ownership of productive means 6

Palme 111
pathological social phenomena 124, 180, 182-8, 193-8, 207-9, 213-17
Payment Solidarity 163
people's attitudes 24
people's capitalism 115
people's satisfaction 110
Perelman, Michael 165
Pfaller, Alfred 150
Pfeiffer, Christian 183
Pierson, Christopher 21, 48, 50, 152
Platt, S. 195
Plaza Agreement 87
pluralism 13, 47
pluralist 13
polarization 177, 212
of prices 63n
political democracy 6
political rights 29
Poor Law 52, 54
private investment 2, 15, 64, 161
private property 29, 200
producers sector 160
productivity 6, 7, 10-12, 214n

249

Wilding, Paul 4n, 13, 15n, 72, 80, 95, 115n, 143n, 167, 187, 225
work incentive 2, 11, 59, 61, 120, 144, 147, 155-6, 177

working-class 18

Zimring, Frank 203

*For Product Safety Concerns and Information please contact
our EU representative GPSR@taylorandfrancis.com Taylor & Francis
Verlag GmbH, Kaufingerstraße 24, 80331 München, Germany*

T - #0116 - 270225 - C0 - 216/148/14 - PB - 9781138630994 - Gloss Lamination